The Yanomami Indians live in small groups of about forty individuals in the depths of the Venezuelan forest. They are to some extent already known to the outside world through the books that have been written, and the films that have been made, about them. In this book, Jacques Lizot, who has lived among the Yanomami for over fifteen years, allows the Indians to speak for themselves. The result is a rich, evocative, and intimate account of the way in which the Yanomami perceive, and feel about, their world.

Presented in the form of stories told by a few key Yanomami individuals, with whose personalities and characters the reader quickly becomes familiar, the book focuses on three areas of Yanomami life: daily experience in the village; shamanism, magic, and sorcery; and relations of war and alliance with other villages. Lizot offers little analysis of the material he provides, leaving it instead to the reader to develop his or her own interpretations of it.

The book will be valuable for teachers and students of anthropology, both for the new and well-documented ethnographic data it contains, as well as for its alternative approach to writing ethnography. It is also unique in the way in which it conveys the atmosphere, talk, noise, smells, images, and flavor of Amazonia and its Indians, and it will therefore appeal to any reader interested in the world's contemporary nonindustrial peoples.

Cambridge Studies in Social Anthropology

General Editor: Jack Goody

55

TALES OF THE YANOMAMI

For other titles in this series turn to page 199

This book is published as part of the joint publishing agreement established in 1977 between the Fondation de la Maison des Sciences de l'Homme and the Press Syndicate of the University of Cambridge. Titles published under this arrangement may appear in any European language or, in the case of volumes of collected essays, in several languages.

New books will appear either as individual titles or in one of the series which the Maison des Sciences de l'Homme and the Cambridge University Press have jointly agreed to publish. All books published jointly by the Maison des Sciences del l'Homme and the Cambridge University Press will be distributed by the Press throughout the world.

Cet ouvrage est publié dans le cadre de l'accord de co-édition passé en 1977 entre la Fondation de la Maison des Sciences de l'Homme et le Press Syndicate de l'Université de Cambridge. Toutes les langues européennes sont admises pour les titres couverts par cet accord, et les ouvrages collectifs peuvent paraître en plusieurs langues.

Les ouvrages paraissent soit isolément, soit dans l'une des séries que la Maison des Sciences de l'Homme et Cambridge University Press ont convenu de publier ensemble. La distribution dans le monde entier des titres ainsi publiés conjointement par les deux établissements est assurée par Cambridge University Press.

Tales of the Yanomami

Daily Life in the Venezuelan forest

JACQUES LIZOT
Translated by Ernest Simon

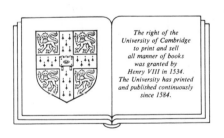

The right of the
University of Cambridge
to print and sell
all manner of books
was granted by
Henry VIII in 1534.
The University has printed
and published continuously
since 1584.

CAMBRIDGE UNIVERSITY PRESS
Cambridge   London   New York   New Rochelle
Melbourne   Sydney

& Editions de la Maison des Sciences de l'Homme
Paris

Published by the Press Syndicate of the University of Cambridge
The Pitt Building, Trumpington Street, Cambridge CB2 1RP
32 East 57th Street, New York, NY 10022, USA
10 Stamford Road, Oakleigh, Melbourne 3166, Australia

Originally published in French as *Le cercle des feux: Faits et dits
des Indiens yanomami* by Editions du Seuil, Paris, 1976
and © Editions du Seuil 1976

First published in English in 1985 by the Cambridge University Press and the
Maison des Sciences de l'Homme as *Tales of the Yanomami: Daily Life in the
Venezuelan Forest*

English translation © Maison des Sciences de l'Homme and
Cambridge University Press 1985

Printed in the United States of America

Library of Congress Cataloging in Publication Data

Lizot, Jacques.
Tales of the Yanomami.
(Cambridge studies in social anthropology; no. 55)
Translation of: Le cercle des feux.
1. Yanoama Indians. I. Title. II. Series.
F2520.1.Y3L592 1985 306'.08998 84-23175
ISBN 0 521 30016 9 hard covers
ISBN 0 521 31451 8 paperback

Contents

The publisher is especially grateful to Professor Timothy Asch for his invaluable assistance in preparing this edition.

Foreword

by Timothy Asch

This ethnography is novel both in form and content. Whereas most American ethnographers have presented analyses drawing on field data to support their arguments, Lizot simply presents the data, in story form, and rarely uses analysis. The absence of explanation of his intent and absence of his field methods forces the reader to search for interpretation within the stories themselves. At first glance, Lizot's stories resemble the ethnographic texts that anthropologists record in the field rather than any of the many kinds of syntheses they have published as ethnographies.

This book can be read at many levels: It can simply be enjoyed, much as a loosely woven novel about a strange group of people may provide an interesting diversion; it can be explored as a challenge to our definition of ethnography and our view of how best to transmit knowledge about the lives of one group of people to members of a very different group; and it can be read as a source of information about the society and culture of the Yanomami.

Lizot's narrative style is easy to read and entertaining. He introduces the reader to many unforgettable individuals and to the affections and tensions that may either bind or divide them. An unusual dimension is Lizot's emphasis on sexual liaisons, particularly among adolescents and young adults. The thoughts, dreams, and attractions of the characters are interwoven in stories about their affairs. Sexuality as experienced by Yanomami from childhood to old age, particularly Yanomami men, is revealed through dozens of incidents.

Another feature of this book is Lizot's translation of many of the endless practical jokes, taunts, and innuendos that amuse the Yanomami. Joking, often related to sex, seems to be a typical ingredient of Yanomami interaction. Inclusion of jokes is unusual, perhaps because humor is so difficult to translate, depending, as it often does, on a subtle knowledge of the language and the personalities involved. A joke devoid of context often loses its humor. Lizot's narrative provides sufficient context for us to recognize the joke, though not always enough to share in an appreciation of its humor.

The book begins with a prologue on the ethnocentrism of the Yanomami;

this is followed by stories, roughly divided into those focusing on sexuality in Part I, on ritual and myth in Part II, and on warfare in Part III, although these themes are interwoven throughout the book. Through the stream of anecdotes, myths, and oral histories emerge Lizot's central concerns about the way the Yanomami think and act within their social universe: who lives with whom, who supports whom, who fights with whom and why; how people explain why they choose to do something or the causal links they make between events; and how myth is incorporated into action. Parts of the book appear to be direct translations of texts Lizot recorded in the field, such as the myth and oral history included in the prologue. The sources of other stories are less clear, containing the purported thoughts, dreams, and emotional reactions of protagonists, as well as descriptions of time, place, and action. By not revealing his own role as selector and interpreter, Lizot leaves the source of creativity ambiguous. Lizot's blurring of the traditional distinctions among fiction, biography, and ethnography is an intriguing aspect of this book.

Lizot does not place himself in his accounts, either as participant or as observer. Only occasionally does he step outside the framework of the stories to provide background or interpretation, and rarely does he include direct reference to his own perceptions or judgments; but when he does, he seems to be reminding the reader that this is not a novel but an ethnography and should be read in a particularly reflective way. Lizot opts to use the approach of the novelist to reveal what is really important to him about the way people interact: their experiences with one another, their dreams, fears, attractions, hates, myths, and oral histories. He does not want us to draw out rules so much as to respond affectively to the material, much as we respond to our own primary experiences.

It is in the shifts from narrative to brief reflection on the events, as well as in the wider organization of the book, that Lizot reminds us that the stories (which seem to reveal ways that Yanomami experience their world) have all been filtered through Lizot. His book suggests that if one lives long enough among a group of people, it becomes increasingly difficult to be sure what impartial observation means or which ideas originate with whom. Lizot and the Yanomami with whom he has lived have influenced one another in profound ways. He does not try to undo that integration; he rarely separates and identifies the sources of ideas and perceptions. Perhaps he hopes that readers will respond to the tales in the book in an unconscious as well as a conscious way and that they too will come to appreciate the substance of ethnography, that subtle interaction between observer and observed in which both are changed.

Not only is Lizot's book challenging in its own right, it is an important contribution to the resources available on the Yanomami, a resource unavailable in English until recently. The Yanomami (known in American ethnography as the Yanomamo) live in southern Venezuela and northern Brazil. They number from 12,000 to 15,000 people and live in approximately 125 villages, which is the world's largest population isolated from the penetration of Western or Asiatic national culture.

I met Lizot on his first trip to the Yanomami in 1968 while I was on a filming expedition with Napoleon Chagnon. Lizot, a student of Lévi-Strauss, had come bearing Chagnon's thesis. He arrived at a Catholic mission across the river from the Protestant mission where Chagnon had begun his research in 1964. When we first met I acted as translator until Chagnon and Lizot realized that their Spanish was better than my French. They agreed to live in different but adjoining areas, which meant they would be working with many of the same people. This overlap has reinforced the complementarity of their writings. Since 1968 Lizot has spent a major portion of his time living among the Yanomami. He speaks their language fluently and shares daily in the pleasures and discomforts of such a life. Perhaps it is this familiarity, as well as a tradition among French anthropologists to emphasize people's thoughts and conceptions of the universe, that challenged Lizot to present his material in its present form.

In 1978 Jean Rouch organized a unique ethnographic film conference in Paris in order to bring together filmmakers and anthropologists who had worked among the Yanomami. Films by Japanese, American, French, Italian, and British filmmakers were shown and discussed by anthropologists from different countries. It became clear that the Yanomami had been used as a mirror for presenting themes central to the foreigners – filmmakers and anthropologists alike – who had worked among them. These works, including some excellent studies by graduate students, reveal considerable differences in perspective. For example, Otto Zerries's work, begun in the early 1950s, represents the systematic tradition of German scholarship. Unfortunately for English speakers, his extremely rich and elegant works on the Yanomami, which contain detailed information on many aspects of their culture largely ignored by other ethnographers, are not available in translation; nor, because of the expense, are they likely to be made so. Napoleon Chagnon, on the other hand, is concerned with revealing Yanomami principles of social organization, particularly of kin, economic, and political relationships, and he overtly characterizes the Yanomami as aggressive and warlike. By contrast, Lizot refrains from any overt characterization and presents the fabric of daily life, the texture of experience, not the abstracted patterns. For example, whereas Chagnon emphasizes the structural bonds between brothers-in-law but leaves the reader to imagine how they actually behave toward one another, Lizot recounts numerous specific interactions between particular brothers-in-law and leaves it to his readers to abstract structural principles. What is exciting is that these two approaches complement one another.

With the publication in 1968 of Chagnon's *Yanomamo: The Fierce People,* which was written primarily for a student audience, and with the production of a series of thirty-seven ethnographic films by Chagnon and myself, the Yanomami have become one of the societies most frequently studied by American undergraduate students of anthropology. Like all ethnography, that of Chagnon reflects the interests of its author, so Lizot's is extremely valuable, giving students an alternative perspective in English. An in-depth ethnography of the Yanomami from a woman's viewpoint would provide another important perspective; unfortunately, one has yet to appear.

Any study of the Yanomami offers more than a glimpse of the oddities of another social system. Lizot's endeavor is to get the reader to appreciate the ethnocentrism of another set of viewpoints, those of his protagonists, and to encourage readers to extrapolate and reflect upon their own ethnocentric views and upon the human propensity to divide the world into "people like us" and "others." He writes in the Prologue: "The ethnic group is the central focus of the human universe; it is humanity par excellence, around which everything must necessarily converge or gravitate." Lizot's choice of a genre characteristic of fiction encourages us to relate what we have previously read. We often respond to fiction affectively and incorporate insights and ideas gleaned from the interactions of fictional characters into our own view of the world. This is even more likely if we believe that the author has managed to distill important aspects of reality, as Lizot seems to have done for the Yanomami. Chagnon, too, asks us to go beyond a simple examination of the Yanomami: He suggests that their society can be viewed as a model of the way human beings may have lived for thousands of years, a model that contrasts with the more romantic and widespread view of the noble primitive.

Perhaps the main attraction of the Yanomami is that their society can serve as an analogy for our own. For example, the taken-for-granted ways that some Yanomami men feel compelled to respond violently to any challenge or threat is not unlike the "macho" reactions of some men at many levels of our own society or, more importantly, the warlike stance between national governments. We have only to read a newspaper to know that we are easily as violent as the Yanomami and that violence is present at every level of our society, from the prevalence of incest among all economic groups to the development of ever-more-violent ways to destroy life on earth – ways rationalized as responses to the aggressive threats and expansionist tendencies of others.

Our world often seems too complex to understand; the individual may seem impotent. However, Lizot's account of a small society can provide some understanding of the human condition. Through his stories we can appreciate the strength with which love and attraction hold kin and affines together, as well as the ways in which antagonism toward another group can be used to strengthen social cohesion within one's own group. Lizot's accounts of the tensions created by incest and adultery, of the use of religion as

x

an aggressive weapon against one's neighbors, and of the ways warfare can escalate can be taken as an analogy to some of our own problems. He reveals how locked we are within our own perceptions of what is possible and what is inappropriate at the human level and at the level of social relationships.

The Yanomami seem trapped by their ideology of aggression coupled with a weak political system that lacks the means to hold large numbers of people together. We Westerners – democratic and communist – with our highly developed social and political systems still behave as though we, like the Yanomami, require hostility toward other groups (in our case other nations) to maintain group cohesion and identity. By examining the Yanomami (among other groups whose lives are very different and yet not so different from our own) we should be encouraged to examine the choices we, in our society, really have, and their probable consequences.

University of Southern California   Timothy Asch

Preface

to the English edition

The educated reader is apt to criticize social anthropology for its excessive abstruseness – and not always without good cause. Yet we must realize that every scientific discipline must express itself through its own vocabulary, its own rules and specific methodology. Admittedly, however, the human sciences in general have needlessly indulged in the excessive use of jargon. Perhaps it is time now to think of improving clarity without sacrificing rigor: Ethnology is often quite needlessly forbidding and opaque, increasingly restricted to specialists and discouraging to the uninitiated.

Such a situation is regrettable. At a time when the last primitives are in danger of extinction – some even say, somewhat prematurely, that there are no longer any primitive societies, and in Brazil the government has made provisions for the deportation and concentration of the Yanomami – an ethnologist should become, temporarily if need be, a spokesperson for and defender of the peoples among whom he or she sojourns; it should be the ethnologist's duty to educate and inform the members of his or her own society and to show in an accessible vocabulary what priceless values are being destroyed forever. Yes, "savages" live worthy lives – neither more nor less worthy than ours. To learn from "primitives" does not mean that we want to imitate them at all costs, nor that we want to go back to a style of life that perhaps we can no longer accept; it means learning respect and deriving lessons that could prove salutary at a time when our own civilization – *Civilization,* as we like to call it – is beset by difficulties that may ultimately be fatal.

This book was written in the field, in 1975, at my encampment of Tayari among the Indians; it is the result of six years of almost constantly sharing the life of the Yanomami Indians of Venezuela. It attempts to fulfill three related concerns: to describe meticulously the material, social, and religious life of an Amerindian society that is still entirely traditional, while reducing sociological interpretation to a minimum by suggesting rather than stating it; to speak of the Indians and only of them; to draw a multifaceted picture, as alive as possible, and rich in clearly expressed ethnographic information. I

xiii

could of course have evoked my own experience of life among the Indians, but I wanted to speak of other things, for strictly personal reasons: I am not yet ready to speak of the terrible shock that this experience was for me, nor of the price I had to pay to become closely acquainted with a civilization so radically different from my own; perhaps I will never be able to speak of these experiences, for I would have to evoke so many harrowing things that touch my inner being. There is a wound that first must heal. Besides, introspective narratives by field researchers have rarely been carried out successfully, and it is as a reaction against excesses in that genre, particularly in France, that I wanted to recede into the background as completely as possible. Nevertheless, it is an obvious fact that I am the one who is observing, reporting, describing, organizing the narrative; the same events could have acquired an entirely different cast had they been observed and told by someone else. Objectivity is at best a relative matter.

It is because I shared for a long time the life of the Yanomami that I was able to write my narrative, in a way and to a degree, from a point of view *inside* their culture. The reader is thus a direct spectator whose opinions are grounded in his or her feelings. This kind of book naturally does without notes and references; it conveys only what I have seen and heard, what was told to me, and what I inquired about. During such a long stay among them, I was able to establish bonds of friendship with these men and women, and they confided in me; I was a go-between in most of the love stories I set down, and sometimes I was a witness. All the ethnographic details, all the beliefs I report have been carefully verified, and even now, four years after writing the book, I find nothing of any importance to change. I was a direct witness to most of the incidents I relate; the conversations, the recollections, the personal secrets, I set down from memory soon after hearing them, or I wrote them down on the spot, or else I tape-recorded them, as in the case of the shaman's initiation and the dreams and dialogues that follow. I did not correct or modify the sometimes personal or passionate interpretations of the protagonists: The way of presenting an incident or a story and of arranging it according to one's fancy is one form of ethnographic reality. Moreover, I purposely refrained from eliminating through some literary device or other the breaks that from time to time disturb the continuity of the narrative; these sequences of life can, without any disadvantage to the reader, give the impression of having been caught by the prying and necessarily selective eye of a camera, a situation that corresponds to the position of any observer, who never receives but an imperfect picture of communal life.

I would like my book to help revise the exaggerated representation that has been given of Yanomami violence. The Yanomami are warriors; they can be brutal and cruel, but they can also be delicate, sensitive, and loving. Violence is only sporadic; it never dominates social life for any length of time, and long peaceful moments can separate two explosions. When one is acquainted with the societies of the North American plains or the societies of the Chaco in South America, one cannot say that Yanomami culture is organized around warfare. They are neither good nor evil savages: These Indians are human beings.

Tayari   Jacques Lizot

Prologue

The stranger had started on his way. He had announced:

> Mother, I am going to hunt the wild pig.
> Go, my son, and kill a great many.

He had sharpened several darts cut from a bamboo stalk and painted their tips with curare, then had gone to a steep rock called "the rock of the menstruating woman." There he had cut a hollow cane to fashion a blowgun, which was obviously not made to last for it came from too soft a stalk.

When he was ready he entered the forest and walked a good while before he was alerted by muffled sounds as of blows. He walked toward the noise and stealthily approached a Yanomami who was busy taking hard-shelled fruits from a heap next to him and knocking them against a large tree root. The stranger remained hidden in the thicket; he watched a long time before loading a dart into his blowgun. The dart streaked into the Indian's eye. The killer then waited for his victim to die before loading him onto his shoulders.

His mother was pregnant. When she saw him return, walking heavily because of the burden he was carrying, she cried out happily:

> Oh, my son has killed a wild pig!

She was rejoicing: She had a passion for human flesh. They quartered the body and boiled it. A young boy was living with them; no one knew who he was. When the meat was cooked they ate voraciously until they had their fill, and there soon remained only bones, which emitted a strange sound when they threw them out. It was something like: *terere* . . . And it could be heard throughout the neighborhood.

Meanwhile, in the great circular shelter, the Yanomami were growing anxious about the man whose return was so long delayed. When they started their search for their companion they suspected a jaguar. Their quest was unsuccessful at first; then they discovered some tracks: recently broken saplings, footprints, scattered husks, and abandoned fruits. They also saw other tracks: the killer's. These sank deep into the ground where it was soft. They followed them and found the strangers' dwelling. The heap of bones filled

1

them with dread: They suddenly realized what had been their companion's fate. They got ready for combat, fastened their arrowheads on their shafts, and scattered. The stranger fought back with his blowgun; his darts made a snapping sound as he blew them out. They killed him and invaded his dwelling. When she saw them the woman became mad with rage; she pulled off her necklaces and their parts scattered all over the ground.

One of them took the foreign woman for a wife. As for the boy, he was adopted and grew up among them, so that they finally considered him one of their own. One day the boy declared that he wanted to go and find fire stones. He asked that a Yanomami boy go with him: His intention was to eat him once they were far away. They went to the place of the stones and started to dig them up. Then, with a stone he had specially chosen for its sharpness, he struck his companion on the head with all his might and killed him. He cut the body into small pieces, wrapped them in leaves for cooking, and did not return to the great communal shelter until he had eaten everything. He was glutted with human flesh. When she saw him return alone, the child's mother asked:

Where is my son?

The young stranger remained silent at first. His only answer was to tap the edges of his incisors with his index finger. Their first reaction was to disbelieve the evidence. Some adult males asked that he lead them to the place of the crime. They found burned-out embers, charred leaves, and loathsome remains. Filled with grief and rage, the victim's father decapitated the young stranger.

This story is instructive concerning the Yanomami's view of their neighbors and of strangers in general – whether Indian or white – whom they frequently accuse of the crime of cannibalism. Ethnocentricity, which is so damaging to our research but so difficult to avoid, is not at all an attitude characteristic only of technological civilizations imbued with their alleged superiority: One can find evidence of it most everywhere if one is willing to recognize it. In order to perpetuate itself in time and maintain that internal logic which enables it to exist, every civilization needs to confer value upon itself and to this end needs to disparage ever so slightly its neighboring cultures. We can perhaps perceive in that need the reason for this almost universal attitude. In an extreme situation, an ethnic group that might have too flattering an image of other groups would be forced to work certain necessary transformations upon itself in order to prevent an unbearable contradiction. What we call acculturation sometimes has no other roots.

We can better understand the tendency of ethnic groups to call themselves by a name that, in their language, means simply "man," "folk," or something to that effect. That is very precisely the meaning of the word *yanomami*. The

2

ethnic group is the central focus of the human universe; it is humanity par excellence, around which everything must necessarily converge or gravitate. For a Yanomami, anything that doesn't belong to his own sociocultural world is necessarily alien, *nabë*. The words *yanomami* and *nabë* form both a pair and an opposition. The *nabë* are first of all Indians of other ethnic groups, but also people of mixed blood and whites, all of whom are lumped together into the same category of creatures who deserve no respect; they are also the enemies, for the stranger is in fact a potential enemy, good only for robbing and attacking, an object of derision, reduced to the level of a subhumanity that is both despised and feared, guilty of the blackest misdeeds.

It follows that the Yanomami accuse foreigners, whites, of a practice that in their eyes truly amounts to an abomination, a hideous crime: eating human flesh. Their religious thought and their mythical world are full of this ever-present threat, this disquieting shadow: cannibalism, whether actual or symbolic. For the Yanomami, every death is conceived as a cannibalistic act; death occurs when the soul has been eaten by a supernatural or human being.

The story that prefaces these remarks springs no doubt from an ideology: It is a product of the imagination, even though some of its elements might have been transposed. It will now be interesting to observe these same Indians as they are confronted by a historical event and to find out how they interpret it.

The following story takes place sometime between 1940 and 1945. Several communities of the present-day central Yanomami, driven back by numerous and enterprising enemies, had just settled in the vicinity of the "river of rains," not far from the swift-running Shitoya, at a place called Thorabë. At that very spot the river ceases to be navigable upstream.

No one knows where the whites had come from. They had traveled upstream in large dugout canoes and were stopped by the rocks. They had traveled a long time to get there: They propelled their boats by paddling and by pushing them on poles that they thrust into the sand. They settled right on the riverbank, clearing an area large enough to build a rectangular dwelling with a gable roof. They had come to extract latex from the rubber trees and began to exploit the surrounding forest. They had enormous kettles under which fires burned at all times.

When we first heard it, the news of their arrival terrified us and we stayed away. But, pushed by curiosity, we grew bolder: We would watch them through the leaves. In those days we had no metal axes, though a few of us owned some miserable pieces of machete fastened to wooden handles with bowstring. But the foreigners used machetes, axes, and knives: We had never seen so many. They also had big dogs that frightened us, but that we would have liked to have for ourselves. One day the bravest among us decided to visit the whites. The first meetings were friendly; in spite of all these objects that we coveted, we did not yet dare to steal. We bartered fruits and manioc, and, squatting down a safe distance away from the big kettles full of heavily bubbling latex, we would throw pieces of wood and balls of earth against their sides, which rang out with a terrifying noise: *tin, tin* . . . From their insides rose a worrisome smoke: It gave birth to the *Shawara* demons who make their way

3

into human bodies where they inflict pain, provoke disease and shortly death if the shamans are powerless to cast them out. Several of our children died; we knew it was because of the kettles and the whites.

Some time later, Karinahusi, Shinanokawë's father, pretended to exchange his son for a large dog that the whites were offering him. The beast was truly desirable: It was big and long-legged, its jowls hung low. In those days we had almost no dogs, and none of those we owned could compare to that magnificent animal. The foreigners had given us to understand that they wanted Shinanokawë to work in their enterprise. At the time the exchange took place, father and son had agreed on a plan: Shinanokawë was to run away as soon as night fell. That did not prove difficult for him; he waited for his masters to doze off, slipped into the forest, and stayed under cover till dawn, vaguely bothered by the thought that a jaguar might be stalking in the vicinity. Then he returned to his people.

After this deception we stayed away for fear of reprisals, but we couldn't stop thinking about the metal tools: We hadn't given up the idea of devising some trick to get our hands on them. We let some time go by before venturing again to the whites' encampment in order to gauge their reaction. When they saw us, they didn't seem angry because of the trick we had played on them. We judged them to be miserly with their possessions, and that irritated us. Previously, at night, men of influence and feared warriors had addressed us at length to incite us to stealing: We shouldn't be afraid of these few miserable foreigners, they said. And besides, those vile kettles caused death.

A group of visitors arrived from Wëtanami; they were our relatives and allies and had lived with us in the same shelter. We had parted because of a quarrel concerning the women. Wëtanami is the place where we got the earthen pots in which we cooked our food; near that site there are beds of fine clay. Taking advantage of the visitors' presence, some young men decided on an expedition to rob the whites. Some spoke to incite them, others to urge caution: They accepted the words of encouragement and ignored the prudent counsels. In spite of my youth – I was still a child – I joined them. When we arrived at the *nabë*'s shelter, I was so frightened that I stayed at a distance. The whites spoke to us in their language, we replied in ours, and there was little understanding. One of the foreigners noticed me and walked toward me; panic swept over me and I almost took to my heels.

My companions did not hurry matters, so as to allay the whites' mistrust. We had taken along some green plantain bananas that we roasted on the embers. We had hidden in the forest a chip of stone to sharpen the stolen machetes. While the strangers went about their business and no longer took any notice of us, we stole metal objects that we hid under water by pushing them into the sand near the bank; it was the dry season, the water was very low. My elder brother signaled to me and said:

Let's go, I have a machete. Let's not stay any longer: I'm afraid.

The men from Wëtanami had taken clothing. That was too obvious; the whites noticed it and wanted everything returned. As we were refusing, one of them drew a pistol and fired on a foolhardy fellow who had lingered behind. He didn't die, but his upper arm was shattered: The injured limb hung limp, oddly turned backward. We ran for our shelter in a panic:

We were attacked by the foreigners!

The older men were furious and wanted immediate revenge.

The moon died. Another "settled" in the sky. One morning a young man went hunting. It was the season when the male curassows sing out morning and night the unvaried notes that attract the females: they "weep," and their moans alert the hunters

4

who post themselves where the birds roost, waiting to kill them at daybreak. So, the hunter set out; it was dark and he waved in front of him a bunch of glowing sticks to light his way. He stopped every so often to revive the fire and listen for noises. He heard no curassow "weep," but at dawn he happened on the whites. As they hadn't noticed him, he took cover behind a tree and shot a harpoon-tipped arrow through a *nabë*'s throat. When he arrived home, out of breath for having run without stopping, he cried out:

I've shot an enemy!

Presently he vomited fat and hair, so he inferred that his victim had died and that he had "eaten" his soul.

We found out later that the whites had left; they had drifted downstream and had abandoned their dwelling. They were never seen again. The injured man's arm took a long time to heal and remained deformed. One can still make out the site of the *nabë*'s dwelling; grass has grown on it.

After Shitoya, last of the rapids, the "river of rains" lazily unwinds its countless loops before losing itself in the Orinoco. Twenty years have passed. Thorabë has changed its name to Karohi and has moved far downstream to escape the murderous attacks of its enemies. The inhabitants have built their dwelling – they call it *shabono* – at the river's edge, on a rise to escape the floods. It is a large circular roof of wood and leaves that shelters all the households, leaving in the center a vast plaza open to the sky. The gardens enfold the shelter; beyond, the forest covers a vast, rolling plain.

PART I

The great shelter from day to day

1

Ashes and tears

It is not yet daylight. The river seems to have stayed its flow. Only a few
eddies quicken the water's surface. Curls of light fog float lazily, almost
motionless. Not a breath of air. Toward morning the humidity had condensed
in the thick layers of foliage overhead: Now it drips down in large, noisy
drops like a steady rainfall. Here and there a toucan spills out the brief notes
of its monotonous song. The morning chill has become more biting; the
Indians stir the fires, and showers of sparks fly up to the roof. The sun, rising
above the horizon, will soon illuminate the tops of the highest trees. The
great shelter of Karohi slowly comes to life: Voices seek answering voices,
children weep, hammocks swing, set in motion by stirring bodies.

Without rising, men sharpen and perfect the bamboo arrowheads they had
rough-cut the day before. For this morning, Turaewë, the shaman, is going
to make curare: They must not run short of arrowheads. That night they
were to abstain from lovemaking; during the day it will be forbidden to bathe
or to eat until the curare maker has finished his work. The poison makes its
demands; to be effective it imposes observance of its rules.

Now Turaewë rises. It is high time if he wants to avoid being overtaken by
the rising sun. With a piece of charcoal he traces circles around his wrists
and arms. Lest the noxious vapors of the curare give the small children sudden and violent diarrhea, mothers wrap a broad band of bark around their
loins. Turaewë takes down a package from below the roof. He tears the wrapping; it contains scrapings from a liana. The shaman pours these onto some
leaves; then he plucks some fibers from his hammock, sets them on fire,
thrusts them into the scrapings, which first flare up and then die down as
soon as the fibers are burned out. The same procedure must be repeated
several times; the heap of scrapings must be stirred until it is dry enough to
burn by itself. When he is satisfied that the scrapings are properly charred,
Turaewë sits down; he encloses the bark between his palms, which he
squeezes between his thighs so as to rub them with greater force; while doing
this he recites the propitiatory invocation:

9

The great shelter from day to day

kushë ha!
toward the celestial disk
where the lightning bursts
you, *shokoriwë,*
close the glans of your penis.
kushë ha! kushë ha!

This is to secure the favor of *shokoriwë,* the Tamandua Spirit. If he sprinkles his urine on the curare, he makes the poison ineffective.

The liana shavings are reduced to powder. Upon the shaman's request, Hitisiwë brings fresh scrapings of another liana, which the young man collected the day before. After these have been quickly dried out on the fire, they are coarsely crushed and mixed with the first batch. Meanwhile Turaewë fashions a cone of leaves in which he places the mixture, while Hitisiwë heats some water on the fire. The cone is fastened onto a stand about fifteen centimeters above the ground, and the shuddering water is poured in small doses from a calabash. Soon a coffee-like liquid drips from the bottom of the cone, along the main rib of a leaf positioned for that purpose: It is the curare.

One after another the men come up to draw their allotted portion of the poison. Then they go home, and, armed with small, soft brushes, they concentrate on painting a succession of contiguous dabs on the arrowheads placed over glowing embers to dry up the liquid. Hebëwë complains of a headache, and his father takes this as proof of the poison's virulence.

Hebëwë is an adolescent about fifteen years old. Despite his headache – perhaps no sooner announced than forgotten – he banters with some boys his own age. They keep their voices low: Excessive noise is detrimental to the curare. Everyone promises to all and sundry that they will exterminate the current archenemies, the *mahekoto-tʰeri.* The Yanomami's curare is primarily intended for warlike expeditions, even if it is sometimes used to kill the big spider monkeys. Most groups have a specialist to make it, but the substance, drawn from a plant with a very localized habitat, is the object of a very lively trade among allied communities. The product used by Turaewë comes from upriver.

On that particular day, the men are so absorbed in their work that they leave to the women the whole task of seeing to the food and firewood. When they have finished painting their arrowheads, the warriors place them with great care into quivers tightly sealed with animal skins.

The following night, Hitisiwë feels feverish; his limbs grow heavy, his stomach hurts. Everyone is asleep; he doesn't complain, and no one takes any notice of him. In the morning he wants to get up, but he is overcome with dizziness and has to lie down again. Two days later the young man has an ugly, dry cough. He can't hold his head erect and speaks with great effort. Worried now, an older brother asks Turaewë to step in. As Hitisiwë can nei-

10

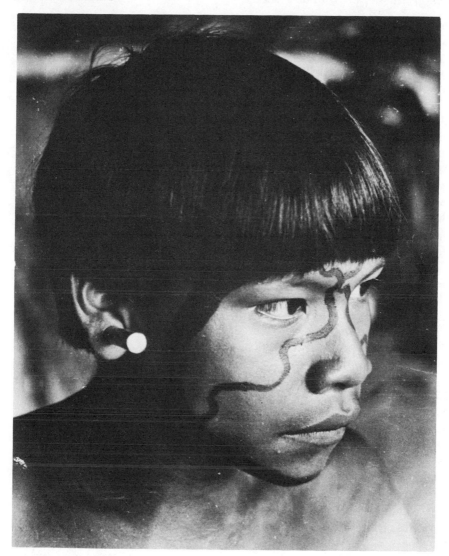

Hebëwë at age fourteen.

ther stand nor sit, they stretch a hammock for him near the place where the shaman habitually inhales his hallucinogens.

Hebëwë's father, Kaõmawë, and Shimoreiwë join Turaewë. These two are shamans of lesser importance, especially Shimoreiwë, whom they mock behind his back: Isn't it true, they ask, that his specialty is treating dogs? A few men who are not shamans also come to sit as spectators or to participate

11

in the taking of the drugs. Resting their heels on pieces of wood, they sit down on logs. Each shaman has someone blow several doses into his nostrils by means of a hollow cane. Turaewë's eyes fill with tears; soon he is under the sway of the drugs. In Karohi he is the most knowledgeable, the most powerful of the shamans, and he will direct the cure. Presently his lips vibrate: They utter the call to the *hekura,* the forest spirits who are his allies in the fight against disease. The summoned *hekura* soon appear. Turaewë himself ceases to be an ordinary man; he *is hekura* and acts accordingly, singing and dancing before the patient while pacing a straight line back and forth with lithe and graceful steps. In this manner he marks out the path of the spirits. The shaman's arms sometimes hang loose, sometimes rise outward, away from his body, or come together above his head. His chant follows the rhythm of his pacing:

> *Tokori* tree
> with whose leaves
> we, the *hekura,*
> paint our bodies.
> You, great white tapir,
> great silvery tapir hidden by the dusk.
> *Tokori* tree, your tender leaves bend down to the water,
> your mouth is clothed in white down,
> your white-downed gaping mouth that blows out the wind.

Turaewë scrutinizes the face of the patient whom he is deciphering. He wants to see what ill afflicts him and saps his health, and he discovers the nasty black bees, the *shāki kë na,* that feed on spoiled meat and offal. Their foul honey has blocked the patient's vital organs and intestines; thousands of voracious mandibles are about to eat his soul. Turaewë, ever watchful, interprets the symptoms; he explains the insects' slow but inexorable work, the tearing bites, the secretion of sticky honey that spreads, enfolds the internal organs, and, even now, is responsible for the patient's deafness.

Now that the illness is named, defined, localized, he must fight it without delay, and, to this end, he must call to the rescue the greatest, the most powerful of the *hekura,* who alone can help achieve the victory of uprooting the illness.

Turaewë places his hands visor-like above his eyes and stares at an imaginary line at right angles to the patient. Standing on his toes, he examines a spot that remains invisible to a man not endowed with his faculties. Suddenly he finds what he is seeking and cries out:

Oh, you, the grotesque! Giant Armadillo Spirit, come to me!

And all around, the spectators laugh at the evocation of that unlovely animal. But the *hekura* is in no hurry; he has not yet left his rocky abode. Turaewë repeats his summons:

Giant Armadillo Spirit, descend into me!

12

When the *hekura* finally appears, the shaman incarnates the animal. He resumes his dance and his chant:

I am the Giant Armadillo Spirit! I am the Giant Armadillo Spirit!

He is near the patient, he crawls under his back. His claws, his powerful limbs dig in and throw out the black bees' gluey honey, free the imprisoned organs and the body from its oppression.

Kaōmawë has called the Spirit of a stone, hard and sharp as quartz, milky as latex: It is *kakuruwë*, that tears, saws, slices, lacerates, and adds its strength to the terrible might of the giant armadillo. When the viscous stuff is fully broken up and torn to shreds, the two shamans lay the patient on the ground so as to move about him more easily. Then they remove the evil honey, banish it to the underworld where it will contaminate a people of strange, hairless beings, the *amahiri*.

When the three shamans are exhausted from the intensity of the battle they have sustained, they order that the patient be taken back to his hearth.

One doesn't make love with a woman who is nursing. The consequence of violating this interdiction is contained in the expression that defines it: "damaging a child." They believe that a new pregnancy would be fatal to the baby: It would die of violent colic. Sexual intercourse is prohibited until the process of weaning begins, when the child is at least two, so that births are usually spaced about three years apart. Whatever the deep and true reason for this practice may be, its consequences work hand in hand with infanticide (not as frequent as is claimed) as well as war to limit the rate of demographic growth and keep it within reasonable bounds. Let there be no mistake, however: The Indians of South America were in an expansionary phase at the time of the conquest, and the continent was far from being the human wasteland that was imagined so complacently. As recently as the 1950s, thanks to the exceptional advantage of their isolation, the Yanomami population was on the increase, and it has been possible to trace in some detail the last stages of their territorial expansion.

Kaōmawë is dreaming that he is about to damage a child. He wants to make love with a woman who is nursing a newborn. The reluctant woman makes as if to withdraw. He begs her:

Don't go away, we'll copulate only once. After that I'll withdraw.
No, my child is still too young. I am stained with the blood of childbirth.
Once only, let's make love only once. I won't come back again.

As he is speaking, he presses the woman's waist between his thighs. She entreats:

Insert only the tip of your penis, don't put it in all the way!

He is unable to control himself: He penetrates her deeply and performs coitus.

13

Later he approaches another woman. Her pubis is adorned with a thick growth of hair, she is plump and light-complexioned: a beauty. He lies down beside her, strokes her genitals, and says:

Let's make love.
We don't value each other enough for that.
We have always respected each other. Today I desire you.

He talks, continues to caress her pubis, and soon continues:

Will you let me fondle your vulva? Let's see if it gives you pleasure.

She doesn't answer but laughs into her hands, which amounts to an acquiescence. He lets his hand drop to her genitals and feels the softness of the vulva under his fingers. He is thinking:

Here I am, handling a vulva; my fingers will smell bad!

An odd feeling wakes him. He opens his eyes and guesses that daylight is near: A slight breeze cools the air, the motmot bird voices its ceaseless *hutu, hutu.* He gets up and goes to urinate at the low side of the shelter. He revives the fire, and the bright flames enable him to see that his bitch is about to give birth. He rouses Mabroma, his wife, to give her the news. Although she is more than four years old, Kerama still sleeps with her mother, who now carefully slides away from her so as not to wake her while leaving the hammock. She glances at the animal and picks up a few leaves that she places under her. They want to witness the birth, but they will have to wait patiently till daylight. In a mocking mood, Hebewë and Kremoanawë observe the scene. Hebëwë scoffs:

They are Yēbiwë's offspring!

They all join in the jesting: Yēbiwë goes into the forest alone with his dog to copulate with it.

Meanwhile the placenta slowly emerges. Tirelessly Mabroma mutters in a low voice:

They'll be males, they'll be males . . .

Indeed, she prefers male dogs. The placenta, however, stops its slow outward progress. The bitch, growing impatient, makes as if to rise; Mabroma shouts at her:

Push, push and stay down!

Finally, three pups are born: two females and a male. Mabroma is only half-satisfied.

The whole family leaves to gather bananas in the garden. The two boys are not going there with the intention of helping their parents; that idea does not dawn on them. They are going in order to suck on sugarcane and to find out whether a papaya or two might not be ripe. When they return to the great shelter, they discover that the bitch has eaten her young. Mabroma, in a rage,

14

beats the animal mercilessly and ties her legs. Like all Yanomami dogs, the poor beast is pitifully thin. She is persecuted all day long. Mabroma's ire grows as the day progresses, so that before long blows and insults are no longer enough to compensate for the loss of the pups. Finally, in exasperation, she picks up a glowing brand and applies it to the animal's genitals. Howls of pain! The flesh crackles and burns, emitting a sickening smell. Kerama, risking a bite, is curious to inspect the wound: She spreads the hind legs and exclaims, amused:

Her vagina is all cooked!

Hebëwë disapproves. He mutters:

When I see Yanomami who behave so cruelly, I feel like being far away from them.

Yet he himself is hardly a tender soul, and not always kind to animals.

Dogs have only recently been introduced among the Yanomami. When the people of Karohi dwelled at Shitoya, shortly after 1940, there were hardly more than one or two in each community. A long time before that, when the Indians were living at Husiwarë, at the beginning of this century, dogs were extremely rare and reached a given local group only after a long journey and through the complicated workings of economic and matrimonial bartering. The dog's late arrival did not prevent its complete integration into the cultural system. It is the cultural animal par excellence; yet it is given no specific name, for it is known by the word *hiima,* which is used to designate any tame animal.

The Indians do not eat the animals they raise, and when this possibility is suggested to them, they declare that only true cannibals are capable of such an action. If such a crime were committed, it would be subject to the same supernatural sanctions and the same illnesses that would punish a murderer who failed to submit to the *unokai* ritual. The Yanomami, like all forest Indians, have tame animals. But they have no domestic animals, and it is probably for the following reason: What good is it to assemble a herd or raise a flock if it is impossible to eat the animals produced? Food received from a human hand is the agent that makes possible the transition from the state of nature to the state of culture; it transcends the original reality. A newborn that has not yet nursed is still of neutral status, a thing in transition; it is not altogether a being, and it is possible to kill it if it displays a patent congenital malformation or if it is not wanted by its parents. Infanticide becomes impossible as soon as the child has sucked the mother's milk even once.

Dogs are cultural animals, even more so than other animals; like human beings they have names, like them they are entitled to shamanistic treatment, and like human beings they are burned when they die. Their ashes are buried, and dogs that were good hunters are honored through a little funeral meal.

The Yanomami are fond of dogs, but they mistreat them and feed them poorly; only their existence counts.

Hebëwë's parents have always had bad luck with their dogs. Formerly they owned one named Ïrahikibowë. They were proud of it: It was an excellent helpmate in the hunt and was unequaled when it came to dislodging a tapir or following the trail of an agouti; it was alert and had a good nose. One day Kaõmawë went hunting with his brother. The dog set off on the track of a peccary; it was baying and one could tell that it was glued to the trail, when it suddenly fell silent. The two brothers searched for it a long time to no avail. It was dead when they found it. From the tracks and the remains they learned that the dog, intent on the chase, had come upon a jaguar busy devouring a tamandua. The cat had left its prey to pounce on the dog and kill it; it was enormous, judging from its tracks and its fangs – as big as Brazil nuts – which had opened a neck wound that was clean, deep, and fatal.

The hunters wept and swore revenge. They began by building a kind of platform in the lower branches of a tree, where they could take cover; then they tied the carcass of the tamandua to a stake, thinking that the cat would come back to feed on it. After a while the jaguar appeared; it was snarling in an ugly way, its tail whipped the air, and it was the dog's body it was after. Kaõmawë pulled his *briki* bow; the arrow flew, but the shot was badly aimed and lost itself among the vegetation. Then the younger brother also let fly; the lanceolate tip sank into the beast's side. It made an enormous leap and disappeared into the underbrush where the brothers were unable to find it: They wanted to sever its head in order to burn it in the central plaza of the shelter and thus destroy the teeth that had inflicted death. Upon their return they burned the dog's body, which they had brought back, and buried the ashes behind the shelter. They gave a ceremonial meal in his honor with meat and boiled bananas.

One day a woman returning from the forest announced:

There's a jaguar over there. We found its bones.

. . . One last time Kerama examines the "cooked vagina" of the hapless bitch, then she joins other children who are playing in the central plaza. There are three boys and a little girl; Kerama is the smallest of them all. The children make fun of one another; they accuse one another of having a big asshole. Each shows the other the anus he attributes to him. The ring formed by thumb and index finger no longer suffices to indicate the size; soon they need their arms. When he runs out of arguments, Haotoiwë spreads his buttocks and shouts at the others, who have banded against him:

Here! Here's my asshole that farts on you!

A large butterfly flutters by; to prevent it from flying away Kerama says to it:

16

Ashes and tears

Mother-in-law, mother-in-law, I'm thirsty!

That's what one must say to catch butterflies. Unheeding, the gaudy wings escape the child's nimble fingers.

Suddenly the children suspend their game and the adults their conversation in order to listen to Morayema quarrel with her cohusband, Mokaukawë. She shouts:

Go on, you with your strutting and showing off! Who'll get your wood when I stop doing it? You'll shiver with cold at night, you'll sneak about stealing logs from those who are asleep. You ugly mug! The child you made me has such a big head that he must have at least two brains.

Let him die and then you'll grieve. And if that misfortune should happen, I'll say: "Look at the hammock in which I sleep, black with grime because you never wash it!"

Your garden is so small that everyone makes fun of it. We, my husband and I, we're the ones who have to feed you.

You know that I can't increase my plot because it's surrounded by others.

Open a new clearing behind the garden.

The quarrel goes on; it exhausts the same old themes constantly rehearsed: It is not the first time that Morayema and Mokaukawë quarrel. Together with Shõnikiwë, they form a polyandrous household. A second husband to Morayema through the good graces of Shõnikiwë his elder brother, Mokaukawë's status forever condemns him to share the fate of those adolescents who do premarital service in the households of their parents-in-law. Indeed, the status of cohusband entails the obligation of providing the household with game and performing the most menial tasks: the same tasks that fall to a young man in the service of his bride's parents. But Mokaukawë is no longer a young man. He keeps a separate household and receives from Morayema cooked food and firewood. His precarious and dependent status forces him to beg the favors of a wife that his brother grants him only grudgingly.

The Yanomami haven't much liking for work; but Mokaukawë is lazy to excess, and this attitude, which is natural to him, stands in contradiction to the special obligations of his status. Hence his irritability, his resentment, and the altercations with Morayema. He is recognized as the father of Morayema's boy, but without the privileges of paternity or the possibility of lavishing upon his son the affection he feels. The mother, who is sometimes brutal with the child, tolerates no reproach on that score, certain as she is of enjoying Shõnikiwë's protection.

In a society where the ratio of women to men is eight to ten and where, moreover, polygyny is permitted, some are unavoidably left out. Some young men prolong their celibacy; others have no alternative but to share someone else's wife. One can easily imagine the conflicts indirectly caused by women and the competition among men for their possession.

When, finally, the voices have died down, dusk is near and Kremoanawë leaves to hunt partridges. He returns as night is darkening, empty-handed.

17

He is walking with measured steps; he can already make out the dark mass of the shelter at the end of the path when he hears whispering and glimpses vague movements in the nearby vegetation. He stops, on the alert. He thinks enemy raiders are waiting in ambush, or else sorcerers who have come to cast evil spells. His hands tense on his bow; slowly he slides an arrow along the shaft and nocks it. He is already sighting, when a voice calls from the nearby shelter:

Rutʰemi! What are you doing?

Right next to him, in the bushes, a voice whispers:

Your mother's calling you.

A female voice answers:

Let's go back.

Kremoanawë understands: it is Rutʰemi and Moriwë hiding just off the path and making love. He says:

What are you doing? Here I was taking you for enemies!

He does not listen to their answer and goes away, half annoyed at his mistake, half amused at the disturbance he has caused.

The lineage to which Hitisiwë and his brothers belong is not native to Karohi. Their father was born among the groups further upriver, where he lived until the age of sixteen or seventeen; he had then come to Karohi to marry Ka- õmawë's sister, had stayed, and had founded a family. Of a person who thus settles within his in-laws' group it is said: "He was captured during his marital service."

Sons-in-law generally prefer to go back to their own group after having spent a year or two in the service of their parents-in-law.

Hitisiwë's father is dead, no doubt carried away by malaria. The main branch of his lineage stayed with the groups upstream, divided among three neighboring communities.

Within two days the young man's state of health has grown desperate: He cannot eat or drink, nor get up or even speak; it is as if his jaws were locked. Since the local shamans were unable to check the illness, the possibility was considered to send for a relative from upriver, a good shaman in his own right, who might perhaps have succeeded where the others proved powerless. The plan is debated, but it is already too late: A heart-rending sob announces the young man's death.

A great clamor rises and soon spreads over the whole collective shelter: sobs, funereal lamentations, endless wails. In a moment the women are near the deceased, sitting on the bare ground; they beat their sides, clap their hands; big tears roll down their cheeks. Soon the men arrive and place them-

18

Hitisiwë shortly before his death.

19

selves in the rear; some sit down, others remain standing, holding their bows and arrows upright in front of them. Numerous fingers run over the now lifeless breast and clutch as if to tear it; others smooth down the hair. The dead man's face is surprisingly relaxed and peaceful. The eyelids have been pressed together. His lower lip still retains the perennial plug of tobacco, revealed by the half-opened mouth. His complexion is pale, yellowish; his hands, hardly clenched, are drawn up on his chest. His two brothers are there; in a grief-stricken daze, they repeat over and over:

Little brother! Little brother!

Their voices are cracked by sorrow and broken by heavy sobs. Hebëwë and Kremoanawë are at their hearth. Their hammocks sway to the tremors of their bodies. They too are weeping:

My brother-in-law! Oh, my brother-in-law!

Everyone expresses his sorrow to the dead man, invoking the kinship that linked them.

A messenger is dispatched without delay to the relatives at Tayari. They soon arrive. There is Mamikiyima and her two sons, Bokorawë, the shaman, accompanied by his wife and his pretty little daughter, and several others. The hot-blooded Ebrëwë strides around the central plaza; he has seized the deceased's bow, snaps the string against the shaft, and brandishes arrows with their tips removed. Others precede or follow him. Each carries an object that belonged to the dead youth and displays it one last time to the whole group. Bokorawë's wife dances and keeps up her funereal lamentations: She is holding two skeins of fishing line, a quiver hangs on her back; but the strap, instead of passing around the neck as is customary, rests on the woman's forehead. Morayema, the dead man's mother-in-law – he was to marry her daughter – holds aloft two packages of rolled tobacco and some cotton armbands. Shõnikiwë, the father-in-law, brandishes a machete.

A whole crowd is milling in the center of the shelter. And it will soon be time to burn these things now publicly displayed, for no possessions must henceforth recall a presence that they will try to abolish in all its material manifestations. Already some have gone to the garden to pull up the magic plants and cut down the palm trees that belonged to Hitisiwë. Shõnikiwë's hoarse voice can be heard singing the praises of his son-in-law:

He was fierce and courageous, fearing neither blows nor pain. He was never afraid, he was always the first to fight the enemies. He was a perfect hunter.

Ebrëwë, still carrying the bow, stops before a narrow passage that opens outside onto a path. He says:

Oh, you, my son-in-law, through this door you will never pass again. This bow that I am carrying and that belonged to you will not be used again to kill game. Oh, my son-in-law, never again will your arrows pierce curassows and tapirs.

20

Yet anger can be sensed hidden beneath the grief. It bursts forth in precise accusations. They need people they can hold responsible for this death. The guilty ones are found: They are the southern Yanomami, the terrible *Shama-t^hari*, the enemies, the *nabë*. It is now established for certain that the youth is a victim of their spells; their evil shamans have sent the *hekura* to bring death to Karohi. Female voices, so high-pitched as to be unbearable, call for vengeance. The men, they say, must show no slackness; they must return blow for blow and death for death. If we do not retaliate ruthlessly, the enemies, emboldened by our weakness, will keep at us and deal us one setback after another: Our tears will not cease flowing. This is what the women say, especially the old ones who have seen many things in the course of a long life.

Indifferent to all this, the little children go on with their games, and at times their high spirits break into the painful manifestations of collective mourning. But the tumult decreases; one by one the adults finally return to their homes. Wishami roasts green bananas; a bunch of fish lies on the coals. Exhausted, Kaõmawë swallows a slice of papaya before dozing off. Mabroma treats her brood to boiled fish and plantain. Hebëwë notices that the three-holed flute he has just fashioned is cracked; he interrupts his tears to make sure that the instrument still works. Everywhere people are eating; night is approaching. The dead man is now alone, his hammock is abandoned. The monotony of daily routine, the automatism of familiar gestures performed without thinking reassert themselves.

Night falls. As she does every night, Mabroma lights a fire next to her two sons, who have their own households. By living apart from their parents and their sisters, the two boys are expressing their need for independence. Hebëwë lies down; he sees Baiwë settle down to keep vigil next to his brother's body, build a fire that is soon burning brightly, fold down the flaps of the hammock over his rigid limbs. A few sobs begin again, soon snuffed out by sleep. Suddenly Hebëwë notices something moving awkwardly between the logs propped up against the base of the roof to provide effective protection against wild animals, enemies, nocturnal spirits, and ghosts. He stirs the fire and discovers a greenish toad. It is called *kunamaru*. The boy begins to speak to it softly, almost respectfully:

Remove yourself, go away, don't stay here: You can see that I'm not sick.

He must at all cost get rid of the beast without handling it roughly. It is said that it goes at night to sit on the chests of sleepers, whom it douses with its noxious urine. The reason one must show it consideration is that it was formerly a famous shaman; and if, by ill luck, one were to kill it or wound it, others would surely come to avenge it.

Peaceful is the night. The sky is cloudless; the moon is in its first quarter and the firmament teems with stars. Far away in the forest one can make out

21

the muffled cries of a flock of agamis. All along the banks of the "river of rains" and in the nearby swamps, toads of all kinds croak frantically. Sometimes one is startled by the mournful song of a whippoorwill.

At daybreak the women have blackened cheeks as a sign of mourning. The process they use to obtain that beautiful, almost lacquered black color that adheres so strongly to their skin remains a mystery. When asked, they all claim that they merely mix their tears with the grime on their cheeks. But it seems impossible that they could by this means obtain that mat black, so well defined, that forms a crust on their faces as if they had used putty. Even on dirty skin, tears only leave yellowish streaks. When it is suggested that the marks they bear on their cheeks might have been concocted with an admixture of ashes and charcoal, the women, even when questioned privately, unequivocally deny it: a jealous determination to keep a secret. Black is for women a symbol of mourning; the white down of birds of prey is exclusively reserved for men.

Shōnikiwë has started to clean the central plaza in front of his home. Ebrëwë and Ubrawë cut small round logs and split big ones. People have again gathered around the corpse, still in his hammock, this time for a final farewell. Funeral dances and lamentations begin again, as well as the display of the dead man's possessions. Mabroma carries her little girl astride on her hip. Bomamoma, the blind woman, leaning on a stick, her large blank eyes turned up toward the sky, loses her way in the center of the plaza because she wanted to participate in the macabre ritual.

And presently the pyre for the cremation is built on the very spot that Shōnikiwë has just cleaned. Ebrëwë sets down a base of round logs arranged side by side, then a framework of crossed split logs in the shape of a rectangle. In the center he places shavings and dry twigs, then gathers embers and glowing coals from different hearths. Vigorously fanned, the fire soon flares up. There remains only to reinforce the framework by sinking sturdy stakes on each side.

Suddenly a terrifying clamor spreads throughout the great shelter. Ebrëwë bangs his machete against the posts that support the roof. Shouting, weeping, and moaning grow in intensity. Everybody crowds around the dead man; the women are sitting, the men are standing and have brought their weapons. Ebrëwë and Kaōmawë untie the hammock in which the dead man is resting and, each carrying one end, place it on the pyre. Flames are already engulfing the corpse, the hammock is already catching fire, when Hebëwë hastily covers the corpse with a layer of logs. Everyone has stepped back, except Bomamoma, who is frantic, having been caught in the thick smoke rising from the pyre. And that smoke is full of the evil demons of disease, the *shawara,* that rise with it, having been released by the cremation. The poor old woman, panic-stricken, doesn't know where to run; she is choking, her hands are groping about uselessly. No one has noticed her plight, except

Mabroma, who orders Remaema to lead her back to her hammock. Meanwhile Kaõmawë destroys the feathered butts of the arrows that belonged to Hitisiwë; he has snapped the shafts, broken the bow, and thrown everything into the devouring fire.

All is peaceful again. One is left with the impression that at times the community is stricken by a brutal amnesia that ends as suddenly as it began, producing this dramatic alternation of excessive despair and feigned indifference. The dissociation between duty, ritual, and daily life is almost perfect: It is strange, inconceivable to our minds. Not all the dead man's possessions have yet been consigned to the fire. The remainder are entrusted for safekeeping to several persons until such time as they will have to be relinquished for destruction. Since everyone vies for that honor, the distribution is accompanied by quarrels and negotiations. Mabroma has insisted that she be entrusted with some lanceolate arrowheads. She proudly shows them to Hebëwë, to whom she says:

These, my son, are your brother-in-law's possessions.

Her eyes, her cheeks are wet with tears, and her voice expresses infinite sadness. Mabroma wraps her son-in-law's possessions in an old piece of cloth and secures them in a small basket hanging from the underside of the roof.

A group of men have gathered to chat at Shõnikiwë's home. Vengeance must be taken on the enemy shamans, but reprisals are put off till later. They criticize the missionary at Mavaca, who wants to take away the small children in order to lock them into a boarding school, who means to impose his will on the Indians and is miserly; the people of Karohi do not want to hand over their boys and bristle when they are given orders. They chat about one thing and another, pass on the news, give their views of events. From time to time, Ebrëwë leaves the gathering to pile up the coals and embers of the funeral pyre. He finds the dead man's skull exposed, a mound of dissolving flesh is on the verge of collapsing. He rearranges things with a long stick, lifting, shifting, and consolidating. Then he adds some wood before returning to his place in the group.

Baiwë has brought back from the forest a *kanaye* log stripped of its bark, about one meter long and twenty-five centimeters across. It will be hollowed out for a mortar in which the charred bones of the deceased will be crushed. The inside is worked with a machete and the sides are hardened in the fire. It is arduous and meticulous work, at which Baiwë, Frërema, and Shimiwë take turns. When the mortar is ready, its inner surface is dyed with roucou and each end is adorned with a strip of white down.

The pyre has gone out by itself. In late afternoon, when it has cooled, the two brothers of the dead man go to gather the bony remains. They squat, depositing the bones in baskets; only their right hands are working, while the

23

left hands rest on their thighs. Finally they sweep the place of cremation, removing all ashes and charcoals. The ground then appears clean, dried by the heat, and hard; the Indians say that it is "cooked," as the soil of a garden is "cooked" for the plantings following the burning of the vegetation, after the spreading of the coals; one wouldn't cultivate a "raw" soil.

The two brothers crush the bones in the mortar, careful to produce a perfectly fine powder that they pour into gourds tinted red with roucou and hermetically sealed with beeswax. Shōnikiwë as father-in-law and Baiwë as elder brother each receives a gourd. A third is put aside: The relatives from Warabawë will come to claim their share of the dead man. Later the mortar will be converted into firewood.

Hitisiwë from now on belongs to the past; he must be completely forgotten. His name must not be mentioned for any reason. The bone dust and the last possessions of the dead man will disappear in the course of appropriate ceremonies. The young man's past existence must be erased; nothing may recall it to the living.

Hebëwë has remained melancholy. He says to his father:

I'm afraid of death. I have a foreboding that I'll never become a mature man; I'll disappear first. Diseases will carry me away, I'll be eaten by a jaguar or bitten by a snake. I know that my life will be brief, and that makes me want to cry. Why must we die? What is it like in the land of souls?

Kaōmawë replies:

We shall die because of the smoke and because of Caiman.

And then Kaōmawë recalls the myth of the origin of fire:

Long ago it was Caiman who possessed fire. He lived in a land inhabited by the "Waika," near a river called the river "of the two who have eaten their tongues." That's where Caiman used to go together with his wife to cook caterpillars without being seen. In those days, indeed, the Yanomami had no knowledge of the use of fire and ate their food raw: One could hear the noise of their chewing. One day, the daughter of the colored partridge, Bokorariyoma, discovered while scratching the ground the remains of charred leaves and a cooked caterpillar dropped by mistake. She brought back her find, and an examination of it led to the conclusion that Caiman possessed fire and that he cooked his food. They agreed among themselves:

We'll have fun and make him laugh!

When Caiman returned followed by his wife, Brueheyoma, a small-sized frog, they gathered around them. Caiman had a package on which he had placed the raw caterpillars he wanted to give away, taking care to place underneath those he wanted to eat himself. They started their games and their pranks, but Caiman didn't even smile at their clowning. They pissed on each other. When it was Hummingbird's turn, he raised his rump and sent a stream of liquid excrement splashing all over the spectators. Caiman was hiding the fire in his mouth; he burst out laughing and dropped it. The Yorekitirawë bird seized it immediately, but he was unable to rise very high, and Brueheyoma threatened to extinguish the fire by pissing on it. That's when another bird, Kanaboromi, came to the rescue and deposited the fire high up in a tree. Caiman gave vent to his anger. This is what he said to the Yanomami:

24

Ashes and tears

Child roasting caterpillars.

25

> This fire that you just took from me, this eternal fire will cause you sufferings: Its smoke will bring you illness and make you die; it will consume your bodies. Your bones will be pulverized. I alone will remain immortal in the cool water where I am going to live.

Kaōmawë went on:

> Our ancestors were immortal; they ceased being immortal when they had possession of fire. Souls leave the body at the time of death. They rise along the ropes of the hammocks and climb up the supporting posts of the shelter to go to live on the celestial disk. When the body is burned, the soul suffers, its nose, its eyes start to glow, but its general appearance is exactly that of the body to which it belonged. In the land of souls, the forest is the same as the one down here; there is plenty of fruit, honey and game; wild pigs roam there in large bands. The souls are gathered together in a great shelter and Thunder rules over them. Lightning is the son of Thunder; his beauty is marvelous; he couples incestuously with his mother. In the dwelling of the souls lives Hera; he is a demon, master of the snakes he wears about his body: They are his charmed animals. Sometimes Hera simulates death; then his mouth exhales a foul stench; his head bends sideways; a vile saliva oozes from the side of his mouth and runs along his cheek. The souls think that he is really dead; they bustle about, weep, and dance in the central plaza. Thunder orders them to build the pyre and burn the body. But when the flames are leaping high and the souls are about to untie the hammock in which he lies, Hera comes back to life and sneers sardonically.
>
> Those Yanomami who in life have been too mean with their possessions do not go into the great dwelling of the souls. Crouching at the edge of a path is a hideously ugly being: It is Watawatawë. He shows their lost souls the route they must follow; they then travel along a narrow trail that curves around a big hill. Behind that hill is a gigantic blaze, the *shobari kë wakœ,* enclosed in a huge new and tender leaf: The souls are drawn to it, they fall into it and are consumed. There is also the underworld of the *amahiri,* who are fashioned like us, except that they are hairless. Their land is like ours; they have dwellings similar to our *shabono,* they practice hunting and have gardens. To their country our shamans send the evil demons they want to get rid of after drawing them out of sick peoples' bodies. The *amahiri* are contaminated by them, and sometimes, to take revenge, they enter our world in order to capture Yanomami souls. We look to them as the celestial disk looks to us: The rays of the sun reach them, for our ground is transparent to them. It is said that other Yanomami living far to the north do not treat the dead as we do. At the meal of the eating of the ashes, they paint their bodies with red ochre, then trace on that background darker motifs with a substance into which they have mixed the bone dust of the dead man. To show their great bereavement, the women strike the men with clubs. The remainder of the bone dust is then mixed with banana soup in a pottery container.

This is what Kaōmawë explains at length to his saddened son.

A month has gone by when it is decided to organize the first meal for the eating of the dead man's ashes. Shōnikiwë goes to his garden and brings back four bunches of plantains that he promptly hangs under the shelter's roof in front of his hearth. As leader of a faction and titular father-in-law of the deceased, Kaōmawë also wants to bear some of the cost of the ceremony. Consequently there will be two long-range hunts and two distributions of meat. Kaōmawë ties seven bunches under his roof: Bunches of bananas thus

26

ostentatiously put up to ripen in the great shelter always indicate the quarters of an important man. This hanging of the plantains signals the beginning of a hunting ritual called *heri* that is regularly associated with a funeral meal.

Four days later the bananas have slightly changed color, indicating that they will soon be ripe. As night approaches, Kaōmawë urges the hunters of his faction to start out no later than tomorrow: The bananas will soon be yellow. He also points out that the birds are wreaking destruction on the plantings, that the gardens are not large enough, and that it is necessary to start working new clearings lest food run short. When he ends his harangue, he turns to his dog, to whom he says abruptly:

> As for you, you mustn't shit here. You must go outside the shelter, or you'll be beaten.

Taking advantage of the last gleamings of dusk, some children are playing with an inflated anteater bladder that they throw up in the air. Others play at war; they act like brave warriors and shoot against each other's buttocks small, sharp-tipped arrows that sometimes stick in the skin and draw blood.

The next morning at break of dawn, two groups of hunters start out; one is led by Baiwë, the other by Shōnikiwë. Both are keepers of a gourd containing Hitisiwë's ashes. One group will proceed upstream along the bank of the "river of rains" so as to reach former hunting grounds; the other will cross the river to head north.

Everyone is disappointed when they return after an absence of five days: there is little game, and the feast will not be plentiful.

While the women hang the cooked meat on a wooden grill – the buccan – over the fires, the hunters refresh themselves, anoint their bodies with roucou and brown dye, adjust their ornaments of colorful birds' feathers, and gather to take part in the inhaling of hallucinogenic powder.

Meanwhile, Shimoreiwë circles in front of the shelter; he takes hold of each post supporting the forward section of the roof, shakes it while invoking the name of Boreawë, master of the plantain. By doing this Shimoreiwë hopes to hasten the flowering of the banana trees: All the important men of Karohi are worried about the insufficient yield of the gardens.

In the meantime, some have gone to gather green plantains, which they peel with their teeth. These are put to boil at the same time as the meat, but in different containers, on big fires set under the high section of the roof or on the perimeter of the central plaza; it is the men who take care of those fires and of cooking the food intended for the ceremony. They had to sort out the caimans from the game they brought back, as these are unfit for funeral meals; so there remains only just enough to fulfill the ritual.

Tears and lamentations pick up sporadically. Baiwë's grief-stricken lament can be heard:

> My little brother! My little brother!

27

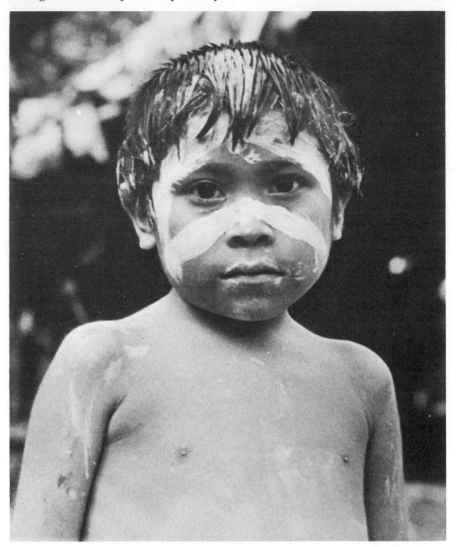

Child with his face painted with clay.

For all this, Ebrëwë's obscene jokes do not let up, nor the laughter they provoke.

Mabroma finishes spinning a big ball of cotton; she contemplates her work with satisfaction and says:

I'll barter it for a dog with "those upriver."

Brahaima spinning cotton.

Ashes and tears

Taromi is intoxicated with *yakōana* drug, as he is every day; this drug is prepared from the bark of a tree. Ebrëwë looks at him with a contemptuous pout and delivers the following judgment:

> He inhales only the *yakōana* drug, which ages you before your time when taken to excess. Look at his buttocks, already furrowed and slack!

Next day everything is finally ready when the sun reaches the zenith. The ripe plantains, now yellow and nicely sweet, are peeled for the banana soup. They are boiled in water for a long time, after which they are crushed with a many-branched stick; the paste is then thinned with cold water until a good consistency is obtained.

The little blood-sucking gnats are so numerous that some people have hung their hammocks high under the shelter's roof in order to escape their pestering.

Baiwë has prepared a basket full of boiled plantains and meat, which he offers to Arusiwë. At a funeral meal, the one who provides the food never distributes it himself. He delegates that task to a person he wishes to honor; sometimes the choice falls on a visitor, on someone who doesn't belong to the community. Arusiwë, quite flattered when the basket is placed before him, cannot suppress a smile of satisfaction. Shōnikiwë bestows the offering on a guest recently arrived from a neighboring community. A general distribution of banana soup is made at the same time, but care is taken that enough is kept for the funeral ceremony.

Suddenly weeping begins again. The men gather and rattle bunches of arrows in their fists; everyone assembles in front of Baiwë's hearth. Ebrëwë fills a large calabash with steaming banana soup; he adds the light gray dust of the crushed bones, which he mixes in with his right hand only. He hands the mixture to Kaōmawë who swallows it in great gulps, without even pausing for breath. Shimiwë and Warami, the maternal uncle and aunt, and Baiwë, the elder brother of the dead man, also swallow the mixture. A similar ceremony takes place at Shōnikiwë's, who is, with his wife, the only one to drink the bones. Those who have consumed the funeral ashes receive no portion of meat: Game would cause them agonizing stomachaches.

All manifestations of grief suddenly cease. Everyone returns to his or her work. They spin, they chat, children squabble. The two half-empty gourds are replaced in their little red baskets: Enough powder remains for a second ceremony. In a year's time perhaps.

30

2

Love stories

The young Yanomami's sexuality is not repressed as long as it remains discreet and limited. In this respect it corresponds to that of the adults. Although they are invested with a unique meaning, the sexual organs are nevertheless organs like any other, and hence subject to playful explorations. Adults speak openly of sexuality and reproductive functions; the role of human copulation and the pleasure it gives are not hidden from children. Everything here is very natural.

Children and adolescents do occasionally indulge in sodomy. They speak of it only cautiously, for like masturbation it is a marginal sexual activity that remains the very private concern of those who practice it; but it does not engender any feeling of guilt, which, like repentance, is rightly banished from Indian morality. Accusations of sodomy are rarely uttered; when they are they elicit only weak protests from the suspects. It isn't worth taking offense, and that is a measure of the slight importance that, ultimately, they ascribe to this activity. One can frequently see boys of all ages simulate it publicly in their games; often brothers-in-law are involved, for these are usually devoted to each other through mutual and lasting affection. Homosexual practices, though more frequent in this kinship category, are not exceptional between brothers or first cousins. If it is scandalous to "eat the vagina" of a sister – that is the Indians' expression for coitus – there is no shame in "eating the anus" of one's brother: Society dictates the exchange of daughters and sisters, but it does not codify sexual practices between persons of the same sex. It must be pointed out, however, that homosexual relations between brothers-in-law are different from relations between brothers. In the first case a shared feeling of friendship binds two young men who exchange women and material belongings and consider each other as equals; a homosexual relationship with a brother-in-law prefigures the future heterosexual relationship with his sister – it is in a way a waiting situation. In the second case the relationship is circumstantial: It can dispense with good feelings and occurs between unequal partners. Within the group of first cousins and parallel

31

cousins, the older have authority over the younger, and it is the first who "eat the anus" of the second.

Like all young Indians, Hebëwë was both precocious and indiscriminate in his early sexuality – the guiding principle being that everything pleasurable is good in itself. Of the gropings of childhood he speaks with discretion but without shame, as of a bygone period. The few people he confides in are the youths of his own age group whom he trusts and who, in many cases, were his confederates.

He remembers that he and other children used to make holes in the ground with their fingers; they moistened the sides with water or saliva before inserting their members. They made believe that the hole was a vagina and that they were making love with a woman. Needless to say, they obtained no pleasure by such crude means. One of them, a bit older, achieved orgasm by simulating coitus with a gourd – one of those that are used to make calabashes. One day, Hebëwë went fishing with Yebiwë. Yebiwë caught a ray; it was big and bore beautiful designs on its back. That species' tail is armed with a powerful spine with which it stings the foolhardy, leaving in the wound a quantity of poisonous barbs that cause excruciating pain. Yebiwë cut off the tail and resumed his fishing. He ran out of earthworms and went to look for more, leaving the child alone at the riverbank. Taking advantage of that moment of solitude, Hebëwë stuck his penis into the ray. It seemed at first discouragingly cold, but he persevered and claims to have experienced some pleasure. Another day, Hebëwë joined a group of adult men who were going to an evangelist missionary's house to ask for various objects. The white was miserly. He haggled over the quantity and wanted the Indians to earn what they were going to take by working or participating in prayers. Hebëwë was bored to death. He went out, loitered about, and discovered some chickens scratching for food. Without giving it much thought, he started chasing them, succeeded in cornering one of them, and took it away into the bushes. What to do with the beast? He tried to copulate with it, but the bird kept squealing and struggling. Losing patience and fearing discovery, Hebëwë broke its skull against a tree and threw it into the Orinoco. He looked most innocent when he went back into the missionary's house.

When they were boys, three "brothers" – Hebëwë, Kremoanawë, and Moriwë – were all courting the young Rut^{h}emi. Of all the girls of Karohi, she was the only one available to them; when addressing her they used a kinship term signifying "wife." The scarcity of potential wives has always been bothersome to the male children of Karohi. To obtain a woman and marry her, they have no other alternative but to commit incest or to perform in a foreign community the premarital service they owe their parents-in-law. That is why so many men of Karohi have settled elsewhere. The rest of this narrative shows clearly enough the consequences of that situation for Hebëwë and Moriwë.

32

The Orinoco near Mavaca.

The three boys were confederates rather than rivals, and they did everything they could to gain the little lady's favors. They succeeded one day in inducing her to go with them into the forest on the pretext that they wanted to gather *hayu* fruits, which are the size and color of cherries and quite delicious. The girl was smart and experienced enough to be aware of their hidden motives, and it is virtually certain that if she consented to go with them she accepted the risks. They first played at swinging on a vine that swept low toward the ground, made a loop, and climbed back up to the top of a tree. They shouted themselves hoarse and swung each other so high that they squealed with fright. Kremoanawë was the first to come to the heart of the matter:

Suppose we made love?

Ruthemi pouted and made as if to refuse; it was an affectation on her part, for she evidently took pleasure in annoying the boys. Kremoanawë wasn't fooled; he drew her aside, away from the trail; then it was Moriwë's turn. The girl was a virgin of course, and they merely rubbed their organs on her vulva without penetrating her. When it was Hebëwë's turn, he pretended to take his time, let the older boys leave first, and remained alone with his

33

Moriwë.

girlfriend. They tarried so long that their absence caused anxiety in the forest camp. The parents asked each other:

Where are they? What are they doing?

Kremoanawë, who had just returned, impishly declared:

They are making love.

Greatly worried, the adults imagined the most improbable accidents. They hurried down the trail after the children, calling to them as they went. They saw them walking back in a leisurely manner, oblivious to the excitement they were causing.

Hebëwë's first true passion was triggered by a young girl from Wayaboto-rewë. Her name was Bawahoma. Her parents having died a long time ago, she lived with her grandmother whom she helped with domestic chores. They had come to spend some time at Karohi. Sometimes Hebëwë went to her in her hammock; in that case he had to be cautious, for the grandmother was jealous of her granddaughter and couldn't bear the idea of her having a lover. Sometimes Bawahoma waited until the old lady was asleep before meeting Hebëwë; then they were certain of being undisturbed, for the boy's parents adopted an attitude of indifference, even complicity – it certainly looked as though they avoided stirring the fire too often, so as not to disturb their lovemaking. During the day they met in the forest. Even now, when he is on the trail, Hebëwë points out the many places where he went with her. Once he had the pleasure of keeping her with him an entire night. They loved each other very much. She was playful; she used to bite him until he bled; she tore strips out of his linen loincloths, so that he lost a great many. On one occasion she said to him:

Let's paint our bodies with roucou!

Don't think of it: The others will discover our relationship and watch us.

Indeed, when two young people paint themselves for each other's sake, they are immediately suspected of being in love. So she confined herself to spreading a little dye on her face.

When they wanted to arrange a meeting, they used as go-betweens children whom they let in on the secret.

One day the grandmother decided to leave; they were thunderstruck at the news. Bawahoma tried to insist that Hebëwë go with her; but that was impossible. Their grief was so deep that they wept. A month or two later, Hebëwë joined some visitors who were traveling upriver to his girlfriend's group, along the "river of rains." He signaled to her as soon as he caught sight of her; she pretended not to notice, and since then he no longer cares for her.

To express how many times he made love with her, Hebëwë shows his ten fingers to which he adds his ten toes, which in a Yanomami's mind is a truly high number. He claims that it was he who took her virginity. When he wants

35

to praise the qualities of her vagina, he asserts that it was as tight and warm as one could wish. To give a more precise idea of that warmth, he extends his hand over glowing embers and says:

She was exactly like that.

It has been a long time now since Hebëwë has lost interest in childish games such as sliding one's penis against the ground, copulating with fish or birds, and masturbating. Even a boy's friendship hardly tempts him now. His desire is focused on women. He has joined the complicated game, both fascinating and dangerous, of masculine rivalry for the women's favors. The only thing that troubles him sometimes is his parents' assertion that precocious lovemaking inevitably causes pubic hair to fall out.

A few days ago a boy of about fourteen arrived at Karohi. His home group is situated far away, several days' walking distance, in a mountainous region on the banks of the "river of honey." He arrived with a group of visitors who spent only one night. As he expressed the desire to remain a while at Karohi, Kaõmawë invited him to stay with his family. Neither the young boy's personal name nor his kinship is known, except that he hails from Bashobëka; and the oldest men of Karohi remember that in the past the ancestors of that group had contacts with their people, and that they even made war against each other a long time ago. This implies that the two communities once had close links of kinship now completely forgotten.

To resolve the problem of the boy's identity, they call him Fama. The word *hama* means "visitor"; by substituting *f* for *h*, they are poking fun at the dialect of the "people upriver." They say at Karohi that these people babble "like parrots"; they are looked upon with a certain condescension: "Those upriver" are in a way the savages of "those downriver." One can see in that attitude both the result of a recent historical process that has produced a slight differentiation of speech patterns, and the influence of the missions on communities located next to the large rivers, while the inland communities, being out of contact with the whites, have no direct access to manufactured goods and are still ignorant of certain usages already adopted by downstream groups.

Not only can the Yanomami behave wretchedly toward foreigners, but they can also be nasty to members of their own ethnic group when these are isolated in a community where they have no blood relatives and thus cannot count on any help in case of conflict. And Fama is a stranger at Karohi. Yet the hosts' attitude toward their young guest is not entirely negative; rather, it involves a mixture of courtesy, generosity, and nastiness. On the one hand, Kaõmawë and his wife, Mabroma, treat Fama well and grant him his share of food, while Hebëwë and Kremoanawë, their sons, show him a sincere affection that grows stronger the longer Fama stays. On the other hand, they can't stop making fun of him or humiliating him in some way.

36

Love stories

Numerous relatives have arrived at Karohi. In the afternoon, children and adolescents, in a merry band, go to the garden to eat sugarcane and papayas. Young Fama, intimidated by the presence of persons he doesn't know, prefers to stay home. Kremoanawë will have none of this and shouts at him in an imperious tone:

Come, visitor, come with us. Don't stay alone; our friends will think that you dislike them!

They proceed slowly under the banana trees. The younger ones dawdle behind, shooting lizards that are warming themselves in the sun. Fama is prudently walking in the rear; Kremoanawë whispers to the others:

We are going to uncap his glans.

Nothing is more mortifying to an Indian than to be seen with his glans uncovered: That is the height of obscenity. On the contrary, decency requires that the foreskin, carefully stretched over the glans, be fastened to the belt with a small string. It is unfastened only to urinate, after squatting down. Not very long ago, young people were still fastening it in this manner at the onset of puberty. Now that linen loincloths are common, they leave their penis free, hidden by the cloth; but the shame they feel upon being seen with their penis exposed is just as strong.

A circle forms around Fama; he looks at the mocking faces, suspects that they are hatching something against him, and flees through the garden. Hebëwë, in hot pursuit, is unable to catch him but succeeds in tiring him enough for the others to seize him easily. Then, Kremoanawë and Hebëwë each hold an arm, Moriwë pins down a leg, Tõhõwë hangs on to the other, and Fama is spread out on the ground, held fast by four strapping fellows. Mabroma walks by at that moment; attracted by the laughter, she comes near. She takes pity on the boy, insists that they release him; no one listens to her. Hebëwë has picked up two little sticks, which he uses to slowly slide the foreskin down. The glans appears, pinkish and moist, greeted by the enthusiastic shouts of the whole laughing band. Fama struggles, cries with rage and humiliation. When they have had enough fun, they release their victim who is in a rage and pelts them with lumps of dirt and pieces of wood. They laugh all the more and shout their pleasure.

When they return to the shelter, burdened by their idleness, they gather at Hebëwë's hearth. In front of them, Wishami busies herself with domestic chores. Her little boy wallows in the dust. Too busy to realize that the boys are watching her, she bends down, legs apart, exposing for an instant her genitals to their sight. They snicker behind their hands and nudge each other. Kremoanawë gets an indecent erection; the outline of his penis is clearly visible under his loincloth. To suppress his erection, he applies pressure to his organ by pushing down on its extremity. Wishami is for him an "older sister," a person with whom he cannot have sexual relations.

37

Night has fallen. Hebëwë is terribly restless: He has noticed the young Kiaroma who arrived that same morning with a group of relatives. Several times he sends Tiyetirawë as an emissary to her and will not rest until she comes to him. Being of a cautious nature, Kiaroma sits down on the edge of the hammock. They chat for a long time: Hebëwë recounts in great detail his exploits as a hunter, whether true or invented. Kiaroma finally lies down beside him. There is much activity all around, and that bothers them; Remaema comes to fetch logs, Baiwë drinks from the kettle resting on the ground, Kremoanawë lingers to drink a mixture of palm fruit and water. This kind of activity always precedes sleep. All is finally peaceful; in the hammock there appears to be resistance, an obscure struggle. Hebëwë's voice, barely audible, is now pressing:

No, right now. Don't go away; right now!

Kiaroma claims that she has an urgent need to urinate. Hebëwë agrees to let her go after she promises to come back to him right away. The girl disappears under the shelter's roof. When she returns, instead of keeping her promise, she slips away to her parents. Hebëwë does not hide his vexation and utters coarse insults.

A few days later an event occurs that will have far-reaching consequences for Hebëwë. It is morning, the sun is still low on the horizon when Ebrëwë returns from Tayari bearing a message from Bosiarima who wants Hebëwë for his son-in-law. For a long time now rumors had been flying, in advance of the official invitation. Hebëwë does not hide his reluctance. A substantial branch of his own lineage has settled at Tayari: He knows he won't be persecuted and bullied as Fama is by himself and his brother. Rather, it is laziness that holds him back and his aversion to change. At Karohi he receives food and firewood from his mother and goes hunting only if the fancy strikes him. His only discomfort arises from the scarcity of women. If on occasion he manages to meet with Ruthemi for a few brief and stealthy moments, they both have to fear the man who is now her husband. He knows some young girls who respond to his advances when they visit Karohi or who welcome him when he visits them at home. If he goes to Tayari to accept the invitation that has been brought to him, he will be compelled to participate every day in hunting and fishing expeditions. A son-in-law must provide his bride's parents with game, carry burdens, cut down forest trees at garden-clearing time, climb up trunks to gather wild fruits, help build dwellings or repair the roof of the communal shelter. The long, idle times in the hammock and the strolls from hearth to hearth will be over for him. He'll receive his food and tobacco from his parents-in-law, but won't be in a position to ask for anything more. At Karohi he is in the habit of requiring of his mother that she cater day and night to his many whims.

That is why Hebëwë is in no hurry to answer Ebrëwë, who for his part

38

does not rush his nephew; he takes his time, pointing out that the father-in-law showed himself very anxious to have him for a son-in-law – he has every reason to think that he will be well treated. The woman that is being proposed to him is worth considering: She is young and attractive, and it is certainly not at Karohi that he can hope to find a wife. If he delays too much, Bosia-rima, tired of waiting, will give his daughter to another. These arguments, reeled off in the course of conversation, finally convince Hebëwë, who suddenly makes up his mind. Without a word, without in any way betraying his innermost feelings, he unhooks his hammock, picks up his bow and arrows, and departs, followed by Ebrëwë. Mabroma has remained silent; two tears moisten her eyes when he disappears.

Hebëwë and Ebrëwë stride along rapidly without speaking. The much-traveled path is wide and clearly marked. The sun is low when they arrive at Tayari.

A spacious shelter rises on the very bank of the Orinoco. It must have rained in the upstream region of the great river whose waters are muddy; on the water-soaked bank, thousands of white and yellow butterflies drink in a flutter of wings.

The whole of the population – a little over seventy persons – is divided into two great lineages, each of which occupies a clearly marked section of the shelter. This twofold partition of the population in the great dwelling is not always the rule; sometimes three or four lineages divide the community into as many homogeneous factions settled regularly side by side so as to cover the whole inhabited space. Hebëwë settles down in the area occupied by his kin, at the hearth of young Tōhōwë. Nothing is simpler: He has only to stand his weapons against a pole and hang his hammock to be at home.

There are many young people at Tayari, producing a merry and friendly activity. Hebëwë, silent as is fitting for a newcomer, has folded his arm under his head and holds his free hand before his mouth in the manner of newly arrived visitors. He watches the children who are playing in the central plaza; divided into two teams, they do battle with long clubs cut out of a soft wood that doesn't cut the skin but can raise welts. The blows are haphazard; those who are struck grit their teeth in order not to show their pain and try to trade blow for blow with their opponent. When they are finished, the children plant their weapons in two parallel rows.

Nearby a group of youths is inhaling a hallucinogenic drug. As a joke, a tall devil of a fellow hails a young boy of about ten and orders him to participate, asserting that it would be cowardly to refuse. The child dares not back away; they blow into his nostrils several doses too strong for him and, stunned by the drug, he collapses, his head striking the ground.

In the east looms a threatening cloud, heavy with rain. Near the fire next to Hebëwë's, Bokorawë, the shaman, sets up his parrot's nightly perch: two fragments of bow shaft linked by a transverse stick. A great woodpecker

39

Woman of Bishaasi (Mavaca).

utters his cry in the nearby forest; Tōhōwë responds with the conventional sentence:

I'm still young, I'm still young!

Suddenly the cloud bursts. It is one of those end-of-day squalls, brief and violent. The wind blows, bending the treetops; raindrops fall increasingly thick, lightning tears through the dense mass of clouds. The domestic agamis tramp up and down the central plaza with their long-legged, jerky gait, heedlessly seeking the water; the large puddles that are forming become for them wading pools where they wallow, beating the water with their wings; at times, they utter the astonishing cry that earned them the name of trumpeter birds. Some women wash themselves under the streams gushing from the roof, others take advantage of the occasion to fill their pots. Hebëwë notices that at the neighboring fire old Yerusi coughs every time she farts. Hisami goes out behind the shelter with a girlfriend; they urinate, standing with legs apart and arching their backs to make the stream of urine spurt as far as possible. At Rubrowë's hearth, an open-work basket hanging too low over the fire suddenly bursts into flame. It contains smoked fish, which now drop one by one. They attempt to smother the flames with their hands, then it occurs to them to douse them with water. The neighbors burst out laughing, amused by the incident.

At long last Hebëwë's bride, Tabrobemi, appears, carrying a bundle of roasted plantains tied with a fiber. She offers this food to her young husband and turns away without saying a word to him.

As a child, Tabrobemi was gravely ill. She was afflicted with one of those endless attacks of diarrhea that all too often put the lives of young Indians in jeopardy; she had grown frightfully thin, had become ugly, and had almost died. She managed to recover thanks to the devotion of the shamans who ministered to her tirelessly. She put on weight and soon had her first period. Despite dull, stiff, and thin hair that earns her the nickname "Baldy," she is now a pretty young girl courted by the boys. Her personality is lively and attractive but capricious. She dissolves into tears whenever someone contradicts her vigorously. Like all Yanomami adolescent girls, she is very devoted to her parents, whom she doesn't want to leave. She is said to behave generously toward the boys whose advances she accepts.

Night falls; the air has become mild again, the sky is swept clean of its clutter of clouds. The disk of the full moon will soon rise behind the curtain of trees. Children chase the fireflies that wander under the roof; they catch them, throw them up in the air to catch them again; some manage to escape. Some men, tired of hearing their shouts, ask that the game be stopped. They are not obeyed. The women intervene; one of them says:

You are going to get them in your eyes!

The children are in no hurry to comply. One can eventually see them leave one by one of their own free will, sometimes taking along an insect that they tie to their hammocks with a string to watch it glow in the night. In order to recognize each other when they move about in darkness, the Yanomami crush fireflies on their chests and shoulders, which thus become phosphorescent. They say that fireflies are stars that fall from the sky.

Tōhōwë sneaks away to Rubrowë's home to be with the beautiful Brahaima, who is visiting. He lies down in a hammock alongside the woman; their bodies are so close that they brush against each other. They chat of trivial things. Brahaima puts her leg on the young man's thighs, and his desire is aroused by that invitation. They go on with their conversation; Tōhōwë is excited and no longer knows what he is saying. Soon a hand is touching his groin; he wants to prevent the expected caress and protects himself with his hand. Intimidated by Rubrowë's presence, he wants to leave, but is asked to stay a while. He is about to make up his mind to make love when the bright disk of the sun slowly emerges, casting its light under the roof.

A deep friendship soon develops among Hebëwë, Tōhōwë, and Erasiwë. Erasiwë calls the others "father," although the age difference between them is only two or three years. They are confederates in all the little details of life, go into the forest together to hunt and fish, share their meals, help each other on all occasions, exchange a multitude of insignificant secrets. As for Tabrobemi, she is rather cold toward her husband; as is fitting, she brings him the food that her parents send him and prepares his daily plug of tobacco; she carefully delouses him, squeezes with her nails or with her teeth the little red pimples that blood-sucking insects leave on the skin. It happens that, in a forgetful moment, she lies down next to him. But she pretends to be deaf to his appeals. In vain he entreats:

Shall we make love?

She invariably answers no.

Since his wife rejects him, Hebëwë's attention turns to the attractive Shubama, married to one of his first cousins named Hishokoiwë, who also hails from Karohi. Shubama shows Hebëwë a friendly mien and throws him burning glances. The youth, seeing these advances, sends Tōhōwë to ask her for a meeting in the forest. She readily grants the favor, and a love intrigue begins behind the husband's back. The lovers meet in agreed-upon places, thanks to the connivance of Tōhōwë and Erasiwë, who help their companion. Each morning Shubama sends word to Hebëwë that they will go together into the forest; they leave each by a different exit, make love, wander in quest of wild fruits to eat. They part when the sun is at the zenith and return to the shelter at different times. Their affair goes on for a whole moon without

42

arousing Hishokoiwë's suspicion. One night they meet behind the shelter to make love under the bushes, which are very dense at that spot. They are so close to the *shabono* that they can make out the conversations. Meanwhile Hishokoiwë needs his wife and notices that she isn't there; he also notices Hebëwë's absence. Does he discover this coincidence himself, or did a friend advise him of his wife's wanderings? To complete their bad luck, Shubama's mother calls in a loud voice:

Shubama, where are you? Come back right away!

Hebëwë, who has heard, says:

It's your mother.
What does that matter? You're afraid?

Hebëwë doesn't want to seem cowardly and doesn't insist. They linger; that is foolhardy. Finally, Shubama goes home to her parents. Hebëwë waits a while before slipping back under the roof to stretch out in his hammock. Hishokoiwë watches them: He has understood; he is aware of their relationship but keeps quiet.

From that moment on, relations between the two rivals become icy. Shubama, closely watched by her parents and her husband, is no longer free in her movements. A rumor is about: Hishokoiwë, no doubt in a show of bravado, has confided to some close friends that he will kill Hebëwë. The young man and his companions deliberate; they take the threat seriously. Rather than being taken by surprise, it is better to anticipate the adversary's move and strike first.

Influential men – the old ones and the leaders of factions – decide to lead the group on a camping expedition to the junction of the "river of rains" and the Orinoco. At that location there are extensive growths of *wabu* trees whose fruits are ripening. Comfortably settled in a temporary encampment, the Indians will eat the products of hunting and foraging and thus give the plants in the garden a respite that will enable them to grow and yield a plentiful harvest upon their return.

Equipped with the bare necessities, the families set out under the trees and arrive at their destination after a night on the trail. The camp is set up alongside a dark and quiet stream. It is the season of "high waters"; on the Orinoco and the "river of rains" swelled by recent rains, branches and tree trunks are carried along by the current. Kingfishers plunge into the water, making an instantaneous transition from flying to swimming and reemerging with glistening fish in their beaks. Sometimes, one of the small fry breaks the surface to escape a flesh eater and streaks along propelled by its vibrating tail. A noisy colony of caciques has hung its nests on the lower branches of a genipap; they are clever mimics of animal cries and their dizzying chatter evokes sometimes woodpeckers, sometimes saki monkeys, sometimes parrots, ma-

43

Temporary encampment in the forest.

caws, or toucans. An old dead tree, undermined by termites and humidity, falls with a crash like thunder.

Hebëwë, Tōhōwë, and Erasiwë share the same shelter: Three poles arranged in a triangle support a trapezoidal roof covered with *ketiba* leaves. It is simple and quick to build and gives good shelter from the rain provided the roof is correctly pitched and the leaves carefully placed.

The three youths, being resolved to take action as soon as possible, wait for a favorable occasion. One morning Hishokoiwë leaves with his wife to look for some palm fruits that he discovered while hunting the day before. He grasps his bow and his machete and, with his wife, who is carrying a basket on her back, steps into a canoe to travel upstream on the "river of rains." Hebëwë and his companions feel that the moment has come. They wait until the shelters around them have emptied. The sun is high in the sky when they take a ball of thread, a few fish hooks, and their weapons; they tell an old woman, who has stayed behind to boil fruits, that they are going fishing.

They follow the bank upstream, looking for the couple. In the low places they are hampered by water that saturates the ground; the thick vegetation, which is often impenetrable near streams, forces many detours. Their mur-

44

derous intent weakens as time passes and as it takes greater effort to move ahead. They hunt small birds, chase monkeys, joke, and are already forgetting the reason for their foray when they are alerted by voices on the river. They listen intently and recognize Hishokoiwë and his wife, who are on their way home. Quickly the youths make their way through a tangle of vines; the current carries the boat along at a swift pace; they must hurry. Hebëwë whispers:

This time I kill him!

He nocks an arrow, bends the bow, and aims. Tōhōwë holds the leaves away from him. The canoe passes in front of them: Hishokoiwë, paddling in the stern, has his back to them as he moves away from shore. The bow unbends abruptly with a sharp snap of the string against the shaft. The arrow streaks out; its lanceolate bamboo tip sinks into the young man's shoulder, but falls out again, stopped by the shoulder blade.

The pain, the surprise are so violent that Hishokoiwë drops the paddle and bellows:

Who wants to kill me?

Shubama doesn't lose her head; she recovers the paddle floating near the canoe and gives such vigorous thrusts into the water that she and her husband disappear out of the aggressors' sight. It was high time: Hebëwë had placed a second arrow onto his bowstring.

Taken aback, the three accomplices no longer know what to do. Hebëwë decides that they must return to camp; whatever happens, he does not want to pass for a coward. They have been preceded by their victim and his wife. When Hebëwë appears, Hishokoiwë's father-in-law, escorted by his brothers, advances upon him menacingly. Tōhōwë and Erasiwë are not directly involved and think it prudent to retire to their shelter. In a moment Hebëwë is disarmed, his arrows are broken, his bow cut into small pieces. Some grasp his arms, brandish axes above his head, and swear that they are going to split it open; others come near to stick him with the tips of their arrows. Some women who have stayed in their hammocks yell insults and shout that he must be killed. Shubama's father deals him two hard blows with his club. Hebëwë, overcome with dizziness, is about to lose consciousness; a black veil passes before his eyes, blurring his sight; he braces himself and remains standing. A trickle of blood from his forehead blinds him, another drips on his neck and down his back. Then his punishers leave him, satisfied with the beating, and he can retire to his hammock. He suffers and says nothing. The people of his lineage have not appeared; he was too obviously in the wrong, and he would have needed his father to defend him.

Tōhōwë wipes away his friend's blood, removes the hair matted in the wound. The scalp has sustained a clean cut, but the wound is not serious.

45

That night, Hebëwë's father-in-law berates him. He has no use, he says, for a worthless son-in-law who makes love with another man's wife and neglects his own, who is so lazy that he does no hunting or fishing. He does not want him any longer and takes his daughter away from him. Let him go away.

At daybreak, Hebëwë rolls up his hammock, borrows a bow and arrows from Tõhõwë, and makes his way into the forest to return to his parents.

When it becomes known at Karohi, Hebëwë's adventure crystallizes rivalries, makes feelings run high, and inflames passions. Rumor and scandalmongering distort the facts and freely exaggerate the matter's seriousness. The two antagonistic factions that divide the community now confront each other openly – especially since one faction is led by Kaõmawë, father of Hebëwë, the aggressor, and the other by Shimoreiwë, father of Hishokoiwë, the victim. Every conflict inevitably unfolds within the structure of kinship ties or within the often underlying pattern of factional oppositions. Parents always take their children's side, no matter what they may have done. An action is never judged according to a moral code; there is never any remorse or regret on the part of the perpetrator. Rather, the condemnation stems from the disruption of a fragile and subtle social equilibrium, from an unfavorable balance between contending forces: If the culprit's faction is in the minority, he won't escape punishment; if it is the stronger, he will remain unpunished. In extreme cases, the social disruption resulting from any transgression is a strong enough sanction to restrain malevolence and aggression. This is true even without armed conflict, for such social disorder causes great tension within the community.

Shimoreiwë delivers a short but virulent public address:

> If my son dies of his wound, we shall have to fight one another; your bodies will receive my deliberate vengeance. If he survives and gets well, we shall part nevertheless. Never more shall I be able to live with people who wanted to murder my child. They wanted to kill him for fun! For fun! There was no other reason. They attacked him treacherously, he wasn't expecting it. You are evil! You are evil!

Mabroma is not far behind in verbal violence. But her speech disregards Shimoreiwë's and is directed against the man who struck her son:

> Shikowei is a thoroughly evil and cowardly man. My son is innocent. He merely defended himself. Since you hate us, we'll go live with my elder brother at Batanawë. We'll seek refuge over there. I am disgusted with you; your cowardice knows no limits. No, I won't stay any longer with you who hate us!

It is the question of coexistence that is raised: The community is on the verge of breaking apart and disappearing as such. The division of a local group into antagonistic factions often prefigures its possible dispersion when a conflict upsets it too violently. That is when the maddest plans are formulated.

46

Love stories

Some people who are less violent, probably less involved, make comments such as:

> Why did Hebëwë take so much pleasure in fornicating with Shubama?

Until now, Kaõmawë has remained silent, waiting for nightfall to let loose with a diatribe that is worthy of the preeminent role he plays at Karohi:

> You want to leave? Go. We won't tell you to stay; I might even leave first. I prefer joining our enemies of Mahekoto and hanging my hammock near "crooked mouth" to looking at your evil faces. Why did they break my son's bow and arrows? Why? Let those cowards go and do this among our common enemies. But they are afraid! Shikowei, you struck my son; come here and confront me in a club fight. Do you think I will let this insult pass without a fitting answer? When you go with us to war, we know you merely follow. Never have you launched a raid on your own initiative: You join others in order to walk behind them. You waste your time, you make yourselves ridiculous, you have never killed anyone, you never shoot an arrow against an enemy. You yourself, Shikowei, who make a show of being fierce and brave, your skin is greasy like the skin of murderers, but it is well known that you have killed no one. Your eyes widened with rage when you struck my son. Go and kill Asiyawë, our enemy: He at least is valorous. We shall confront each other with clubs, do not doubt it. You will hit me perhaps, but do not hope to remain standing. Strike me with your club or your axe, it does not matter, I do not fear you. We shall fight each other. Long ago, you boastfully told the people of Witokaya that you wanted to kill me; they reported to me that you wanted to stretch me out on the ground! I waited, but in vain. I shall join forces with those of Witokaya, who are my kin, and we shall make you run. You claimed long ago that you were going to kill the people of Batanawë, and you did not even wait a moon before visiting them and asking them for goods. You are nothing but a liar, a braggart. At Tayari the women howl with rage, their lips are twisted with spite: Let them be quiet or let them goad you into showing some courage when facing the enemies. For you are only cowards, that is what you are! Shikowei, I know very well that you are in the habit of craning your neck to look at the warriors lined up in the central plaza, ready to strike at the enemies. Will you join them? You caused my son's blood to flow; you must now fear my blows. Do not go and live on the opposite bank of the Orinoco where you might hope to escape us; stay where you are, remain at Tayari. As for me, I prefer joining our enemies and forming an alliance with them if they grant me hospitality. There are among them men to whom I say "father," "brother," or "son": They are my kin. Do not blame me for that alliance; you are not unaware that, despite the war we are waging, your women have continued their visits to Mahekoto, sometimes betraying our plans. No, do not go away, stay at Tayari; continue to hang your hammock there, enlarge your garden. I shall be among the warriors who will attack you. Scrape and plane your bows, make them flexible and fit for battle: Twist the strings. Straighten your arrows! When you see us in our black paint, your eyes will widen with fear, you will remain in your canoes, irresolute, no longer knowing where to go ashore.

The quarrel is at that stage when another affair is discovered: incest between Moriwë – a "brother" to Hebëwë – and Hiyomi. The two young people have been hiding their lovemaking for a long time. They have brief meetings in the forest and lie together in the same hammock when the others are asleep. Moriwë "eats the vagina" of Hiyomi, even though she is a "mother"

47

to him. Now he wants her for a wife and settles her at his hearth, thus openly revealing the incest he is committing.

Disapproval is discreet and indirect at first. One morning, very early, before dawn has whitened the sky, Frērema exclaims in a loud voice:

What is happening? Why is daylight so late in coming?

Moriwë is aware that the allusion is aimed at him and that Frērema refers to a definite event. The story is told that in the mythical times of the Yanomami ancestors, some young men indulged in incest with their sisters. Then, daylight ceased, a deep gloom prevailed in the shelter; it lasted so long that fuel was exhausted. They shivered with cold, the fires were about to die, they crawled on all fours groping about to find twigs. A few who were innocent ventured out of the *shabono* and discovered that there was daylight outside. While they were walking away, the others changed into sloths and the darkness lifted.

Mabroma privately disapproves of the incest but refrains from any public comment. Drawing a moral from the situation, she points out to her sons:

What they are doing is impure. Those who succumb to incest do not burn when they are cremated.

The two brothers merely make fun of Moriwë, whispering among themselves:

Your brow is oily, you are incestuous!

Moriwë has stopped saying "mother" to Hiyomi since he is making love with her; and she no longer says "little brother" to him as before; they use nicknames or avoid being precise. By giving up their respective terms of kinship, they are fictitiously abolishing the blood tie. They do, however, conform to the correct usage when addressing each other's relatives: Hiyomi says "elder brother" to Moriwë's father; and Moriwë's little sister still says "mother" to Hiyomi, even though the young woman is about to marry her brother. Only the terms used by the culprits to address each other are ever affected by the manipulation of the vocabulary of kinship; frequently, it is an evident contradiction in the partners' mutual form of address that leads to the discovery of an incestuous relationship.

The Yanomami disapprove of incest but don't always take it seriously; everything depends on the personalities involved and on the local political situation at the time a case comes to light. It is a common joke to say:

My mouth alone says "mother" [or "sister"] to her; the whole lower part of my body says "wife."

It is the rare individual among the Yanomami who has not, at least once in his life, "eaten the vagina" of a forbidden relative: a "sister," a "mother-in-law," or a "mother." The culprits are not always discovered, nor is there necessarily any violent condemnation when they are. It is unusual to see a youth riddled with machete cuts for having made love with a "sister."

Love stories

Tension rises during a drug-taking session. Moriwë is among a group of young men, as dazed as most of them, when Wakamoshiwë, with tightened jaw and green mucus dripping from his nose, leans toward him and whispers:

Incestuous! Incestuous! You are incestuous!

Moriwë is not in a condition to understand. Turaewë, who did hear the insult, waits until nightfall before coming publicly to his son's defense:

Why are you whispering! What are you saying? Won't you stop speaking nasty words? I have kept quiet so far, but I'm tired of hearing what is being whispered about. Enough! Leave my son alone. You mention incest? Don't you know that only the brave commit it, for they fear neither spiteful words nor punishments? Others would have hidden in the forest, but he reveals himself because he doesn't fear you. Be quiet, you ugly mouths distorted by envy. Those who have a well-shaped body and attractive features are incestuous. My son is here next to me; don't take it into your heads to throw arrows at him or to strike him on the head. You talk of leaving, of separating yourselves from us; I too shall go live apart so as not to hear you any longer. I shall go downstream on the "river of rains" and open new clearings there. Meanwhile, be quiet and stay still.

Next morning a quarrel breaks out between Natoma and Moriwë's mother, who asserts that Hiyomi is incapable of restraining her sexual appetite and couples with anyone, even if he is a child or a close agnate. Natoma, Hiyomi's brother's wife, answers smartly:

They have been making love for a long time. Hadn't you noticed it? Don't say that you didn't know, when they were embracing right next to you. Didn't you see them get up at night? You gave birth to an incestuous vermin, for this concerns your son.

The shouting rises to such a pitch that, carried away by anger, they yell out their personal names in order to insult each other.

Seemingly indifferent, Moriwë keeps quiet. He picks up his fishing line, a paddle, and a knife and heads for the dock. Hiyomi remains alone, weeping in her hammock. She waits for Moriwë's parents to leave for the garden to gather manioc; then she rises, takes her belongings out of a bag, and spreads them out, angrily lacerates a piece of cloth, breaks some stone bead necklaces. Natoma has guessed that she wants to leave; she comes upon the scene to retrieve the objects that belong to her: a pot and a dilapidated calabash. Stung by curiosity, a few women come and sit down. Meanwhile, Hiyomi wraps whatever she wants to take with her. Mabroma makes a timid attempt to detain her; she does not listen, unhooks her hammock, and leaves. One can hear muffled sounds in a canoe, then the splash of water struck by a paddle. Kokobirama hastens to pick up the strips of cloth strewn about the ground and seizes a piece of manioc cake left in a basket.

It is high noon when Moriwë returns. He does not seem to notice his wife's absence. He takes down a few ripe bananas, breaks off a piece of cake, and lies down. Hebëwë waves to him from afar as an invitation to come to him. When Moriwë has come near, Hebëwë informs him of the latest events and of Hiyomi's flight. Moriwë is anything but talkative; he returns to his fire, makes sure that his arrows are straight by sighting along the shafts, and straightens them in the heat of the embers that he stirs back to life. When he leaves, a woman says:

> Why go looking for her? Let him leave her where she is.

Moriwë thinks his wife went to Wayabotorewë, to her second older brother; he therefore takes the trail that leads to that group. Although he studies the ground closely, there are no footprints to indicate a recent traveler. He goes on until he comes to a muddy and swampy area where obviously no one has passed for a long time: The only thing left to do is to retrace his steps. He is near Karohi again when he meets the fugitive in the vicinity of the garden. She agrees to come back to the shelter, realizing that, with enough stubbornness, the quarrel will eventually subside.

Their determination bears fruit; people pretend to ignore them, unkind remarks become rarer. Every day they leave together, go fishing, gather fruits and caterpillars. Moriwë clears a plot in the forest to establish his garden. While he cuts the vines and saplings, she sits down a little distance away and weaves the basketwork for the household. By doing this they give economic independence to their association. Under normal circumstances, each family can indeed provide for all its needs; food comes from forays into the forest and from the plantings in the garden; a couple is quite able to manufacture all the things required for material existence.

Time passes. One moon dies, another appears and waxes in the sky. Karohi enjoys peaceful days again; all seems strangely dull after such great agitation. The incestuous marriage is now tolerated: Moriwë and Hiyomi have won out.

Furthermore, news comes of Hishokoiwë's recovery, and rumor has it that Hebëwë's father-in-law, forgetting his resentment, wishes his son-in-law to return. The causes of discord have disappeared, and there is no longer any talk of separating.

Hebëwë idles about in great boredom; every day he stuffs himself with hallucinogens. As he is looking for a woman, he thinks that he could very well take advantage of Hiyomi. By indulging in incest, Moriwë opened the way for him. In Yanomami terms, they are first cousins to each other, sons of brothers, that is to say, "brothers," hence entitled to the same women. Hebëwë wants to forget that Hiyomi is a "mother" to him and wishes to remember only that she is the wife of a "brother." He won't rest until he puts his idea into execution and keeps turning around the couple, seeking a favorable occasion. One night, Hiyomi goes down to the river to wash; Hebëwë follows her. She is fascinated by the idea of having a lover; she offers no resistance and they couple. Suddenly a light shines on them. It is Moriwë who was suspicious and now descends upon them holding at arm's length a

50

handful of burning leaves. Surprised at the moment of orgasm, Hebëwë retreats. While he is walking away, he hears Hiyomi's cries as Moriwë beats her.

Meanwhile, at Tayari, the friendship between Tõhõwë and Erasiwë has continued after Hebëwë's departure. At the next hearth live Bokorawë and Yerusi, and Hisami their grown daughter. Yerusi's cohusband is Ayawë, Tõhõwë's elder brother. Ayawë lives somewhere else in the *shabono;* he sometimes appears at day's end, lies down near Yerusi, and stays there for long moments, silent and almost motionless, occasionally cradling on his body the household's last-born child. His discretion is exemplary. Ayawë and Tõhõwë participate in the economic activities of the Bokorawë family. In truth, only the older youth is actively involved. Tõhõwë does only as much as he wants, and in exchange for the irregular work he contributes, he receives from Bokorawë a portion of his food: roasted bananas, a little fish or boiled meat, fruits according to the season. Tõhõwë shares with Erasiwë, who in turn offers him a portion of the food he receives from his father. An absolute solidarity unites the two youths in all the activities of daily life.

Tõhõwë was only a small child when he lost his father and his mother. He was raised by each of his older brothers in turn. A youth of generally pleasant disposition, he is obliging and willingly complies when his help is solicited; such qualities are appreciated at Tayari. His rages, however, are uncommonly violent; he breaks and tears anything that comes into his hands, first his own belongings and then other people's, for in his blind passion he no longer fears anyone. Afterward he retreats into an absolute and persistent silence that nothing can break. He refuses all food. These attacks indicate in Tõhõwë a sensitivity that is almost pathological, but that reveals both his delicate nature and his fragility. As a child he was almost ugly. Adolescence refined his features and gave his body firmer, more harmonious lines, while the texture of his skin retained all its smoothness and beauty, and his complexion kept that dusky shading so highly valued by the Indians.

Tõhõwë was about twelve when he arrived at Tayari. He had previously lived at Wayabotorewë and at Karohi, where his other brothers still live. He used to go about completely naked. He remembers that it was Makokoiwë who came to gird around his hips his first loincloth of red linen with the fragrance of new fabric; he took great pleasure in wearing it. He used to masturbate; he would spit into his hands and imitate the thrusts of coitus which, for young Indians, masturbation must imitate as much as possible. Then came puberty. His interest first turned to "green" little girls; he persuaded several to go with him into the bushes, where he would rub his saliva-coated penis against their vulvas or their lower bellies. He says that this practice makes the penis hurt. He carefully observed the color of his first sperm: it is said that those whose sperm is yellowish engender only children

51

Tōhōwë shooting fish.

doomed to die young. He was surprised that it was rather colorless. He believed for a long time that women, like men, had only two openings: the anus and the vagina that also serves as the urethra.

At Tayari, his nickname is "Bearded One," even though he has hardly any beard. Often, adults tease him by saying:

> You, "Bearded One," you pluck the hairs from your chin before dawn and you hide them all day only to replant them at dusk.

Since Hebëwë's departure, his wife, Tabrobemi, turns around Tōhōwë. She spends most of her time near him, using as her excuse the visits required by her friendship with Hisami. She stealthily casts burning glances toward the youth. They play together in the company of other adolescents. They make noise, chase and bite each other, splash each other while bathing or roll about in the sand. At first, Tōhōwë is unaware of the feelings he arouses in the young girl's heart. At no time does it occur to him that there could exist between them anything but a good companionship. While she is in his age group, she is a "daughter" to him, namely, a woman with whom he cannot have a sexual relationship. Their kinship allows them to be free with each other without arousing suspicion and to prolong their ties of friendship. Indeed, it is Tabrobemi who, falling in love first, displays the greater eagerness and is more enterprising. Tōhōwë, on the other hand, shows himself most ingenuous.

Tōhōwë discovers the place that Tabrobemi occupies in his life when she goes away for several days with her parents on a fishing expedition to the swamps. Without realizing it, Tōhōwë had grown used to the constant presence of the young girl. He feels an odd malaise, wants to see her right away. He finds this separation unbearable and loses his appetite; he can't drive his girlfriend's image from his mind, and he no longer takes an interest in anything. For a while, he entertains the mad notion of following her and proposing that they run away and live together in the forest. At a loss for what to do, he abandons Erasiwë for a while to settle down at Tabrobemi's hearth, where he makes friends with the girl's brother, a boy of about twelve, transfering to him the affection he feels for his sister. He sleeps with him, offers him many gifts of food, and can contemplate at his leisure Tabrobemi's quarters, nursing the illusion of her diffuse presence that his acute sensibility perceives as real.

One morning she returns, loaded with fish and fruits, with bunches of flowers inserted through her ear lobes and her skin dyed red. Tōhōwë can hardly hide his emotion. Presently, her little brother offers him, no doubt at her bidding, a smoked fish clothed in a green leaf. Tabrobemi is not far behind, bringing genipap fruits that she wants to prepare for a skin dye. Tōhōwë pierces holes in a piece of metal with a nail to make a grater; she is working, but her eyes are insistently fixed on him as if to convey her feelings. The fleshy husks of the fruits are grated and pressed; when spread to dry on the skin, the juice leaves a dark blue tint that lasts several days.

Next day the entire group goes to a camp in the forest near a place where *morē* fruits can be found in abundance. The trees that grow these fruits produce only every fourth year; to account for this oddity, the Indians say that Thunder is their master and that he delays their flowering as long as possible. In order to compel Thunder to make the trees produce, the shamans undertake the voyage toward the celestial vault where he lives. They find him there and, by tripping him into the water, give him such a fright that he grants them their demands: The flowers appear, and soon the fruits.

Tõhõwë and Erasiwë want to stay together in the same hut. They enlist children to gather the leaves for the roof. As they march through the forest, they knock against a nest of wasps hidden under a large leaf. The aroused insects sting those in front and put the whole group to flight. When they regroup, the children wait for the wasps to calm down, then they challenge each other to see who will have the nerve to crush the nest with his hands. Valiant as always, Erasiwë steps forth. He warily approaches the nest as closely as he can, and, suddenly thrusting his hands out, he crushes the insects. Some have managed to escape and sting him; but he stoically stands fast and protects his eyes with his hands. The children scatter. When they return, carrying armfuls of leaves, Tõhõwë discovers an amphisbaena – a kind of limbless lizard, blind and harmless, whose body is ringed with black and white stripes; it spends a part of its life underground. The Yanomami, who class it among the snakes, are convinced that its bite causes fatal bleeding. Tõhõwë starts when he sees it, and the children form a circle around it at a prudent distance. They observe the animal's awkward crawl and play at hindering its laborious progress by throwing obstacles in its path. Erasiwë remarks:

A tall and strong Yanomami must have been killed by an arrow, for this is a good-sized snake.

The Indians believe that an amphisbaena comes out of the spinal column of every man killed in war. They hold that this lizard is in contact with the underworld where dwell the *amahiri;* indeed, it is not unusual to see one emerge in the central plaza, but the dwelling where it appears is never that of the human being from whom it came. When one sees it, one asks:

Who are you? Where do you come from?

If it has friendly intentions, the amphisbaena makes high-pitched noises:

ei, ei, ei!

If it remains quiet, it is advisable to distrust it.

Twilight has come. On the horizon, a fiery glow casts blood-red highlights on the clouds and the high treetops. The shamans see in this portents of doom; they assert that the redness of sunset comes from diseases that are

54

released by a demon and spread to contaminate human beings. The redness darkens and turns to purple. Slowly night spreads out, a moonless night as dense as the darkness of a cave. The evening meal is eaten by the light of the fires: a soup of *morē* fruits, which look like small brown olives, and roasted plantains. When the fruits are crushed in water, fragments of dark skin adhere to the fingers. It is difficult to remove them, and the Indians believe that they cause moles: The fragments that are inadvertently swallowed reappear on the surface of the skin. Tōhōwë, who has a mole on his left cheekbone, preferred cutting it out rather than endure the taunts of the other boys, who are always quick to make fun of other people's flaws. Since it keeps coming back, he must remove it time and time again. Young people also get rid of warts by rooting them out with a string. Better to bear the pain and the bleeding than to expose oneself to jeers.

Tōhōwë and Erasiwë are finishing their meal when a go-between appears, sent by Tabrobemi. She sends word to keep a hammock empty; she will come in a moment, accompanied by Hisami. Tōhōwë's happiness is dampened by apprehension; he desires her, but he knows that he is going to commit incest. The flames of the fires have subsided, leaving only embers glowing with a shimmer that makes them look alive. The girls arrive, chattering like two birds, vibrant with liveliness and suppressed laughter. Hisami carries under her arm a miserable hammock of grimy cotton that she hangs under the low part of the hut. A light breeze drives the acrid smoke of the embers in that direction, making the area uncomfortable. Tabrobemi settles down in the hammock that was left empty as she had requested. Tohowe feels his heart beating in his breast; an imperious desire grips him and makes him bubble with impatience; his fear of incest vanishes on the spot. He would already have joined her but for the fires that have been stirred back to life by chilly sleepers and flame up again, casting shards of light in their direction.

Around them conversations cease, people are falling asleep, some snore; Tabrobemi grasps Tōhōwë's arm and draws him near. He goes to her. Nearby, Hisami and Erasiwë converse to give the impression that all is normal. Tabrobemi arches her back in order to facilitate a deep penetration; they are face to face, her legs are wrapped around his, and her hands apply pressure on his back. Tōhōwë feels his lover's pleasure as he notices a contraction in her movements and in her neck. They rest next to each other contented.

She says:

You must eat, you know that you must eat.

He complies; between his fingers he crushes peach palm fruits into the water in a calabash, and in long draughts drinks this beverage that smells of hazelnut.

The Indians do not know the reproductive function of the testicles and think that sperm, produced directly by the food that is eaten, comes out of

55

the lower abdomen. That is why, they say, it is so difficult to get an erection when one is hungry.

Tōhōwë's vigor has returned when he comes back to Tabrobemi for renewed lovemaking. Hisami makes impatient noises, but they beg her to wait a little longer. Erasiwë is sleeping when they finally part. The two girls then slip silently away in the darkness, taking care not to rouse the dogs curled near the fires.

In the morning, Tōhōwë recounts a dream he has had:

> I was widening the opening of a bees' nest lodged in a tree trunk. I was throwing away the honeycombs that contain the bees' excrement and putting aside those with the eggs, which I wanted to roast and eat. I lowered my eyes and noticed Tabrobemi at the base of the tree; she was looking at me. Without making a sound, solely by the movements of my lips, I made her understand that I wanted to make love. She agreed by nodding her head. I climbed down and said: "Let's go into the bushes." We went to sit down, and I added: "Let's make love now." But I heard noises of broken twigs coming nearer; I was afraid someone was approaching, and I said: "Let's forget it for today, someone is coming."

Marvelous days now begin for Tōhōwë. He meets with Tabrobemi every day in the forest. With the connivance of Erasiwë, Hisami, and Yebiwë, he arranges nocturnal assignations. When the group returns to the great shelter, they must increase their precautions lest their incestuous love be discovered. One evening, Tōhōwë as usual instructs Yebiwë to arrange a meeting with the young woman outside the shelter. She is with Hisami; they hold each other by the waist, giggle, and seem to be having a very good time. Yebiwë calls her, speaks to her for a moment, and she slips away between the logs of the roof to disappear into the thickets around the shelter. A little later, Tōhōwë also leaves, loudly announcing that he is going to defecate. He goes to meet her. Exhausted perhaps by too much sexual activity, he does not immediately achieve a proper erection. They linger. When they are finished, it is the young man who returns first. At the edge of the path he finds Hishokoiwë and another youth seeming to be waiting and on the lookout. Tōhōwë wants to ignore them, but when he reaches them they say:

> You are incestuous!
> What kinship term do you use when you address her?
> Don't you say "daughter" to her?

He despises them too much to answer and continues on his way. Unheeding, Tabrobemi follows too soon; they seize her and drag her to the riverbank, though she defends herself vigorously. Tōhōwë hears her cries and her sobs; he can't be unaware of what is happening. He knows that they won't release her before possessing her. He hates them but does not flinch.

Yebiwë and Hisami are a married couple. The age difference between them is at least thirty-five years. Yebiwë is an older man; his wife has not yet performed the ritual of the first menstruation after marriage. Hisami still lives

56

at her parents' hearth; she visits her husband only on occasion. Now it happens that, for several days, she has obstinately withheld her favors and draws away from him as soon as dusk approaches. Tōhōwë sees in her attitude the result of insults he has witnessed; a few days ago, some boys invited Hisami to go and make love with them. She refused, and in their disappointment they said to her:

> We are young, all of us. You prefer to "have your vagina eaten" by an old man with furrowed buttocks!

Hisami's mother is aware of her daughter's reticence; she keeps warning her:

> You must not be afraid of your husband or you will fast become an old woman.

So say the Yanomami of women who fear their husbands.

In return for the help he gave Tōhōwë with his love trysts, Yebiwë in desperation asks him to draw Hisami to him. So Tōhōwë calls the girl; he claims that he wants to report a conversation to her. When she leans toward him to listen, he seizes her by the hand and waist and carries her to Yebiwë's hammock where he forces her to lie down. She yells, cries noisily, struggles, and keeps saying a little stupidly:

> Watch out! Let me go!

She makes such an uproar that Yebiwë prefers to let her go.

It is night; everyone is asleep. Tōhōwë is awakened by a need to urinate. It is probably the bananas with which he stuffed himself all day long. Half-asleep, he wants to set his feet on the ground but almost steps on Yebiwë unaccountably squatting below him:

> What are you doing there?
> I heard a rat and I wanted to kill it.

At daybreak, Tōhōwë looks in vain for his tobacco plug, which he was quite certain to have left on a log. He suddenly understands that Yebiwë was stealing it when he went to urinate. He does not hide his dissatisfaction: Tobacco is scarce at this time.

Several times, Bosiarima sends word to Hebëwë that he is welcome again. The trouble between Hebëwë and Hishokoiwë is forgotten, and nothing hinders his return to Tayari. Hebëwë would comply if people at Karohi weren't warning him against a premature return to Tayari. He shouldn't show any eagerness, so as to shield himself against the unkind remarks of the women, who are always ready to recall unpleasant memories. Bosiarima pretends to be surprised at his son-in-law's delay; through the good offices of visitors who travel from one group to another, he contrives to send messages. He lets it be known that no one will find cause to criticize Hebëwë's return, since he himself is taking responsibility for it; he promises that his daughter will live with Hebëwë. This last reason proves conclusive; on a sunny morning, Hebëwë sets out toward Tayari, where he arrives without delay. He is reunited with his two friends. An embarrassing moment occurs when Tabrobemi arrives with her hammock on her shoulder in compliance with her father's assurances. Hebëwë is about to tell her to hang her hammock under his, then he thinks better of it and considers how awkward it will be for his wife and himself to live in the constant presence of the two youths, and what a temptation it will be to have this young girl living next to them. When it comes to women, no Yanomami has faith in his neighbor; prudence dictates distrusting even the best of friends. Everyone knows his own mind and consequently the minds of others. Taking all this into account, Hebëwë sends his wife to settle down at Yebiwë's hearth: Yebiwë is alone, and that is where they will live.

For Tõhõwë, Tabrobemi's obedience to her father's commands is a heartbreak, a betrayal. Not for an instant does he imagine that she might be suffering as much as he, that she is being asked to submit, not to choose. Hebëwë's unexpected return entails a break, a great disappointment for which Tõhõwë and Tabrobemi blame each other. A terrible sadness takes hold of Tõhõwë: Tabrobemi is now a wife; she will never again be entirely available for amorous intrigues. Hebëwë, who doesn't suspect anything, lies down next to his friend, happy to be with him and to banter in the old familiar way. Tõhõwë hides his grief and makes a show of good fellowship.

In his bitterness, Tõhõwë refuses to give Tabrobemi a present he had promised her. He no longer condescends to speak to her and assumes an air of total contempt. He takes advantage of Hebëwë's dazed condition following a drug-taking session to let Tabrobemi know how disappointed he is:

> I'll never again be your friend. I'm vexed and angry. I promised you some white beads; you won't get them; you can stare at me all you want to entreat me.

She replies:

> Your resentment is useless.

Tõhõwë goes to extremes; he is unjust, but he has been hurt, and his disappointment blinds him and clouds his mind.

Besides, the show of indifference that he has sworn to uphold does not stand up to time. If they must both adjust to Hebëwë's presence, they will so adjust. Presently, Tõhõwë sends his lover the promised beads and a piece of cloth. This gesture immediately dissipates the constraint they were feeling. In late afternoon, Hebëwë and Yebiwë go fishing. Tabrobemi and Hisami approach Tõhõwë, sit on the edge of his hammock as long as daylight lasts, then lie down in it as soon as darkness falls. The lovers take pleasure in their reunion, in recognizing the smell of their bodies and feeling their warmth. They chat for a long time, oblivious to passing time. They are about to come close for a lovers' embrace when Hisami warns them of Hebëwë's return.

Quickly, the girls jump out of the hammock and pretend to be interested in the catfish the fishermen are bringing back.

Cautiously, Tõhõwë and Tabrobemi resume their secret meetings, helped by their confederates as before. They are clever enough not to arouse Hebëwë's suspicion. One evening, however, Hisami's foolishness nearly ruins everything. They are together near the same fire. Tabrobemi and Hisami are lying head to toe in the same hammock, Tõhõwë and Hebëwë in another. The two girls are so excited that they keep bursting out in irrelevant, hysterical laughter, shout obscenities, and kick over the household utensils. The uproar is so great that they are asked to calm down. They refuse to listen, so that Tõhõwë rises in exasperation and presses Hisami's temples between his fists. He squeezes so hard that she bursts into sobs and shouts:

Leave me alone, Tabrobemi "vagina eater"!

Tõhõwë is thunderstruck. He knows that Hebëwë has heard but wants to show that he is not afraid. He goes back to his place in the hammock. Hebëwë merely says:

So that's it!

He is silent for a moment, then continues in a low voice:

Were you afraid when she talked?
No.
I won't be angry with you if we remain good friends.

3
Women's lives

The heat is unbearable. The hammocks, swollen with prostrate bodies, sway imperceptibly. All around the shelter a multitude of banana trees of all species make up the garden. One can recognize the plantains with their beautiful leaves delicately fringed and stained blood red, the *tabitabirimi* with their light and fragile leaves that flutter in the wind, and the *baushimi* with vaguely yellowish leaf stems. One can also recognize the sturdy and violet-tinged stems of the *rōkōmi*. New leaves are unrolling their scrolls. Next to the shelter, where the roof ends almost at ground level, rise a few *rasha* palms with their thorny trunks and their beautiful, shiny green fruits hanging down in thick clusters. The rustling of the palms in the light but warm and moist breeze spreads like a slight shudder over the surrounding vegetation. Nearby, the edge of the forest raises its thick curtain, beyond which rings out the ear-filling chirping of the cicadas. Remaema listens to their singing and, modulating her voice to theirs in order to hasten the ripening of the rasha, of which she is fond, she murmurs:

Red-redden, red-redden!

For it is said that the cicadas announce the imminent ripening of the *rasha*, which they thus celebrate in their own way.

A hunter comes home, walking with hurried steps under the oppressive sun, a curassow swinging on his back, the bird's white down stuck into his earlobe plugs. Some young people squabble, overflowing with magnificent insolence. Near Remaema, a young mother is carrying a newborn in her arms, a faint smile revealing her regular, even teeth; she playfully rubs her index on the infant's vulva, sticks a tuft of hair on her pubis, and says:

That is how she'll be when she is grown.

A woman is spinning and chatting with Mabroma; Hebëwë is puzzled, sensing something unusual; he tries to count his neighbor's toes, while she chatters without paying any attention to him. He places one finger opposite each of the woman's toes. Then he discovers what is odd about that foot: it has an extra toe. To arrive at that conclusion, Hebëwë had to concentrate all his attention. The Yanomami's numerical system is rudimentary: one, two, and more than two. To count larger quantities they use their fingers and, if necessary, their toes. One can overhear statements such as: "Many visitors arrived yesterday: there were two men, two more, one more; women, I could make out two and one more; there were as many children as women" – all this said with the tangible aid of the fingers. Such approximations suffice. Still, Hebëwë is endlessly amazed by his discovery; he eagerly reports it to his older brother, and the two of them promptly have their fun at the poor woman's expense.

Kaõmawë, his wife, and his four children are visiting relatives in a neighboring community, Wayabotorewë. Kaõmawë had heard that there would be a feast there; since the hosts were said to be well provided with marvelous hallucinogenic seeds, and since he found himself in dire need, he decided to go there in order to obtain some. These seeds are collected on wild trees that grow in high, shrubby savannahs. It is the famous *yopo*, which reaches the forest communities through long chains of exchanges along often complex commercial routes. When Kaõmawë arrived with his family at the collective shelter of Wayabotorewë, he was given a friendly welcome. He was immediately offered tobacco and food, as prescribed for visitors. There are many persons there whom Kaõmawë calls "brother-in-law" or "son."

Hebëwë was born nearby, at a site called *makorima*. In those days, Wayabotorewë and Karohi formed a single community. One day, Kaõmawë and his brothers decided to clear a new garden on the very bank of the "river of rains." The first harvests from that garden were excellent, and since the place was attractive, they decided to move there. But the others refused to join them and preferred to remain on their old site, which they found comfortable. They separated without any quarrel – which is not always the case when a community divides – and continued to maintain good neighborly relations.

When the leader of a faction makes a decision, he commits only himself and those who are closely tied to him. The others do as they please. Yanomami "chieftains" exercise only moral authority; they can rely only on their prestige and on the possibility of rallying others through persuasion. They cannot use coercion, nor can they compel would-be rebels. Even in warlike expeditions, participation is optional and depends only on the prevailing moral code: the obligation to display one's courage or to avenge a relative. A group's cohesion is weak, and there can be many disagreements. The entire political interplay within the settlement is a fragile and subtle balance between the different lineages that make up the group, the factions, and the maneuvers of individual leaders. Any of a number of circumstances, such as divergent interests, competition for the possession of women, or adultery, can destroy this balance. Then occur club fights, separation, sometimes war.

Kaõmawë is relaxing in his hammock when he is called to care for a sick

Bawahoma.

child; the shaman inhales the drug already prepared for him and is soon *hekura*. His chant says:

> He tears the down from the harpy eagle
> and though he took but a little,
> he covers his whole head with it.
> The *hekura* dance and sing;
> they hunt toucans
> to weave wreaths
> with the feathers.

The child is sitting quietly. He nibbles a manioc cake while the shaman draws the demons of disease out of his body.

Meanwhile, Hebëwë and Kremoanawë have eyes only for Bawahoma, who lives at the next hearth. She is a beautiful young girl; her face is round, her breasts firm, her back describes a graceful curve. She is giving final touches to her toilette with studied deliberation. A slender, polished stick pierces her nasal septum. Two shorter ones are implanted at the corners of her mouth, another in the middle of her lower lip. When she speaks or eats, all this waves about oddly, like the bristles of a porcupine. Being an orphan, she lives with her maternal grandmother, who needs her for domestic chores. That is why Bawahoma is still unmarried. The old lady can't make up her mind to marry her off; so as not to lose her, she watches her jealously and keeps her away from boys as much as possible.

The two brothers turn around the young girl so busily that they provoke

Women returning from the wood-gathering chore.

the old woman's anger; she is so furious that she spoils a bundle of fish cooking on the coals. The youths do not spare her their jeers; they say that the grandmother is jealous of her granddaughter as a husband is jealous of his wife:

> She suspects her granddaughter is being unfaithful to her. How is that possible?
> Perhaps the grandmother is marrying the girl.
> What would she say if we lured her into the forest?
> You would be beaten.

As evening approaches they notice the two women's absence and ask each other what they are doing: Where are they?

> Bawahoma is escorting her man on a partridge hunt, for he, like any jealous husband, cannot bear to leave her at home alone.

63

The great shelter from day to day

Next day, the women leave for the forest. They cross a part of the garden before reaching the cool shade under the forest canopy. They walk in single file, without hurrying; the carrying baskets on their backs rock in rhythm with their steps, and fat, whimpering infants ride on their hips. Little girls run swiftly back and forth between them. They seem to be strolling, as if they had nothing to do. They soon leave the trail to make their way according to the accidents and obstacles of the terrain. One wonders where they might be going; but since they are perfectly familiar with the terrain, they always know where they are. An old stump in the last stages of decay, a knotty root showing above the ground, a leaning tree trunk studded with thorns, all is familiar to them. They reach the bank of a rivulet, where they sit down to chat at their ease. One of them takes her seat on the lower branches of a tree leaning over the water, unwinds a fishing line, and casts it with a casual yet precise movement. A swarm of mosquitoes swoops down on them, and one can hear the sharp report of slaps on bare skin. Sometimes, an insect bloated with blood rises heavily; they follow its flight and squash it with a leaf so as not to dirty their fingers.

The fisherwoman catches a few small fish that she throws on the bank where they thrash about a long time before suffocating. A few of them then conceive the notion of going to a nearby water hole, almost dry at this time. They wade into the mud up to their bellies, pushing before them a long screen of vegetable fibers in which they ensnare the fish. As soon as a fish comes to the surface of the dirty water, they stun it with a stick, catch it, and break its backbone. Some fish, long as eels and with narrow heads, disappear into the liquid mud where they cannot be found. The women methodically cover the whole pond in this manner, without ceasing their merry chatter. Then they clean the catch piled up at the water's edge and make neat bundles with leaves and vines.

Tired of the relentless pestering of the mosquitoes, they prefer to resume their walk upstream along the brook that feeds the swamp. Presently they notice a place where the ground has been disturbed; they bend down and recognize a nest of those big termites called *oshe* that they are fond of nibbling together with roasted plantain. They cut some slender rods with which to probe and scratch the ground to uncover the uppermost tunnels. One of them finds a deep hole into which she pushes a reed. The soldier termites bite the reed with their powerful mandibles and remain attached to it; one has only to pull it out in order to catch them. But the termites are too few: The women soon lose interest and resume their walk and their chatter.

For a while now the conversation has been all about the incest committed by Brahaima and Makokoiwë – a scandal that is causing quite a stir. One moon ago, Brahaima went to live for a while at Tayari. It was rumored that Bokorawë wanted her as his second wife; but she had no sooner arrived than an intrigue began between her and Makokoiwë, Bokorawë's son. They ran

64

Soldier termites, whose heads can be eaten.

away into the forest to enjoy their lovemaking, resolved to ignore the inevitable criticisms and quarrels. As they are making their way under the trees, the women find it opportune to recall that Brahaima is free to make love since her husband died and that her sex drive is unbridled.

She used to take her hammock into the forest and attract even children with whom she would make love.

Now she has her "vagina eaten" by a "son." She used to call him "my penis," as one does a child. He called her "mother." Now they fornicate together and want to forget their kinship.

She won't burn when she is cremated. The bodies of those who indulge in incest do not cremate well; the fingernails don't burn, and the eyes remain untouched in the flames; only the hair ignites easily. It is necessary to add more and more wood to complete the job. She's an anteater woman, she's a sloth. She will change into one or the other of these animals, just as they themselves changed into beasts after indulging in incest.

He had just been initiated as a shaman; now he is lost. The *hekura* who had come to dwell in his breast have been driven away by the stale odor of sperm and genitals. The ill-smelling exhalations of her vagina repelled them; they went back to the rocky abodes that they had left to come to him. He still calls out to the *hekura*, he still thinks he is a shaman; but he is deceiving himself to no avail: His breast is empty, his power is nonexistent.

65

Cooking meat.

The file of women makes slow progress. From time to time they point out ripe palm fruits to one another, and then they are sorry that they forgot to bring their machetes. Once it happens that the one who is walking in front blunders among some wasps and gets stung. She flees laughing, protecting her eyes with her hand. The others cautiously walk around the nest.

The fisherwoman obstinately casts her line into the water whenever a halt gives her a chance. By persevering she catches enough fish to provide handsomely for the noon meal. One moment they are quite alarmed: They have recognized the reptilian movements of the terrible *Bothrops atrox,* whose bite is sometimes fatal. They are tempted to chase and kill it, but caution prevails. Sometimes one of them pulls down a beautiful vine, straight and smooth, that she will use to fashion a carrying basket or some other basketwork. They bend down to gather dead wood, break it, and smell it; if it is dry they keep it, reaching over their shoulders to place the bits of wood into the baskets on their backs.

The sun is at the zenith when they return. It is time to prepare the meal: The men are about to return from the garden or from the hunt, and the children are hungry. In the central plaza some boys play at burning the grass; Hebëwë singles out one of them, whom he asks to come near. His name is Yimikakiwë – ear – because his ears are indeed large and stand out from his

66

Hiyomi.

head. Hebëwë makes him dance before him, orders him to pull on his ear-lobes with all his might; he laughs and urges him on:

Pull, pull hard! See the women who are looking if you are afraid of them. Dance and pull again, they'll know that you are brave.

Meanwhile, Kaõmawë has obtained the drug he wanted: a whole packet that he has carefully wrapped and tied. The family will leave tomorrow to return to Karohi. Kremoanawë and Hebëwë were unable to foil the grandmother's watchfulness, and Bawahoma remained unreachable; helpless and furious, they pursue the old woman with their sarcastic remarks.

Downstream, but at some distance from the Orinoco, can be found the old site of Korita; hunters who go there on occasion can still make out the traces of the former settlement. That is where Hiyomi was born hardly more than twenty years ago; she grew up and spent a happy childhood there.

She must have been ten years old when, one evening, a girlfriend came to lie down next to her. They were in a merry mood and chatted far into the night. Suddenly, Hiyomi felt her companion's hand on her genitals; she laughed but made no move. The other put her mouth to her ear and suggested:

Let's make love!
No, I don't want to.

Try. Don't be afraid; you'll see it's nice.
No, women are not attracted to one another.

The other girl insisted so much that she finally consented. She discovered then that prolonged fondling could give pleasure. She learned how to recapture the sensations she experienced with her friend: She could bring about her own body's enjoyment. She would go off alone to rub her vulva softly against a hump on a tree trunk, or she would invite her friend, or others whom she would initiate in turn.

She had no sooner had her first period than she was married off to a man who already had two wives. Hiyomi happened to be the youngest, the prettiest as well. The husband could not openly show his preference for her; he feared the jealousy of his main wife, who ill-treated Hiyomi and burdened her with unpleasant tasks. Usually, the first wife, the oldest, enjoys a kind of precedence over the others in the household; she is the one who oversees the women's domestic chores – provided, however, she is not too old. In that case her sexual value and economic worth can fall to nothing; she is then almost abandoned by the husband and must depend on her children for food; people shamelessly make love in her presence.

Hiyomi was deflowered without subtlety. She experienced little pleasure from furtive couplings; so she had to look for something that might satisfy her better. She reverted to her former practices and secretly met with those youths of the community whom she found most attractive. But what anxiety! She had to take elaborate precautions: Her husband was so cruel and violent that he would surely have killed her if he had discovered that she was making love with others. One day, when she was alone in the garden, letting her imagination roam, full of sexual desire and fantasies, she wanted to masturbate. Her glance settled on the banana shoots that were thrusting out of the ground like tongues. She scanned the surroundings and took a few turns around the garden to ascertain that she was all alone. Then she squatted, introduced into her vagina the slender tip of a shoot, and began the rhythmic movements of coitus. She was in that position, feeling the first sensations that precede orgasm when, suddenly her heart jumped: A youth was standing nearby, looking at her. She was ashamed and nonplussed. He broke out into a smile, pleased with the advantage he had over her, then he proposed:

Let's make love!

She agreed and they went to take cover under the tall trees.

Her husband died. She mourned for him without regret. She did not love him. The youth who had surprised her in the garden wanted her for a wife. Hiyomi's brothers opposed the match. The two lovers then decided to flee into the forest. They took their hammock and some matches, but they forgot to bring a machete. It was the height of the rainy season; the streams were swollen, the forest flooded and infested with mosquitoes. So as not to be

68

discovered easily, they walked as far as they could. They put up a shelter, breaking saplings with their hands and feet, cutting vines with their teeth and splitting wood by pounding it on the ground or knocking it against old stumps. Everything was wet and saturated with humidity: The fire smoked a long time before catching; they took turns blowing on it or fanning it with folded leaves. They had nothing substantial to eat; during the day they wandered in the rain looking for wild fruits; they had to settle for unworthy quarry. They spent their nights making love. With little food or sleep, they could last only as long as their passion sustained them. When material constraints and sexual weariness became too strong, their relationship soured and they decided to return. Hiyomi was abandoned at the shelter's entrance; her companion placed himself under his relatives' protection. She came back to her brothers soiled with mud, exhausted and famished. Her skin was mottled with insect bites, her legs and feet were torn by thorns and bleeding. To punish her they burned her thighs and buttocks with coals and struck her on the head with logs. Her breasts, her shoulders, her back, and her thighs were covered with blood. They did not bother to feed her.

Her widowed status made her free, but her misfortunes continued. This is what she says concerning subsequent events:

I was a widow. My older brothers kept thinking about the gourds that held my husband's ashes; this made them sullen, and they refused to give me to another. Yet Akahimi's husband, who wanted me for a second wife, kept asking for me and was furious at meeting constant refusals. My younger brother had sided with him; they appeared one day armed with clubs, determined to fight if they did not receive a favorable answer; but my elder brothers stood up to their adversaries. To avoid a direct clash, each side took hold of one of my arms and tried to drag me away. They pulled so fiercely that the skin of my wrists gave way and I shrieked with pain; but no one cared. Akahimi's husband and my younger brother failed; they were unable to take me. They did not, however, give up pestering us, my elder brothers and myself; my younger brother and his allies fought against us with clubs and were again defeated; my elder brothers were very brave, they feared no one. Mad with helpless rage, my younger brother tried to make us leave by setting fire to our roof. My elder brothers set fire to the rest of the *shabono*, uprooted their adversaries' tobacco, corn, and manioc plants, and cut down their banana trees. Akahimi's husband did likewise in our garden. We had nothing left to eat, we no longer had a shelter, and at any moment we had to fear being shot. Life had become impossible; that is why Natoma's husband, his family, and I came to Karohi, while my other elder brother and his family went to Wayabotorewë. We no longer want our younger brother; we hate him, some day we'll kill him.

Such was Hiyomi's life: a woman's life. Time has passed since her incestuous marriage to Moriwë: The disturbances, the scandal provoked by their union have subsided. The stinging comments have ceased. The couple can now live peaceful days. Not long ago, Hiyomi discovered that she was pregnant. Now her belly is slightly rounded and her nipples have taken a darker hue. Happily, she speculates about the future child's sex. As she prefers a boy, she is on the lookout for omens: If twigs become entangled in her toes when she is walking in the forest, she concludes that she will have a boy; if the bananas she is roasting on the embers split lengthwise, she deduces that it will be a girl. She catches a grasshopper, pulls out the long hind legs, which she places on the coals, saying:

It will be a male, a male, a male!

Should the legs burn with a crackling noise, she asserts:

It is a boy's voice!

And she is happy. Should the legs remain mute, then she keeps quiet and thinks it will be a girl. It does not matter that the omens conflict; she multiplies her experiments and interprets them according to her wishes.

Near Hiyomi, who is daydreaming, Moriwë's sister is playing with a tame mouse; through its ears, which she has pierced, she has threaded pendants with alternating blue and red beads. Sometimes she handles the mouse too roughly and it squeals with pain. When the little girl is distracted, the beast slips out between the upright logs that close off the low end of the roof against the outside world. The mouse cannot be found for a long time, and the child weeps, thinking the animal is lost.

Hiyomi joins the women who are going to the garden to bring back some plantain. Kremoanawë follows her at a distance. When she is alone, he goes up to her, grasps her by the arm, and wants to pull her aside to make love. She points out to him:

Don't you see how my belly is?

He does not listen, and a struggle begins: Kremoanawë wants to take her by force. She manages to free herself, abandons her carrying basket, and runs back to the shelter shaken by a fit of sobbing. She has had enough both of men who want to use her and of a husband who is forever suspecting her. A destructive rage takes hold of her; she tramples the beautiful calabashes that she was polishing so carefully the day before. Mabroma wants to soothe her; Tʰēõma invites her and comforts her.

Tʰēõma can understand Hiyomi: She is not happy either. She had accompanied her first husband to Krauwë, where he resided; she was treated so brutally that she feared for her life and took refuge at Karohi. When the young men of Karohi saw that she was young and without protection, they took advantage of her one after another. Frērema was the most determined; he wanted her to be his wife. He mistreated her and beat her cruelly, and she learned that to defend herself she had to make him pay for the blows he gave her: Sometimes she refused to go into the forest and ignored his threats, sometimes she stopped preparing meals, or else she broke some household utensils.

After the birth of their first child, Frērema did not stop suspecting her of

70

adultery despite the fact that she was forbidden to have sexual relations. Contrary to custom, he insisted on taking her with him on a long-term hunting expedition. She had to accompany him on the long marches; one day, tired of carrying the child and dragging herself after the hunters, she took advantage of a halt to run away. She came back to the camp, where she found Moriwë, who was ill and had stayed behind to watch over the meat grill. He was still a child then. He thought: Why is she coming back alone?

She sat down in silence and warmed herself at the fire. She was carrying her child, held against her by a strap of bark. Suddenly Frērema appeared, seething with rage. He seized a harpoon-tipped arrow by the butt and sank it into her thigh; he struck her with a burning stick. She narrowly avoided his finger about to tear her earlobe. She protected the crying baby as best she could; at one point, frantic with fear, she shouted to Moriwë:

Take my child! Take him quickly, he is going to kill him!

But Moriwë was not about to get involved in a quarrel that did not concern him, and he was afraid. He didn't budge.

Such were the beginnings of her marriage to Frērema. Since then, she has learned how to gain respect; hence she is beaten less frequently than before. She has two children: a little girl now eight years old named Boshomi – little turtle – and a one-year-old son. Frērema, who respects the prohibition against sexual relations during the entire nursing period, cannot make love with her; he sodomizes a young boy and has an affair with Ritimi, whom he meets in the forest. Tʰēōma is jealous of her younger and prettier rival: She denounces her publicly and exasperates her with cutting remarks. Yesterday, Ritimi in a fit of temper broke her bead necklaces; in revenge, Tʰēōma burned her on the pubis with an ember.

Although women suffer under male dominance, they do have means of coping with it. They form mutual-help groups informally led by one or more old ones who guide them in searching for fruits, collecting frogs or insects, or hunting for crabs. These matrons are experienced and can give good advice. The women have their own little secrets, their own magic practices, their own domains; they help one another, and they are irreplaceable in the economic life of the community. The old ones who are no longer sexually attractive can have a role in political affairs: In the event of exchanges with visitors, they urge the men to be less generous; during internal quarrels or armed clashes, they incite to violence, call for vengeance, and stimulate the males' aggressiveness. The wiser ones are respected counselors to their husbands.

Hiyomi is watching the progress of her pregnancy. She has taken out her earlobe plugs, which custom forbids her to wear henceforth. She must avoid looking in the direction of the dock where the canoes are moored: The glance of a pregnant woman causes wood to split. In bygone days, when the Yano-mami were still cooking in clay pots, expectant mothers were not permitted to handle the pots for fear they might crack. Hiyomi and Moriwë avoid eating the biggest fish: Their spirit, or rather the vital principle that inhabits them, can take possession of the fetus and torment it to death. Like all pregnant women, she dislikes the taste of certain foods: Fish generally is nauseating, roasted bananas suddenly acquire an unpleasant taste, drinks made with the fruits of *hoko* and *kareshi* palms have the stale odor of the newborn. Moriwë shares his wife's distastes; he thus participates in her pregnancy.

One morning, pains and uterine contractions warn Hiyomi that birth is imminent. Presently, her waters escape, the pains increase. She stays in her hammock until she feels the time has come. She sends word to Moriwë's mother and Natoma, her brother's wife, then slips out through the narrow passage opened near her hearth at the base of the roof. She avoids the immediate neighborhood of the shelter, soiled by human defecation, urine, dog feces, and household garbage. She takes the path toward the forest. The other women hurry after her, accompanied by two little girls. No man may join them; it is said that if a male witnessed childbirth, he would be panic-stricken.

They have to wait a while before labor begins. Then Hiyomi squats down, leaning back against a large tree trunk. They place under her a handful of hastily gathered leaves. The child emerges from the womb. Natoma, who is an expert midwife, lightly massages Hiyomi's abdomen with one hand, while the other hand attends to the baby's delivery. When the child and the placenta have been delivered, Hiyomi, who is fainting and losing blood, wants to go home. A little girl is quickly dispatched to fetch Moriwë. He comes, supports Hiyomi, and helps her walk. The return trip is arduous; several times she thinks she is going to faint or fall. Moriwë breaks off some twigs with which he gently strikes her shoulders in order to help her regain some strength.

Natoma has cut the umbilical cord with a reed splinter; she has smeared blood on the child's lips so that he will later learn to speak more quickly; she has scraped off the mucus that covered his body. Now she uses some *komishi* leaves to wrap the placenta. She hesitates, deliberating whether she will wedge the package in the fork of a tree, stuff it into the abandoned burrow of a paca or an armadillo, or simply throw it into the river. Then she remembers in time that Hiyomi's children die soon after birth; in that case it it wise to bury the placenta: They say that this promotes the infant's survival. Before leaving the place, she throws some freshly dug earth onto the bloodstains at the spot where Hiyomi gave birth.

Under the shelter's roof, Hiyomi is sitting on the ground, her back resting against her hammock; to facilitate the discharge of blood, she has placed a log under her crossed thighs. When Natoma returns and she learns that she has a son, she cheers up a little: Her wish has been granted. Natoma keeps

72

the newborn close to her body, near a fire she keeps burning brightly; she entrusts him to his mother only for nursing. In the afternoon the slanting rays of the sun reach under the roof; to protect the child, she erects a screen of banana leaves balanced on a horizontal pole.

By the following day, Hiyomi has already regained much of her strength. Natoma has given her child back to her and, like all Yanomami mothers, she stuffs her dark nipple into the grimacing little mouth every time the baby cries. She insists on giving him the right breast, because he is a boy. Girls are associated rather with the left side. Other food taboos are now added to or substituted for the earlier ones: The mother for a while abstains from eating caribe fish so that the baby's tongue should not decay; anteater and tapir meat are expressly forbidden to the father: The first would cause the son's death, the second would give him skin lesions.

Because she doesn't want to lose the bit of umbilical cord left on the child's belly, Hiyomi twists a cotton thread around it and ties it behind the baby's back. In a few days the cord will be dry and will naturally separate from the navel; she will then secure it in a leaf and hang it on the rope of her hammock. Later yet, she will tie it to a "ghost tree" (*bore kë hi*) and, holding her son upright in the carrying strap, she will walk several turns around the trunk: The child will stop being irritable and will be assured a long life.

At night the infant sleeps against his mother's body; by day he rides on her, secured by the carrying strap, or is held in her arms. His urine and defecation run down her body in long streaks that she patiently wipes away. Their skins are always pressed together in a living contact that perpetuates the shelter of the womb. The little Yanomami stop sleeping with their mothers and get their own personal hammocks only after they are completely weaned, around their fourth year. Then, the heat of the fire replaces for them the warmth of the mother's body, for which fire becomes a substitute; there is from one to the other a kind of continuity, an undefinable relationship which makes the separation – or rather, the transition – more acceptable. For fire is a living domestic element; its abiding presence is almost human. In the Indians' minds, the warmth of bodies and the warmth of fire are equivalent, interchangeable. They cannot do without the gentle, life-giving warmth of a fire that burns throughout the night; to them it means much more than protection from the cold or hostile elements: It is a profound, fundamental need. Even after they have been separated from their mothers, Indian children remember that the contact of warm skins is something enormously pleasurable; hence the sensual enjoyment they derive from lying several in the same hammock. They find in this practice reassurance, security, assurance of friendship, and sensual gratification.

Yanomami children are little tyrants who enjoy the most absolute permissiveness on the part of the adults. Except in the southern communities, they are very seldom punished or beaten. Their only apprenticeship consists in learning the qualities required of a warrior people: They must develop physical endurance, get used to pain, become imbued with the idea that vengeance must always be taken, that every violence suffered must be repaid. The moral code is structured around two complementary virtues: On the one hand, one must exchange food and possessions with friends; on the other, one must take vengeance for aggressions. The endemic state of war in which the Yanomami live is merely a consequence of actually practicing these principles. Society as a whole, the local community, and not only the parents, present living examples of these principles and force children to submit to them.

The imperative rule is to "return blow for blow." Should a little boy inadvertently knock down another, the second child's mother enjoins her offspring to strike the clumsy playmate. She shouts from afar:

Avenge yourself; go on, avenge yourself!

Should a child bite another, the victim's mother comes running and urges him to stop crying. She immediately exhorts him to take revenge. If he hesitates or if he is afraid, she herself places the culprit's hand between the victim's teeth and commands him:

You bite him now! You must take your revenge.

If it is a blow with a stick, she places the stick into her son's hands and, if necessary, she herself will move his arm. In this way, the harmless conflicts between children sometimes degenerate into bloody clashes between adults when the parents take sides and the quarrel escalates.

Hiyomi, stretched out in her hammock, enjoys the idleness of the torrid hours of the day. Sitting near her, Mamobrei has herself deloused by her husband. Her little girl wants to climb on her, but does not manage to settle down comfortably. She is frustrated and begins to whine; Mamobrei tells her with a smile:

Be quiet, you are going to attract the jaguar. You'll be eaten!

She nevertheless spreads the hammock so that the child can make herself comfortable. Changing her mind, the little girl immediately gets up again and goes to uncover the pot that contains the household's drinking water. She plays at pouring the liquid into a gourd, spills some of it, and dirties the rest so as to make it unusable. She is not scolded. When she is tired of the game, she approaches her mother again, grumbles, and by her gestures makes her understand that she wants to sit on her lap. Mamobrei helps her climb up; she then stops her antics, clutches her mother's breast, and begins to suck hungrily.

Some distance away, Boshomi and Marauwë are playing with a doll. They have a large green plantain that they are carrying in a strip of cloth. At the

74

narrow end of the fruit – the end opposite the stem – they have inserted a thin, polished twig like the ones that women wear through the septum, which confers a sex on the toy.

The baby bird that Boshomi was trying to raise has just died from being handled too much. The little girls want to burn its body; they therefore take some coals from the neighboring hearths. They build the pyre with twigs that they pick up all around them. When the bird is burned, they carefully collect the tiny bone fragments: They insist that they will eat them during a funeral ceremony.

Kremoanawë and Utʰëkawë return from the hunt exhausted. After leaving early without eating, they walked all morning and into the afternoon. Their quest for game was fruitless. Without even glancing about him, Kremoanawë collapses into a hammock. His features are drawn by fatigue, his stomach tormented by hunger. He remains quiet for a long while, then calls out loudly:

Remaema, I'm thirsty! Bring me a calabash of water!

He receives no answer in return. He scowls, repeats his demand in a more imperative tone. When he is tired of waiting, he sends Utʰëkawë to the water supply. When Utʰëkawë returns with a calabash brimming with clear, fresh water, he announces:

The isolation screen has been erected for your sister.

This means that Remaema is having her first menstrual period. Kremoanawë turns his eyes toward his parents' quarters. In a corner, near the base of the shelter's roof, in front of the propped-up logs, rise the fragile, leafy walls of an isolation booth where the young girl is hidden from sight. Within the tight area thus screened off, a fire burns brightly and one can vaguely make out her presence.

As soon as the news reached her, Mabroma hastened to gather the little twigs of "menstruation leaves" (*yɨbɨ kë henakɨ*). These twigs come from a shrub hardly two meters high; when in bloom, the plant produces modest, dark purple flowers that appear at each leaf joint out of a fused calyx. Upon noticing her first menstrual flow, a girl immediately notifies her mother who, without delay, builds an isolation booth that will hide her from the sight of men. If she remained exposed to male eyes in her condition, the whole community would be threatened with dire perils. In the mythical times of the ancestors, the Yanomami had to bear the consequences of their ignorance or negligence, and the narrative of these events – the myth – fully justifies the fact that the ritual should be fulfilled exactly as prescribed and without any delay. During drug-taking sessions, Turaewë often tells the following tale, which he claims to have learned directly from the mouths of the *hekura*:

The great shelter from day to day

A feast was being prepared. Messengers had already been sent to invite the guests who were camping near the circular shelter. When night came, the women assembled to fulfill the *heri* ritual in the central plaza. A man shouted:

All the women without exception must sing and dance.

Then, a young girl who was secluded in a booth of leaves because of her first menstruation pushed the twigs aside and came out. She had heard the command and thought that it was also meant for her. She picked up the first song:

> *naikiē kere, naikiē kere,*
> *nakba kara, nakba kara*

She had hardly uttered these words when water began to ooze on all sides, the earth became so soft that everything was sinking into the ground: persons as well as things. An old woman began to implore:

My son, exhort the *hekura* to ward off the catastrophe! We are sinking! Call them!

Soon only the tips of the supporting posts remained visible. They had all sunk into the ground where they had become rocks.

The human community is threatened with sinking into the underworld and with petrification if people do not observe the obligations of the ritual. As will be seen, the prescriptions are more stringent for the secluded girl.

As if to better underscore her return to the state of nature, Remaema has to give up the cultural elements – including clothing and adornments – that are connected with cultivated plants. Tobacco is allowed provided it is *nosi*, namely worthless, tasteless, and without effect after having been washed clean by endless sucking. She has replaced her cotton hammock with a coarser one made from crushed vines. She has shed her little loincloth and undone the twisted threads she was wearing crossed on her chest or coiled around her limbs: She is now completely naked; she has even taken out her earlobe plugs. She is forbidden direct contact with water: For drinking she uses a hollow cane that she pushes deep into her mouth beyond the teeth, for the teeth would loosen if they came into contact with water. She has a little pointed stick to scratch herself; if, through forgetfulness, she should use her nails, the hair on her body and scalp would fall out and lesions would spread over her skin. To revive the fire she does not blow on it but uses a fan. She may speak only in a whisper. Prepubescent girls may come to her to chat, but the sound of their voices may never be heard outside. Her diet is severely restricted. Boiled foods and meats in general are prohibited, as well as bananas and sugarcane. Her daily ration consists only of a few plantains roasted on the embers or taro roots; she eats this meager pittance by stabbing into it with a twig. Her only gastronomic enjoyment is sometimes to suck on the shell of a crab, a pleasure she prolongs as much as possible. These various obligations as to her behavior all contribute to isolating her from everything. She urinates in the middle of her quarters and defecates into leaves that she bundles together for her mother to throw out.

It is said of a recluse that she has a "value of humidity" if it rains copiously during her seclusion. Girls who are fond of *yubuu na* – a liquid condiment made from the ashes of a bark – all fall into the category of those who have a "value of humidity." The Indians say that any lunar cycle is accompanied by good or bad weather; women are like moons in this respect; their menses, too, are a periodic element. This similarity is underscored in the language: Of a lunar crescent appearing in the sky and of a menstruating woman sitting on a log that she is staining with her blood, one says: *a roo,* she is settled, sitting.

Though free to go into the forest, Moshawë, Remaema's husband, is nevertheless subject to the same rules of behavior and to the same restrictions as his wife. He sleeps in a bark hammock. He may touch neither water nor honey. He is, however, allowed to rub his body with "menstruation leaves." Sometimes he goes out a moment for a bowel movement. If he wanted, he could go for a walk in the forest, but being extremely cautious, he prefers to stay put for fear of accidentally doing something forbidden. Tradition tells of a man in his situation who was eviscerated and changed into a bee because he tried to collect honey. The men of Karohi all remember an incident in which they almost perished. They had gone hunting. The husband of a secluded woman, weary of his inactivity, insisted on joining them, promising that he would not step into the water. They walked upstream along the bank of a brook, looking for game. The clear water flowed over golden sand spangled with shiny particles of mica. They walked slowly, carefully scanning the surroundings, probing with their bows into eroded places in the hope of discovering the lair of a caiman. The man was following at a distance, keeping to the bank. Pressing onward, they noticed the tracks of a caiman in the sand; the feet had left clear impressions, and the tail had traced a regular furrow in the middle. The tracks led them to a place where the bank was high and the water deep; they were certain they would find the beast there. They started digging. The other man watched them work at first, then, forgetting the prohibition, he came down into the water to help them. Several men who had slipped beneath the bank to work more comfortably suddenly had the impression that the ground was giving way beneath them: The earth wanted to "swallow" them. Their eyes became red as if they had been rubbed with pigment. They would have disappeared underground if Turaewë, the shaman, had not been with them. He uttered these words:

ushu, ushu, ushu!

The *hekura* hurried to their rescue and everything went back to normal: The ground became firm again under their feet. But they had had such a fright that they preferred abandoning the search and returning to the communal shelter. They had almost been changed into rocks.

There is a striking resemblance between the ritual for murderers and the ritual that a couple must observe when the wife has her first period; indeed, the same word, *unokai,* defines the two situations. If one looks for the common element, there is no doubt that it is blood. In isolating a murderer and a young woman, society merely protects itself against a stain and avoids contamination; it wards off a danger. This horror of blood has a culinary consequence: Game must be boiled for hours before it is eaten; rare meat, even if only slightly pink, would be promptly rejected; the thought of eating it provokes disgust and nausea.

For Remaema seven long days thus pass in seclusion. She is thin and dirty. One morning, Mabroma undoes the twigs that surround her and paints her with roucou; then she goes into the forest, taking the "menstruation leaves" with her and fastening them with a vine upright against the shaft of a *mraka nahi* tree. Meanwhile, Moshawë has bathed by splashing a potful of water over his body.

Another twelve days pass before the ceremony that marks the fulfillment of the ritual. Remaema, who now eats normally, has recovered her strength; her body is plump and fleshy again. Wishomi, Hiyomi, Rut^hemi and Mamobrei lead her into the forest. With a splinter of the traditional reed, Mamobrei shaves the top of her head; her body is rubbed with roucou, as well as the patch of skin laid bare by the tonsure. On that background, they draw winding lines that coil over her body; the shape of her mouth is accentuated by a dark line that passes over the lips. Through her earlobes they thread tender young palm leaves of a very pale green color, which they lacerate and cut into thin strips. Around her waist they wind a skein of cotton thread lightly reddened by rubbing. Cotton threads circle her arms, wrists, calves, and ankles; to the armband is affixed a bunch of palm fronds regularly thinned and shortened. Now Remaema is magnificent; it is as if her body were made heavier by the adornments and the heady perfume of the plants and dyes. She radiates a sensuality that is both provocative and charming; her face shows a muted joy, which her eyes express in their unaccustomed sparkle.

Remaema enters the great shelter; she crosses the central plaza with calm and confident steps and returns to her parents' area. All around her a holiday atmosphere has arisen: she knows it is in her honor. The men are adorned, their skin is embellished with dots, circles, Saint Andrew's crosses, with broken or wavy lines. Faces exhibit similar motifs that encircle the eyes and spread over forehead, chin, and cheekbones: It is simple but graceful. In their armbands of cotton or birdskin, they have threaded a colorful assortment of feathers; here and there a red macaw tailfeather rises above someone's head, tall and alive as a flame. Pendants swing from earlobe plugs: lacy, glittering breasts of blue cotingas, irridescent spoils of tanagers. Remaema, sitting proudly, surveys the scene. She has now risen to the rank of woman; she is no longer a "green" girl (*ruwë*), she is now "mature" (*tatʰe*); her menstrual blood has so testified.

The taking of hallucinogenic drugs has begun. Gray, green, olive powders make the rounds from one nostril to another. Some men, suddenly overcome by nausea, get up to vomit in the central plaza; the emaciated dogs then approach and lap up this unexpected treat. Others, with watery eyes, spit out a thick saliva that they have difficulty detaching from their mouths. Kremoanawë is dizzy. He sees fantastic landscapes bathed in orange, red, carmine, or scarlet light. The shelter has convulsions and buckles grotesquely. Suddenly a bloody whirlwind arises and submerges everything, both objects and living beings. Uncanny and frightful figures take shape and dissolve again: A headless man is pursued by a many-limbed being who is quickly replaced by a man crowned with a quarter of a head. Sometimes these creatures are swollen like balloons, sometimes their skin is covered with repulsive blisters. Kremoanawë feels his nose lengthen and a sense of dread takes hold of him. At times noises are particularly sharp and each sound is distinct, at other times a heavy silence reigns and time is abolished. He is unaware of the thread of green mucus that hangs from his nose like a stalactite.

Young Yabiwë, under the influence of the drugs, says anything that passes through his head, spouts obscenities and insults, utters the name of a dead person. The others pretend not to hear him. Yet when night has fallen, Kasikitawë confronts the youth; he claims that he was insulted and is looking for a quarrel:

> You offended me; let's have a club fight right away. We are going to hit each other on the head. You heaped ridicule on me; you thought I wouldn't hear because of the drugs!

Indistinct voices clash in the darkness. Kasikitawë and his brothers provoke Yabiwë's father, who is supported by Kaõmawë. Kremoanawë is excited at the thought of a fight; he is already clutching the club that every young Yanomami keeps near at hand. He shouts:

> Stir the fires; let's have some light, let the flames rise. Stop talking of fighting, it is time to act. As for me, I do know those of Bishaasi: Those people are truly valiant; they fight one another for less than this and don't make speeches.

Shimoreiwë answers:

> I don't fear a fight. I fought a good deal in my younger days.

And Kremoanawë replies, not too loudly:

> You are lying, your shaved head bears no scar.

A female voice yells:

> Fight, take some drugs.

No one stirs or steps forth; soon everyone falls asleep.

79

Kremoanawë adorned for the celebration.

Unhappy Hiyomi. Two moons have passed through the sky since her child's birth when he falls ill. She notices whitish adhesions in his mouth: It is thrush, which the Indians attribute to the *hemare* fruits, which, they say, "gnaw the tongues of infants." (The seeds are eaten cooked; the tree that produces the pods is a *Theobroma,* like the cocoa tree.) The little child begins to waste away and, perhaps because of the thrush, he has diarrhea. His face soon becomes livid, his upturned eyes are no longer moistened by the movements of the eyelids; they are coated with dust and assailed by voracious little gnats. The shamans take turns at his side, without success: They are unable to check the progress of the disease.

One night, Turaewë has stayed very late to sing his chants. His beautiful deep voice booms out, accompanied by the piercing chirping of the crickets. He is suddenly still, and heartrending sobs break out, echoed by the forest: The child is dead.

Hiyomi remains prostrate till daylight, holding the dead baby against her. In the morning she gives a banana to her favorite parrot and breaks its head as soon as it is sated; she wants to show her grief through this gesture. Around her, the women wear the signs of mourning. After a while, Natoma takes the little corpse, whom she ties against her breast with the bark carrying strap, then she goes to weep and dance in the plaza. Moriwë silently performs his duty; he erects and fires the funeral pyre, puts his child in a basket, and thrusts him into the flames. Natoma then throws the carrying strap into the fire.

The bones are collected at the end of the day and wrapped in leaves. Moriwë will crush them the following day in one of those thick and tough shells that contained Brazil nuts. That day also, well before dawn, the women and children will go to purify their bodies in the river during a collective bath: The smoke of cremation is particularly dangerous in the case of a young child. The arrows and the dogs must also be taken along to be washed; if this were not done, the arrows would miss their marks and the dogs would no longer find and follow the scent of animals. Later, the bone dust will be consumed in a banana soup, but no meat will be eaten: Indeed, everything is done as if to dissociate the hunt from the calamity that is the death of a newborn.

Shortly after these events, news comes to Mabroma that her brother has just been killed in a warlike expedition. She immediately goes into public mourning and blackens her cheeks. She will go to Batanawë with her family – she hails from that community – to claim a funeral gourd. They must first stop at Tayari to pick up Hebëwë and ask about the trail they must take. Mabroma hasn't visited her cousins for a long time, and since war has broken out with Mahekoto, a long detour is necessary to avoid meeting an enemy party. The infrequently traveled trail they have to follow is difficult to recognize. During the journey Kaõmawë and Mabroma take turns carrying Kerama. Sometimes Mabroma sets her on her carrying basket already filled with the family's hammocks and provisions, and sometimes Kaõmawë carries her with the help of a strap across his chest. As for Hebëwë and Kremoanawë, they stride briskly in front, carrying only their weapons.

They spend their second night in an old encampment of Batanawë. They have made considerable progress toward their goal. Soon they will reach a well-traveled, hence wider and clearer path. It is said of these decayed encampments, of a collapsed dwelling, of a dried-out vine, of an abandoned garden, that they are "old women." The camp where they are halting was set up near a stand of mauritia palms. The swamp where these particular trees are growing takes its name from the poisonous rays that infest it. It is so dangerous to collect the fruits that have fallen into the water that the Indians have given it up. That day they have a dinner of roasted plantains accompanied by the tough meat of a toucan killed by Hebëwë. The latter complains of a toothache as he is chewing. He says:

My teeth are gnawed by palm worms.

The Yanomami believe that these larvae cause tooth decay.

After the frugal meal, quite worthy of a trip through the forest, Kremoanawë goes to defecate. He climbs on a tree trunk; under him flow the clear waters of a brook. His father sees him and says:

You musn't shit into the water; those who do this can no longer warm themselves.

This belief harks back to the myth of the origin of fire: Before stealing coals from Caiman, the Indians ate their food raw and defecated into the water. Kremoanawë moves a small distance away. As he suffers from diarrhea, he farts loudly. Hebëwë snickers and shouts:

Your farts are funky like a woman's!

The other youth ignores him; when he is finished, he chooses a sapling with a smooth round trunk and rubs his rump up and down against it.

Mabroma has a dream. She sees Kremoanawë thin, yellow, and sickly: It is a bad omen. As soon as she is awake, she makes the youth get out of his hammock. He insists that he wants to sleep longer; she doesn't listen to him, gathers a handful of leaves with which she deals him little blows on the shoulders, arms, buttocks, and calves while uttering the following formula:

shabo, shabo, shabo . . .

By performing this timely action, she is warding off the risk of disease announced by the dream. This practice is peculiar to women and is used to exorcise a host of misfortunes: When an enemy raid is feared, they beat the supporting posts and the low part of the shelter with branches so that the enemy arrows will not reach their targets; when they go camping in the forest

82

to escape an epidemic, they perform this rite in order to mislead the *shawara,* who will lose the fugitives' track.

The little group is approaching the goal. Mabroma is filled with sadness; it has been a long time since she has walked these paths, and scenes from her childhood flood into her memory; she is thinking of her brother. Ahead of them, the trail climbs a steep hill through a tangle of vines; she points out on the right a ravine strewn with boulders and says:

There is the way to Titiri.

They are now moving along a path muddy and slippery from constant use. They reach a brook that winds its way under some skimpy trees, and they stop to wash. The boys bathe, redden their skin, and arrange their feathers; Kaõmawë merely rubs his wet skin. Mabroma does not wash: She is in mourning and her cheeks are blackened. Nearby they cross a vast banana garden before reaching the *shabono* whose gigantic circumference shelters more than two hundred people. Shouts and whistles greet their arrival. Mabroma remains frozen with surprise: Her brother recognizes her and looks at her, no doubt waiting for her to approach and sit next to him, as is fitting.

She steps forward, on the verge of tears, and confesses:

I was told that you were dead.
Those who said that are liars.

II

The magical powers

4

The path of the spirits

Rikōmi was born at Karohi, where his father and his brothers still live. He went to Botomawë to marry two sisters and remained to live there among his allies after fulfilling his marital service with his parents-in-law. He is rather short compared to the average Yanomami. His body is muscular without being massive; small eyes, cruel and cunning, shine in his round face; his gestures are quick. He is sensitive on questions of honor. In his adopted community, he is esteemed and respected for his qualities as a good hunter and courageous warrior. He is still young and has the stuff of a future leader. His undertakings are always well thought out. He is a man on his way up, a fiery and prolific orator, a worker who knows how to be generous. He has recently arrived at Karohi to receive from his fathers his initiation as a shaman. That is a hard trial; but if he succeeds, the status he will acquire will further reinforce his aspirations to play an active role in the political affairs of his adopted group.

Every day since his arrival, Rikōmi has been scouring the forest for the bark of the *Virola elongata* tree, from which a powerful hallucinogenic drug is prepared; he dries this bark and crushes it to a fine powder before pouring it into a long, narrow tube tightly sealed with the skin of a toad. After a solitary quest that takes him each day farther afield, he finally manages to complete the filling of the bamboo tube. Nothing henceforth prevents the start of the ceremony of which Turaewë will be the grand master, assisted by Kaōmawë and Shimoreiwë.

Turaewë does not want to delay the beginning of the initiation. He is already pulverizing seeds of *Anadenanthera peregrina,* another hallucinogenic substance that he is going to mix with the drug prepared by the novice. The three shamans can be seen painting and adorning themselves: They will officiate together during the first session. Turaewë anoints himself uniformly with red ochre from his mouth to his chest. Rikōmi's skin is speckled with regular dots; Wakamoshiwë hands him earlobe plugs in which he has inserted pendants of the most brilliant blue, then he sweeps the place where Rikōmi is to sit down.

The magical powers

Now the shamans step forth, each carrying an inhaling tube. They deposit the magic powders on the upturned bottom of a clay pot. Meanwhile, Rikōmi has moistened his plugs with saliva before inserting them through his ear lobes. He has secured his armbands of curassow skin and passed over his head a necklace of stones. He sits down when the shamans are near him and immediately adopts the position prescribed for all the active phases of his initiation: His legs are spread, and his arms, propped behind his buttocks, keep his torso upright.

He is seated under the high part of the roof, somewhat in front of the most forward supporting posts, at a place customarily devoted to the great events of social life: shamanic exercises and cures, drug-taking sessions, exchanges of goods, and consumption of funeral bone dust. The low part between the two rows of posts that support the sloping roof is the place of family life and domestic activities. Farther back, beyond the upright logs set at the edge of the forest, is the dumping ground for household refuse and dog feces; that is where one goes to urinate. From the central plaza to the forest – looking from the inside toward the outside – one can make out a series of concentric rings within which specific activities are carried out. Each of these rings is in turn divided transversely, each segment being occupied by a particular lineage and subdivided among different groups of first cousins. But that is not all: The great shelter, the *shabono,* also reflects the Indians' conception of the universe. The central plaza is the celestial vault, and the low part of the roof is a replica of the low part of the sky – conceived as a convex structure – where it meets the disk of the earth. When a shaman goes on a trip between the different levels of the universe to recover a stolen soul, to "eat" a little child, or for any other reason, the dwelling is for him a convenient geometric representation where he can orient himself perfectly. This exact convergence of the social, religious, and cosmological orders makes a microcosm of the Yanomami dwelling.

Turaewë then gives the signal to administer the hallucinogens. Six times the oblong knob fastened with resin to the end of the tube is introduced into Rikōmi's nostrils to discharge its magic dust. Then it is the shamans' turn. Women and children who have stayed in the vicinity must now withdraw, the women because of the vaginal odor that they spread around them, which displeases the *hekura,* and the children because of the powers that are going to manifest themselves here, which they will be unable to bear. Dogs and a tame parrot are also driven away; they are impure and their excrement can pollute the earth. After remaining silent a long moment during which he collects himself and seeks inspiration, Turaewë intones a melodious song while his arm rises slowly and his forefinger points toward the earth. The great *hekura* are summoned to appear:

Moon Spirit! Spirit of the Whirlpool! Vulture Spirit! Come down into me!

These are not the spirits that will first come into Rikōmi, however, but the little folk, the minor spirits: These are the ones that are first guided toward him. These beings have no power of their own; they are only the attendants of the great *hekura* – elements of the dwelling that is being erected for the *hekura* in the novice's breast, parts of the ornaments that the *hekura* use in their dances. These minor spirits who pave the way for the superior beings are the aphrodisiac woman, the one who has "value of palm leaf," the one who has "value of *kumiti* leaf," the tail of the ocelot, and so forth. A crowd of them swirls all around Rikōmi.

Rikōmi is intoxicated with drugs and unconscious. Nevertheless, fresh doses are blown into his nostrils. A stream of dark mucus flows from his nose and spreads on his chest. Presently it will dry there. It is said of these thick crusts that they are the *hekura*'s excrement, and they must not be wiped away.

When he is treating a patient, Turaewë's gestures move upward, for he must uproot from the body the demons that contaminate it. Now his movements are reversed; they channel the *hekura* and direct them toward his pupil's chest.

When the shamans were uttering their first songs, someone had blocked the exit directly in front of Rikōmi; now they grasp their machetes and go to reopen it ceremonially. Then, beginning at this opening to the outside, they pull out the grass and clear the ground of debris, dead leaves, and twigs, thus tracing a path that ends exactly between the spread-out legs of the initiate. From now on, the shamans will use only this path in the course of their functions, and their constant comings and goings will soon give it the appearance of a busy thoroughfare diametrically crossing the central plaza. In the rocky abodes where they dwell in the forest, the *hekura*'s attention will be caught; they will be attracted, guided toward the opening reserved for them, led on this new path by the shamans who will embody them, and sent into Rikōmi's chest, their new dwelling place. It is not adult *hekura* who will answer the shamans' exhortations, but children who will develop inside the human habitation thus assigned to them and who will bestow increasing power upon their master as they grow in strength.

Turaewë lifts Rikōmi's chin and, showing him the path that has just been marked out, shouts in a strong and persuasive voice:

> Look, my son, look! This is where they will come from. Look carefully, there is the path of the spirits, and now they are coming toward you!

Then they lead toward the novice the Moon Spirit, the Darkness Spirit, the Spirit of the Whirlpool, the Milky Way Spirit, the *witiwitimi* bird, the *mārāshi* woman: The active phase of the initiation is beginning.

All of a sudden, a young child, still unaware, is about to cross the path of the *hekura* where Turaewë is busily officiating. On all sides, voices tell him

The magical powers

to turn back. Bewildered, the child hesitates, scowls, and runs sobbing into his mother's arms. Some time later, it is an absentminded woman who is told much less gently to go back by a whole concert of jeering voices. But these two examples are salutary; during the whole time of the initiation no one else makes such a mistake.

Unperturbed, Turaewë goes on with his instruction. At one point he throws a handful of arrows before Rikōmi. He is embodying the Moon Spirit, a powerful and frightening cannibal who is advancing with measured steps to take possession of the body that is assigned to him. But the power of the great *hekura* is such that the initiate cannot withstand its contact; he collapses flat on his back, his arms spread out. Then, in a peaceful moment, the secondary spirits resume their gyrations around the body, so perfectly still that he hardly seems alive. The anxiety that has gripped the community abates when Wakamoshiwë, who has stayed behind Rikōmi to help him and to drive off the bloodsucking insects glued to his back, sets him upright again and corrects the angle of his legs and arms, which he replaces in the proper position.

The initial phase of the ceremony is drawing to a close. The pupil must now repeat the sentences uttered by the master. Already, an imperceptible transition is occurring within Rikōmi; he is leaving the domain of prosaic reality and, under his initiator's direction, he sees opening before him the marvelous universe of supernatural spirit realms, of demons, of superimposed transparent worlds, humid or burning. Through the message of the shamans, a superior reality heretofore hidden to him is revealed, full of flaming colors, uncanny shapes, strange and terrifying beings who are given to devouring souls, but who are ready to obey him meekly if he knows how to tame them.

Standing next to the initiate and leaning toward him, Turaewë nearly brushes against his face and chants a sentence. He rises, withdraws a few steps, and commands:

Repeat what you have heard.

Rikōmi repeats the sentence perfectly, and the master's face lights up with pleasure. There remains only for the shaman to give the last words of advice:

You must always answer me thus. Keep your eyes in that direction: There is the path of the *hekura;* from there they will come toward you. You will speak softly, without excessive haste and without raising your voice. Bring your heels together more, don't you see that your legs are too far apart!

Then begins an endless dialogue that will go on until the end of the initiation. The instructors are going to take turns with the novice. Turaewë sings:

The path is strewn with white down. They are walking toward you and your body will weaken from their presence.
I hear the voices of the *hekura* on the path.
My son, here comes the black jaguar.

90

Shaman singing to the *hekura*.

91

Stuffed with drugs, half-unconscious, Rikōmi thinks he hears the word "rock" (*këki*); he is mistaken:

The rock of the black jaguar rises in the distance.

He should have said:

Here comes the black jaguar.

Unperturbed, Turaewë goes on:

His mouth is framed with stripes of a lighter color.
I hear his growls on the path [another mistake].
My son, is the *bore koko* bird hoarse? You must answer exactly.
I speak like the *bore koko* bird.
The *hekura* dance, rustling the palms that their arms wave in front of them.
The palms of the dancing *hekura*.

Turaewë dances his way along the path, imitating the *ushuweimawë* Spirit. Rikōmi identifies the song and says:

The *ushuweimawë* bird speaks through my mouth.
Look, my son, look at the *hekura*: a feather from this bird adorns their pierced lips.
We are the ceremonial Spirits; we are coming to merge into you.
They are here! My son, they are coming, following the path that has been opened for them. They are dancing, their arms are bearing the light palms, their steps are graceful. Pay attention to the noises they make. But now, the *eeeeri* birds are gathering on the ground.
The *eeeeri* birds are gathering.
They are still young, and their breasts are without down. On the hill where they live, deadly charms grow in profusion. Come, let us dance, we are the *hekura!*
We are the *hekura* who are dancing.
They are shaking the tail of an ocelot.

Rikōmi is again mistaken:

I am the voice of the ocelot.
My son, haven't you the impression that the whole shelter is beginning to tilt? Look, on the horizon rises a gigantic tree. The *hekura* are there, putting out their tongues heavy with white down. Before them, the roots, covered with the same down, creep over the ground and hinder the dance. We are the *hekura,* we want to come to you!
Am I deceived?
My son, keep your head steady, do not turn your face toward the other Yanomami. A moment ago, the Sloth Spirit left my breast. He is going to seek for you the free *hekura* who wander in the forest. Already I can hear them making fun of his awkward gait, but his wife is answering their banter and they are starting out.
They are starting out and are walking toward me.
We will still be very young when we get here, but we shall grow within you.
We are a whole crowd.

Again Rikōmi hears wrong. He confuses "to assemble in great numbers" (*tirirou*) and "to sing and dance like the shamans" (*tirurou*). Thus he answers:

We are going to sing.
We are sewing end to end the skins of black toucans. My son, behold this astonishing thing: The red tree answers the songs of the *hekura*.

92

Nowhere else do I see such a tree. If it answers the *hekura,* it wants to be *hekura* itself.

It repeats their songs.

Human beings have been adorning themselves with birds' feathers and painted decorations for a long time. They went away to rouse the magic tree to song. The rock where dwell the *hekura* has folded its arms on its back. We come, still feeble, to knock on your chest and make you weak. The red waterfall rumbles and leaps into emptiness. You must answer, my son!

Rikōmi has fallen silent, too weak to answer. A woman's voice shouts from the other side of the shelter:

Answer! Repeat the songs!

Turaewë does not stop. Drenched with sweat, he continues his dance:

Your silence offends us, we are going to leave. Go on, my son, you must answer them. Our calls ring out for you, our lips are adorned with light and sinuous lines. Repeat this, my son! Do you wish to deceive the toucan woman who wants to come here? They are here, they are dancing! Look at them! Answer! Already the smell of the paintings that cover their bodies makes you lose your wits; they make you unconscious. We are approaching, we are singing and dancing.

Turaewë, Kaōmawë, and Shimoreiwë have officiated in turn. Only afterward do they let Rikōmi lie down in a hammock of vines stretched between two free-standing posts stripped of their bark; the initiate must not be in direct contact with any part of the shelter: His isolation must be absolute. Like persons who must submit to the *unokai* ritual, he is forbidden to eat game, fish, and bananas. He is allowed only roasted plantain and taro roots. He may not drink water, and he quenches his thirst with bits of sugarcane that are parsimoniously dealt out to him. He stays in his hammock between the sessions with his instructors. He relieves himself into a hole next to him and moves about only in a crouching stance. Neither children nor women may approach him; only Wakamoshiwë watches over him. No fire burns at night; only in the morning, a little before dawn, do they light a brush fire next to him. It is the rainy season, the sky is overcast, and so the nights are mild. That is why they say that later, when Rikōmi is a shaman and he calls to the *hekura,* the chances will be great that it will rain.

During his sleep, Rikōmi dreams of fantastic beings and landscapes. A vast number of streams run through the forest, as near to one another as the veins of a hand. A whole population of tapirs is following them downstream to reach a waterfall so high that the mere sight of it makes one dizzy. Below, in the roaring and foaming water, a turbulent crowd of birds are bathing; they are covered with soft down, and their quills are still unformed. Between the rubbery boulders clothed in moss rise the fragile shapes of the *tokori* trees, and their branches are covered with small white feathers. Another vision replaces the first. Rikōmi has shot Kaōmawë with an arrow; his victim's blood runs over his chest and flows up again, tracing a long sinuous path. Around them unfolds a fabulous landscape. Roucou trees covered with red

93

pods are bending under the weight of innumerable capuchin monkeys. Beneath a tangle of acaulous plants, of creepers and tendrils, opens the path of the *kowahito,* a people of water demons personified by the wild rabbit.

Because of the dazed condition produced by drugs, fatigue, and fasting, Rikōmi confuses his periods of sleep and wakefulness. If he talks in his sleep, he thinks that his voice belongs to someone else. (The Indians say of such dream talk that it "makes like a ghost!") He has the feeling that someone is shaking him by the arm; but no matter how much he casts about him with his deadened eyes, he sees nothing. He knows then that the *hekura* are near him, that they surround him. He hears moans. A volley of arrows almost kills him. Garrulous parrots chatter on top of a heap of dead leaves. They take fright: A child leaps toward them, only to be snapped up by a jaguar. He feels himself transported into a vast savannah covered with short grasses; macaw tails unfold their feathers and wave in the wind, looking sometimes like clusters of high, narrow flames, sometimes like glowing coals. An animal comes out of the mist; it looks like no other, but irresistibly suggests a great anteater, and it wallows in the middle of a mud hole. At one end of the muddy surface, the banks narrow gradually and an unruly torrent is formed. The contrast of appearances between the still, misty, and vague mass of the mud hole and the lively, powerful presence of the water induces in him a feeling of oppression. Suddenly, someone invisible shoots a headless arrow against the beast. The anteater collapses and dissolves in the liquid, sending up a shower of mud. This disquieting vision dissolves; he is now sitting on a steep rock. Some *hekura* come to him, but he does not recognize them. They call him by name, saying to one another:

Is this not the one we were seeking?

They hang bead necklaces around his neck. A *hekura* spits out the magic plants that float in lumpy saliva.

From time to time, he is dragged to a session of songs with the shamans. They stuff him full of drugs. He is annihilated: He no longer has a will or even an existence of his own. His mouth speaks without his willing it, his body remains in the proper position because it was so placed. Macaws with bulging eyes bellow things to him that he does not understand. Day after day, however, the ceremony takes its course. At night or in the afternoon, never in the morning, the shamans channel toward him the multitudinous beings that inhabit their magical world. They show him the blaze in which the miserly are consumed and the great dwelling of the souls in the sky. They continue to bring into his breast the different parts that make up the dwelling of the *hekura.*

To the usual substance – bark and seeds – they now add cultivated plants of the genus *Justicia,* which are psychedelic and aromatic. The path of the

94

spirits, constantly trampled by the shamans, is now impressed on the central plaza, and the violent late afternoon squalls are not sufficient to erase it.

On the third day, Turaewë has led the powerful Electric Fish Spirit into its new abode. The chanted dialogue between the master and the novice continues:

Tiri, tiri, tiri! They are advancing towards you.

The *hekura* are going to merge into me.

Here are the cannibal spirits: the Moon Spirit, the Night Spirit! The sides of the mountain are peopled with macaws.

The sides of the mountain are peopled with macaws.

We are dancing for you, our earlobes wear jaguar eyelashes. We are the wind: Listen to it blowing against your chest.

I hear the wind knocking against my chest.

The blue-tinted water of the fall topples into emptiness and its roar is deafening. Our pubic hair exhales delicate fragrances. The Toucan Woman Spirit is dancing toward you with a rustling of palm leaves.

The Toucan Woman Spirit advances toward me.

They are bringing for you all the magic objects. Diadems of purple feathers are waving on their legs. The bluebird takes its flight. The rocks sparkle with unknown lights. Garlands of crimson beads hang from our pierced lips. I see the Jaguar Spirit readying itself for you. The Macaw Spirit is near.

The Macaw Spirit is near.

But I am overcome with dizziness, my mind is failing. The *hekura* are carrying me, and I see on their backs the slender tongues of toucans that they have tied one to the other. My son, do not stay prone on the ground, unmoving and silent before them!

Rikōmi has indeed fallen silent. His unhinged body is lying on the ground.

On the fifth day, the novice is crowned with the *watoshe*. It is a diadem of woven palm leaves covered with the white down of birds of prey. This headdress is the symbol of the Jaguar Spirit, which from now on is dwelling in Rikōmi's breast; it is the token of his future power. The *watoshe* is also an ornament of the *hekura*.

It is on the eighth day that the ceremony culminates and comes to its conclusion. Early in the morning, the three shamans go into the forest to cut down the trunk that will be used to prepare the *bei kë maki*. The foliage and the undergrowth are still dripping with the morning dew. They are looking for a small tree of the *morē* species. The trunk they choose is as thick as an arm. All around, within a radius of two meters, they cut the vegetation and clear the ground of dead leaves. Kaōmawë then pulls out a little packet wedged between an armband and his skin, and each of the shamans takes two or three doses of the drug. They beat the air all around in order to drive off the evil spirits and the enemy shamans who may be hiding there. Kaōmawë intones a wordless invocation. Then, together, they invoke the Moon Spirit, shake the tree from which fall some dry leaves and other debris, and rub the bark with their hands to remove the moss. They keep on singing

Stripping a tree of its bark.

while they strip the shaft of its bark, starting at the bottom. When they are finished, Shimoreiwë cuts a deep circular groove at the base, taking care to leave untouched the heart of the wood, so that the trunk will not topple of itself. Then all three grasp the tree with both their hands and shake it until it gives way; they carefully lay it on the ground and cut off a segment about two meters long, which they take away.

During the shamans' absence, the women have picked up all the dog feces they could find in the central plaza. The trunk is entrusted to men charged with the task of preparing it. They sit down outside the shelter. The bare wood is dyed with roucou, then three black wavy lines are drawn from top to bottom, and dots of the same color are placed between the loops. The trunk will be inverted to become a mast, the thinner end being sharpened to penetrate the earth. At the upper end is affixed a bouquet of parrot and *mãrãshi* feathers. Around this bouquet hangs a wreath of pale green *waima* palms, finely shredded and barred with a line drawn with roucou. The entire mast is then clothed with a layer of white down that almost totally obscures the red background and the black designs. The *bei kë makɨ* is ready. It symbolizes the rock, emblem of eternity, where live the *hekura* who have no end. It is in rock that the free spirits of the forest dwell. Captured by the shamans, the little *hekura* enter the breast of the man who is meant to become their

96

master; that is where they will grow into adults. They are eventually freed by the death of their mortal host. This liberation can have cosmic effects if their master was a great shaman: The sky darkens, blinding thunderbolts are unleashed, rain whips the leaves. Then people say: "A great shaman has just died." The *hekura* scatter; they leave for uninhabited rocks. It happens, however, that one of them goes to dwell with another great shaman. Of the *hekura* who undertake this transmigration from one body to another, it is said that they are *habrabɨwë*. When they reach the shaman they have chosen to inhabit, the *habrabɨwë hekura* announce and introduce themselves. They say: "I come from the breast of such-and-such [they mention the personal name] where I was before."

. . . Meanwhile, the masters of the ceremonial have renewed their ornaments. Turaewë has wound the tail of a saki monkey around his brow, reddened armbands clasp his biceps, his pectoral muscles are marked with thick lines, and in his hand he holds an arrow with its lanceolate point covered with white feathers. Many people adorned with gaudy feathers, their bodies painted, have come to sit in half-circles to the left and right of the novice. He is gorged with drugs; his emaciated body is pitiful to behold, his upturned eyes are lifeless; from his half-open mouth hangs a long filament of sticky saliva, and his chest, belly, and thighs are stained with dried streaks. His answers are barely audible, and it seems that each sentence he utters might be his last.

But all the shamans of the group are roused to action and contribute to this last phase of the initiation. One can see them standing, shielding their eyes with their hands, staring into space. They fear an attack by enemy shamans bent on destroying the *bei kë makɨ,* thus wrecking the initiation and reducing to nothing so much effort and so much accepted pain.

As soon as they are told that the mast is ready, the shamans go out. They soon reappear. Turaewë, arms extended, is carrying the *bei kë makɨ.* They advance step by step on the path of the *hekura;* their progress is punctuated by frequent pauses. The shamans do all they can to make their appearance frightening: Their bodies are deformed, their faces are grimacing, and their tongues, thrusting out of their mouths, flicker in all directions. When they are near Rikōmi, Kaōmawë orders the assistant:

> Blow some more drug into him!

These fresh doses deprive Rikōmi of all reactions. He can no longer pronounce a word. In order to maintain him in the proper position, Moriwë and Hebëwë each hold one of his legs, while Wakamoshiwë supports his back. Between his legs, they quickly dig a hole in which they plant the foot of the mast; Turaewë draws on the ground imaginary lines that radiate all around it. He says:

Shamans carrying the painted mast toward the initiate.

These are the roots!

Exactly above the *bei kë maki,* now standing upright and shining, they hang a palm leaf barred by a line drawn with roucou.

Shimiwë is the Spider Monkey Spirit; he is walking about, on the alert, his hands shielding his eyes, when he suddenly detects a foreign presence. He has recognized Sebretowë, sent by the *shamatʰari* to undo the initiators' work. A violent and confused struggle begins. The shamans of Karohi unleash a multitude of fiery bolts by means of the inhaling tubes now converted into blowguns. Resheshei is the Whirlwind Spirit; he prances in the central plaza, whirling his two arms in order to absorb the intruder. Kaõmawë is the

Final phase of the initiation.

Tarantula Spirit with stinging hairs. The whole dwelling is occupied, defended. The enemy is riddled with darts, overwhelmed by itching stings, cleft in two and finally routed. At that moment, Turaewë briefly imitates the flight of the hostile shaman who, crippled from so many blows, creeps toward the outside, scratching himself. Resheshei, overexcited, exclaims:

> He had come to destroy the dwelling. He almost succeeded. I did say that we had to be on our guard. I saw him slip by, near his goal, at the moment when he was about to act!

After this easy victory is won, the interrupted ceremony can proceed. And the multitude of the *hekura* advance toward the mast. The Oriole Spirit comes first, immediately followed by the *waroo* Snake Spirit who haunts the dwellings of the *hekura* in familiar companionship. Here comes Woodpecker, who flutters to and fro, intent on digging his shelter in the wood (the shaman's forefinger is now a beak); busy with his work, Woodpecker suddenly realizes that he is near the ghost. He starts and is so frightened that he flees; staying away but an instant, he gathers his courage and timidly resumes his work. Here comes the Caiman Spirit, carrying a bow on his shoulder and staring stupidly about him with his globular eyes. Here also comes Ghost, master of the bananas and the plantain; he is miserly and mispronounces his words. The plantain woman rounds off this heterogeneous host advancing toward the *bei kë maki*. Turaewë embodies all these different characters in turn, with consummate mimicry: His spare gestures caricature the animals exactly.

It is all over. Only the mast remains to bear witness to pain. In a few days it will be taken away and fastened, together with the *watoshe,* to the trunk of one of the biggest trees in the forest. Rikōmi is eating normally; he will regain his strength. For a long time he will not be able to approach women. In them lies the danger: How many before him were unable to resist the temptation, and the *hekura,* driven out, went back to their rocks! He must withdraw when an animal hide is singed, for the *hekura* abhor the smell of scorched flesh. He is advised not to go into the forest, in order to avoid the many cobwebs that hang across the trail. He takes his first bath using the water from a pot.

For a few more days, he has a single afternoon session with his teachers. He learns from the mouths of the *hekura* the songs that he must know: These are his personal songs, the ones that distinguish him from the other shamans. On the second day, Turaewë sends upon him the Wild Pig Spirit; the shamans then rub their brows with ashes and put out the neighboring fires by scattering them. Then it is the Sloth Spirit that is called. Rikōmi can finally consider himself a real shaman. He tries out his songs and his dances: He is himself *hekura.*

At night, the spirits are all around him. They murmur into his ear: "We

100

know that one of us is going to come into you, one of the most powerful." Rikōmi expects the coming of the Jaguar Spirit, the Milky Way Spirit, or some other equally important. He must answer when they address him; he then purses his lips and makes them vibrate. This is the way of the shamans when they communicate at night with the supernatural world. His dream activity is also intense: He sees all sorts of waterfalls with waters of many colors, a host of beings whose heads are covered with down; he crosses the path of horrible macaws, heartrending voices hurt his ears. He says:

> When I am awake, a breeze surrounds me: It is the *hekura* who are moving about. I see them only in my sleep; they emit a kind of sustained buzzing. If they face me, blinding lightning flashes in front of me.

When he utters his call, he can detect this perfumed breeze that surrounds his body. He knows that *they* are there, he feels *them* climb up the side of his leg, swirl around his kneecap, reach his thigh, rise above his hip. His stomach suddenly feels oppressed, then this both subtle and irresistible breath glides over his chest and whirls near his head. He can hear their song: "*a rērērērērē* . . ."; this is the sound the shamans make with their tongues at the time of the first call. A tube protrudes from his mouth; its lower end is sunk into his side. The breeze hesitates and finally rushes into the tube, thus gaining entry into his body. Magical trees have grown in his chest. The marvelous tube, the trees, these are the possessions of the *hekura*, furnishings of their world. They have brought with them the aromatic dyes. All are there; Rikōmi sees them only at night. The parrotlets skip from branch to branch and sing: "*brē, brē, brē* . . . " The *kreōmari* toucans speak with their hoarse voices: "*kreō, kreō, kreō* . . . " He can hear them clearly. These are not ordinary birds, but *hekura,* of course, who are there for him, distant, but brought near by the dream vision.

Enormous boulders, dizzying mountains, immense rivers, landscapes unknown to him appear. The *hekura* teach him their names. They whisper: "Here is such a rock, such a savannah, such a river." With them he enters the underworld of the *amahiri,* where he meets a great anteater with powerful arms who wants to embrace and crush him. The amphisbaena crawls beside him; it raises its white head and dances. The *hekura* tell him: "Be patient, we are preparing for you a magical tree. We shall come and scrape your throat, and you will spit out substances that will give you power." He tries to spit them out as some shamans do, but only succeeds in bringing to his lips some milky saliva. It is still too early. Thanks to the *hekura,* the exquisite perfume of the dyes wafts out of his body; it is they who sprinkle him with their nourishing nectar, sweet as honey and red as blood; but they have not yet made up their minds to grant him the use of the magic plants.

A moon passes. Rikōmi has extended his stay at Karohi, both to take advantage of his masters' teachings and to avoid being tempted by the presence of

101

his pretty wives. He has gained new strength. Notwithstanding many prudent counsels, he is resolved to take part in a great hunt. It has been raining for several days, and the forest is flooded. Several times the hunters wade through depressions where the water reaches their waist. Frērema loses his curare points when he falls into a water hole. In the evening, the hunters prepare the game, which they cure on a grill; they singe the pelt of the monkeys before gutting them. Rikōmi kills a tapir; he asserts that the *hekura* guided him in finding and following the tracks. Besides, he had had a premonition in a dream. But he had to carry an enormous haunch of meat over a considerable distance, and his weakness reappeared. He almost fainted under his burden; he felt overcome by an inexplicable weariness. He complains that his body was deformed by the load. Like the others, he eats *kumato* fruits picked up while on the trail, but a ball forms in his throat. He coughs, but the mucus does not come up and is as if glued to the bottom of his windpipe.

Upon his return to the collective shelter, he narrates the events of the hunt to Kaōmawë, tells him his mishaps, and describes how he feels physically. The shaman examines him a moment, then pronounces his diagnosis:

Cobwebs came to stick to your face: They could have blinded you. They will remain if you aren't careful and your *hekura* will lose their eyes. As for your sore throat, it is the evil *shamatʰari* shamans who are responsible: they have closed the tube that descends into your chest in order to bar the way to the *hekura;* hence the discomfort you feel. You were very foolhardy to go into the forest so soon.

Kaōmawë takes drugs. He utters his call to the spirits and dances. With the edge of his hand he slays the maleficent beings that beset the young shaman. With every blow, he shouts:

Wakrashi! Wakrashi!

Rikōmi feels relieved, his throat is cleared. He can again feel the soft breeze raised by the passage of the *hekura.* They begin to speak to him again: "We shall make our path go very high into the sky." His anxiety abates: He is cured. As a last manifestation of his illness, the tobacco he chews tastes unbearably bitter.

Rikōmi walks toward Turaewë. The two shamans chat for a long time, speaking of their experiences. What Turaewë tells Rikōmi is part of the oral instruction he gives him informally. This time it is Rikōmi who speaks first:

The path of the *hekura* is visible, luminous; there arises from it something like a fiery breath that makes the air heavy and almost unbreathable. One does not see the *hekura,* one feels the wind they raise when they move. During the hunt from which I just returned, I scattered the *hekura* who were in me.

Ordinary men are unable to recognize them. Yet the wind tells us that they are there.

I see them only at night, when I close my eyes.

One can see them only then.

Their paths become luminous for me. I am sleeping, they approach and summon me to answer them. They suddenly wake me by shaking my arm or pulling on my ankle.

They wake you.

I get up and stir the fire.

Those who are not truly shamans do not hear them. He who is really a shaman hears a kind of buzzing: *bouu* . . . during his sleep, and this song echoes, rebounding off the celestial vault. He opens his eyes and says to himself: "I am going to see them now!" The parrotlets sing: "*brē, brē, brē* . . . ," he knows that it is they. A cool breeze then glides along his legs.

The kneecap is their *shabono*.

That's right. The big toe is their main path and the other toes their secondary paths: They all converge on the kneecap.

During the hunt, I made the mistake of touching a piece of meat hung on the smoking grill. Yet I do know that they abhor everything that smells scorched.

There is in your body a long tube hollow like a bamboo. One end is inserted into your hip, the other is set flush with your lips. Below your throat, the *hekura* have placed a hollow sphere through which your breath must pass.

I saw the *hekura* walk on a rotten branch; I was passing right underneath.

Indeed, it was they; but they were not friendly toward you. The strong odors of the smoking grill, the smell of singed hair, of scorched meat near the fire, all this drives them off. Yet they did seem inclined to approach you.

They give off a heady perfume; it comes from the dyes and the magic plants they carry with them. Suddenly, I stopped smelling these aromas, my nostrils no longer perceived them.

When one is at the end of the initiation, it is advisable not to hunt. If a flock of toucans takes flight and one of them lands near you, then all the others immediately follow suit. Be sure not to frighten them: Stare at them fixedly and continue on your way, you can be sure that they are *hekura*. Of course, there are those you drove away during the hunt; but don't be overly concerned, I foresee that those were not the good ones. The others remain, who came into your breast while you were lying in your hammock: Those are truly yours, they are in you, rocking lazily in their hammocks.

If they should happen to desert their hammocks, I would prefer giving up or beginning the initiation over again.

Some shamans die, killed by some evil charm. If the *hekura* they set free should transmigrate into your body, you must be sure to refuse them or repel them: They would make you ill of a disease from which you would never recover.

I had this dream: A shaman was inhaling an unknown drug; soon he started to spit out the magic plants, the objects belonging to the spirits. At his feet lay the bamboo from which the *hekura* fashion their fire bolts. There was at that spot a waterfall so high that its water became foam while it was falling; at its summit the toucans came to roost; they too carried the magic substances in their beaks.

If you can see this, it means that you already are a true shaman. If you go near water, its level rises all at once; you are suddenly in it up to your lips, and the demons that live in it enter your breast to mingle with those who are there already. Then you have enough power to fight against other shamans. I like to listen to the toucans' song; they appear when I sleep and sing: *yaukwē, kwē, kwē* . . .

Like Omawë's child, I shall be a hunter of tapirs and I shall kill many. I shelter Omawë's son in my breast, for he is a *hekura;* he did not flee like his father and did not change into an evil demon. I caught a glimpse of him in a dream: He was raising his head and carried lanceolate arrowheads in his clenched fists.

103

In that direction rises the Kanae rock. It is very high. Toucans roost at the top. They are all *hekura* and carry in their beaks the purple ornaments that they have just spit out. A long time ago, I too believed that I could bring to my lips these magical objects, but I could not do it. The toucans of this world are distressingly ugly; only the others are magnificent – they are as red as the blood in our veins and their breasts are covered with down.

The moment I utter the call to the *hekura,* my breath no longer passes through my chest. It takes the path of the *hekura:* It follows my leg, swirls around my kneecap and continues its way up to my mouth; it becomes identical to the breeze produced by the movements of the spirits. My breath is fragrant with the exquisite perfume of the charms. How afraid I was during this last hunt! So great was my exhaustion that I thought I would drown.

When you wish to leave the shelter, go with several persons, but be content to follow. When one walks at the head of the group one does not think about the things one should consider. If rain threatens, you must immediately cut leaves and take shelter. Stay in the middle of the group, let the others sit on the perimeter. Thus you won't get wet. When you set out again after a shower, the wet leaves flap against your shoulders and splash you; they undo the *hekura*'s down. When drinking, do not dip your lips into the water, but use a leaf or drink from the hollow of your hand.

I drank the stagnant water of puddles. Since then, when I try to spit out the marvelous objects of the *hekura,* what comes into my tongue is something like the milky juice of plants.

Normally, it accumulates at the back of the throat, with the consistency of honey. Our ancestors who lived at the beginning, in legendary times, those were great shamans. They would fold their arms on their chests, put their heads inside and stay like this without moving: The *hekura* would then come of their own volition, without having to be called. When they ceased being immortal, the *hekura* carried them on their shoulders; they started them breathing again, and the most handsome among them came back to life. One day, a jaguar killed a dog running on the track of a tapir; it took its head off with one bite. This dog was an extraordinary hunter; thanks to it, its masters never lacked meat. Its owner was overcome with grief. He was a very great shaman, and he thought that the *hekura* would bring the animal back to life. He placed it on a rock and sang out to the spirits, who hastened to respond. Then the head reset itself in its place, exactly as before, as if it had never been severed from the body. The dog arose: It was alive. So it was in the days of our ancestors. As for me, my fingers remained powerless when it was a matter of making my child well again. Since then, I am filled with an anguishing doubt, I no longer have faith in my powers.

I have heard this tale before. When he died, he changed into a *hekura*. He was about to enter my breast when I drove him away with the acrid smell of singed hair.

Long ago there was a powerful shaman. The Yanomami were being decimated by a man-eating jaguar, so that they all believed their death was near. They thought: "Sooner or later I shall fall prey to the beast." This famous shaman went hunting and killed a tapir. He asked for help with the quartering. He was thinking: "Let *them* eat the intestines of the tapir. As for me, I would prefer the liver of a turtle." While they were transporting the bloody hunks of meat, he went looking for a turtle. He was alone and was attacked by the man-eater. Since he harbored the Land Turtle Spirit, he changed into that animal: His head drew back between his shoulders, his mouth became tiny and horny. The jaguar tore his chest but could not break his neck. The beast kept at him, and his hair was wet from its slobber. An outstanding hunter happened to pass; he heard the confused noises of the struggle, approached, and killed the jaguar. They returned to the shelter together. The shaman preceded his savior and announced: "Totorifanawë, the Turtle Spirit, granted that my head was not exposed!" The others looked at him: They were just finishing their meal of tripe. In those days lived the truly great shamans. Those who are living and copulating nowadays have only an ounce of power left.

If a new shaman makes love, he loses all his *hekura*. He is "empty."

That is it exactly; those shamans can only begin tracing the path of the spirits all over again. Only a new initiation can give them back what they have lost and enable their nostrils to smell the perfumes of the magical dyes.

It is the smell of smoked game that drove most of the *hekura* out of me.

Your nose will again fill with sweet odors. You will not go near women: These pleasures are forbidden to you. When they arrive, the *hekura* are not always well disposed. You must be patient. They settle down in time and become friendly. They help you bring back stolen souls; thanks to them you don't lose your way. You can repel the demons of disease; they enable you to recognize them by their smell. Each one has his particular odor, and their hammocks are impregnated with it; it comes from the *watota*, which they all possess. A high-quality hallucinogen enables you to see and name the one who has just stolen a soul. You think: "It is so-and-so who is guilty!" And it is your turn to hurl your familiar *hekura* after him. Shamans who are too old have been taking drugs for too long; they have no sensitivity left and lose their way. Not so with you. You say at the first try: "Here is the right way!" The others, the old ones and those who do not know how to see, hesitate and remain perplexed: "What could it be?" When young men come to me and ask me, "Initiate me!" I immediately pick up the ornaments of the *hekura;* they purify my body. I say: "Inhale this!" I call the spirits. I send them day after day into the young man's breast. I warn him: "You are going to feel as weak as a sick man." I first send into his body the ornaments of the *hekura* and the elements of their new dwelling. I take a great deal of drugs, and I command the Sloth Spirit to scour the forest and herd toward him the free *hekura* he finds there.

One feels them approaching by the wind they raise, but also by the various odors that rise from their bodies. One can make out the smell of the oriole, that of the *yei* palm or of the *rasha* palm, that of the *morē* tree or the *momo* tree. The moon smells of old things and garbage. The hammocks smell scorched. When one lies down, there is dizziness, the posts of the shelter totter as if they were about to fall.

This happens when the *hekura* carry you on their shoulders or in their arms. Some men pretend to be shamans. These lie or deceive themselves. In reality, they are empty. Only yesterday, the *hekura* sent by Teteheiwë almost killed Kokobirama. I found them out in time; they had already sunk their hooked claws into his flesh and were about to carry his soul away. His soul would have died if I had not driven them off. It is always the *shamatʰari* shamans who come here to kill; the *waika* are too weak and never appear:

Night has fallen gradually. Sparks fly up from the stirred embers. Hebëwë's body is shaken by hiccups; to make them stop, he repeats tirelessly:

An old woman has "eaten my vagina" [women in this case insert a vine into their nostril].

The pleasant warmth of the fires induces a voluptuous drowsiness.

105

5

Spells

They are setting out into the forest early in the morning to gather the *morē* fruits, which look like dark olives. Kaōmawë is walking in front, looking up to scan the trees and determine whether the fruits are ripe. When he points out a trunk to Hebëwë, the youth climbs up, carrying a coil of vines around his feet, and cuts the branches, which fall down noisily. When he is finished, he lowers his machete tied to the end of a vine. The women then gather around to pick the fruits, which they put into leaves rolled into cones. Tiyetirawë has no liking for this task; he is busy in the vicinity killing small birds that he then carries on his back. Sometimes his arrow remains caught in the foliage, and then he addresses to the hummingbird the propitiatory formula:

Hummingbird, hummingbird, give back my arrow!

Then he throws pieces of wood to make it fall down, or else he climbs the trees.

The carrying baskets are full. Hebëwë, weary of the gymnastics demanded of him, leaves his father and the women to go home by another route. He asks Tiyetirawë to accompany him. They are walking upstream along a river when Hebëwë leaps onto the bank and creeps through the dense undergrowth. Presently he stops short and draws his bow; his arrow sinks into the shoulder of an otter; but the badly secured arrowhead loosens from the shaft, and the animal carries it away in its mad flight. The two youths give chase and catch up with it at the moment when it is about to set foot on dry ground and make its escape. Hebëwë strikes with his machete, but the blow only scratches the animal's tail; it falls back into the river and swims underwater. They follow its course by the air bubbles on the surface, until the otter takes refuge in a hollow under the bank. The hole is deep, but Hebëwë does not give up. He sharpens a stick to use as a throwing spear and tells Tiyetirawë to poke into the hole with his arrow. He laughs and admits:

When I saw it, I thought at first that it was a *yahetiba* [an electric fish]. Then I glimpsed its head.

They are about to give up the chase when the animal's head suddenly appears. Tiyetirawë raises his bow; his arrow lodges into the beast's back,

Young fisherman.

while the spear, vigorously thrown, glances off the tough skin. The otter goes back into its hole. The feathered butt of the arrow protruding out of the water moves to and fro, then stays still; Tiyetirawë wedges that butt between the string and the shaft of his bow and pulls it toward him: The arrow comes easily, but that is because it has lost its harpoon tip and the shaft has been mangled. The otter had rid itself of the arrow by biting through it; only the tip has remained implanted in its flesh. The youths wait a moment; they have no more tipped arrows, but Hebëwë keeps his spear in readiness. One last time they methodically explore the bank with a long pole, but the otter remains hidden. Tiyetirawë says:

> It is dead.
> No, it would have struggled before dying and we would have seen the disturbance in the water; it is huddled in a hole and won't come out for a long time. Let's leave.

On the way home, their path crosses the garden before reaching the shelter. Whole bunches of bananas have been left unharvested. Rotting fruits are strewn all about, and swarms of wasps and black bees come to feed on them. There happens to be a glut of bananas, and they are being used in the shelter as missiles in interminable mock fights; children smear them over their bodies and hair. Hebëwë and Tiyetirawë pick up a few and suck on sugarcane; then they loiter in the gardens and gaze at the thin, round strands of the hunting charms, which have been tangled by the wind.

These charms are all plants of the genus *Cyperus*. Their bulbs, when dried over a fire and fastened to the arrowheads, are supposed to ensure the success of the shots. Each plant has a specific use: One is for hunting partridges, another for curassows; one is for toucans, one for armadillos, and another is for small birds. They all look alike, and only the owner's expert eyes can tell them apart. As they walk by, the youths notice the aphrodisiac plants, the aromatic "leaves for women," the plant for "making children grow," the one that gives fortitude for working in the gardens, and the one that ensures a successful incest.

The terrible *aroari këki,* which can be used to kill, also belongs to the genus *Cyperus*. Hebëwë looks at it from afar: He fears it and does not want to reveal its existence to Tiyetirawë. His father brought it home from a long voyage upriver among the *waika,* where he bartered a cotton hammock for it. Every owner of an *aroari këki* knows its properties, its history, its origin; this plant is a being respected and feared, and it is kept only if its properties are confirmed in practice. The man who gave it to Hebëwë's father spoke at length in a low voice, extolling the power of its spell and explaining that it was potent and that it had already killed at least three persons; he asserted that with such an ally, Kaōmawë could exterminate his enemies. Kaōmawë was impressed, even though he knew that there is always a certain amount of exaggeration in such claims. The man then reverently dug into the ground to bring up a few detached roots and bulbs, which he immediately wrapped in a leaf before handing them to Kaõmawë. Upon his return, Kaõmawë buried his plant secretly to prevent others from stealing it, as well as to conceal his thoughts of murder.

A myth tells that it was Opossum who first used a deadly substance for purposes of black magic. One day, as he was working in his garden, two female visitors arrived at his hearth, where they were welcomed by his mother, the Mushroom Woman. She sent a child to the garden to tell Opossum the news; he came running, already painted and adorned, to sit in his hammock and strut before the young women, who were very beautiful; but everything smelled foul, and they held their noses. The Mushroom Woman drew a muscle out of her own thigh and offered it to them, saying: "Eat this tapir meat!" They refused it because of its fetid odor.

After a while, Opossum asked them to go and prepare some tobacco on the site of an empty hearth a short distance away. They went there. The place belonged to a man named Honey; everything smelled good, everything was beautiful and pleasant to look at. Honey soon appeared: His skin was neither too light nor too dark, but appealingly dusky, and his body was magnificently painted. They immediately forgot Opossum and gave their preference to Honey.

Opossum was jealous and conceived a fierce hatred against his rival. That night he prepared a deadly charm with the hairs of a red rodent – the *bëna* – which he fastened to some darts. At the break of dawn, armed with a blowgun, he posted himself near a path where Honey appeared followed by the women who were courting him. Opossum loosed his poisoned darts; Honey fell and expired. When the body was cremated in the central plaza, the coals changed into honeybees. At length, suspicion focused on Opossum; he was forced to flee, and his fright was such that he grew feathers and flew away. He took refuge in a rock cave, but was discovered. All the birds in the vicinity tried to excavate the rock, but their beaks bent under the stress; only the toucans, with their massive beaks, managed the task and made the enormous mass of rocks fall on Opossum. His blood spread out into puddles where the birds came to paint themselves: The curassow covered his beak with it, and it has been orange-red ever since; the colored partridges traced a circle around their eyelids; the toucan dipped in it the base of its tail which, since then, has been amaranthine; the kingfisher rubbed his breast with it; and the macaw made spots with it on his feathers. When they were all painted with Opossum's blood, Toucan assigned to each a rock as his dwelling place: From now on they were *hekura* and immortal.

Thus Opossum is the originator of black magic in a tale that sets him in opposition to Honey, who is associated with fire since the coals of his funeral pyre changed into bees. Indeed, Opossum is the antithesis of Honey: He connotes decay – his mother is the Mushroom Woman; he is one of the most despised animals, a foul-smelling beast unfit for human consumption; he is repulsively ugly, with his naked tail and dull, thin coat; eager for meat, he is bold enough to come near human dwellings to kill tame animals. Finally, his habits are strange, and it is said that the female's belly splits to give birth to the pups. He is an ambiguous being: When afraid, he flies like a bird; he evokes the rainbow, which the Yanomami call boa; and it is the blood of that reptile, and not that of the opossum, that, in other Indian cultures, is at the origin of the diversification of birds.

The *bëna* of the myth is used only rarely and locally, for that rodent lives only in a few mountainous regions. The *aroari këkɨ,* on the other hand, is cultivated everywhere; its bulbs are harvested, cut into small pieces, and dried over a fire to preserve them. When the time comes to use them, these fragments are crushed on a rough stone or a perforated tin, and the powder thus obtained is distributed into cotton capsules fastened to palmwood darts. During the whole time of the preparation, the sorcerers (*ōka*) are isolated and speak in low voices lest the poison lose its virulence; they keep their faces as far away as possible from their hands to avoid breathing its noxious fumes.

They leave at night, after painting their faces black in imitation of the warriors. They work covertly and do not engage in any public ritual. It is said that during their walk, they inevitably meet a *Bothrops atrox* snake that they hold fast at the head and tail with sticks. They break its venomous fangs, set it free, and, as it crawls away, throw two peeled sticks at it. The fangs, slipped under the cotton on the darts, mightily reinforce the virulence of the plant poison. A person who dies as a result of a snakebite is said to be a victim either of the spells of the *ōka* or of the black magic of the shamans, but not of the animal itself. The name of *Bothrops* (*aroami*) and that of the evil spell (*aroari*) stem from the same root.

When they are near their goal, the *ōka* shoot their darts with a short blowgun; the one who sends his dart the least distance or whose shots are the least accurate is eliminated: He goes on with the sorcerers but does not participate directly in the attack. It is considered an excellent omen if a leaf happens to bend on its stem during this trial. The spell may also be tested on a band of spider monkeys; when the poison is violent, the monkeys fall dead instantly.

The *ōka* conceal themselves near the edge of a busy path with their blowguns loaded. When an enemy appears, they wait until he is moving away from them before shooting a dart over his head, without really trying to hit him: That is enough to kill him; and they therefore flee without verifying the outcome of the expedition. Sometimes unforeseen obstacles arise on the way: The quiver holding the precious darts is lost, the fragile blowgun is broken, or some other incident occurs. Such bad luck is attributed to the perspicacity of the enemy shamans, who are held responsible for the failure of the raid.

One day, some men of Bishaasi went to kill enemies at Batanawë. Kaōmawë narrates their expedition:

They traveled upstream along the "river of the *shanishani* trees" and reached the "river of the agoutis"; there, they took a trail that angled away from the river and brought them near the *shabono* after following a ridge. They took their positions at the edge of the trail. They were not kept waiting very long before a hunter appeared. He noticed some debris of fruits falling from a tree and came stalking around with his nose in the air, trying to make out what animal was feeding. It was a parrot. The hunter shot his arrow, but the bird flew off with heartrending cries. While the man was looking for his arrow, the witch doctors "blew" their poison onto him. The victim immediately showed the effects. The man became hot, he undid his cotton belt and slung it over his shoulder; as his fever was rising, he walked to a brook and squatted down to drink directly from the stream; his thirst was unquenchable. He was weak, and already he was stumbling over the roots and holding onto the trees. But he was able to return to the shelter. Contrary to custom, the *ōka* waited; they heard women weep, and a shaman announced:

Sorcerers "blew" *aroari* on him!
From his song they understood that he was calling on the *hekura* to burn the spell that was consuming the patient: The poison creates a fire inside the body, which can be quenched only by the superior fire of the *hekura*. There was a moment of silence, then the sorcerers heard the women's lamentations and their funeral songs:

Yaiyo, yaiyo . . .

The shaman had failed, the victim had died, and they rejoiced in their own hearts. After a moment, they whispered:

Let us go; they are going to seek revenge and will come looking for us.

They left, avoiding the middle of the path so as not to leave any identifiable footprints. They returned to Bishaasi and underwent the *unokai* ritual for murderers. One of them was called Hukushatatama.

Hebëwë and Tiyetirawë have lingered in the garden a long time; they have eaten their fill of fruits. Everything is peaceful in the *shabono*: Women are chatting and spinning cotton in their hammocks, men are taking drugs. Kremoanawë has been fishing and is returning with a catfish. Hebëwë is glad to see him and, though he is stuffed with vegetarian food, declares that he would like to eat animal flesh.

As a general rule, the Yanomami draw a sharp distinction between vegetarian food (*nii*) on the one hand and, on the other, meat (*yaro*) and fish (*yuri*), which are classed in the same category of foods. To be hungry in general is *ohi;* to be hungry for meat or fish is *naiki*. One must have shared for a while the Indians' diet to appreciate these distinctions fully and to understand that one can be sated with vegetable food and still feel a strong desire for animal food.

The fish that Hebëwë covets is not yet cooked. Animal flesh is eaten only after long boiling. Some kinds of game may be left to cook for hours. In the case of animal food, cooking among the Yanomami is always done to excess. Their horror of blood has already been noted. Felines, harpy eagles, all predators that feed exclusively on raw meat are not only wild beasts; they are cannibals (*naikiri*) and are therefore classed among the supernatural beings who are eaters of souls. If a man were to commit the extravagance of consuming imperfectly cooked red meat, his body would become covered with hideous lesions, and sooner or later he would die.

Even domestic animals do not escape the dangers that threaten those who feed on raw flesh. On this score an edifying story is well known at Karohi:

A piece of raw fish had been thrown away because it was soiled with dirt; a famished dog came up to eat it. Someone warned:

Drive him away, or something will happen.

The animal's master replied:

Nothing is going to happen.

The dog swallowed the fish, and his behavior immediately became abnormal: He started spinning around like a top, tried to bite his tail, and ran about in ever-larger circles. He was tied up as a precaution, but he bit through his bonds and resumed the same behavior. He was finally swallowed by the river where he had fallen like a stone: He had changed into a fish. From then on, when the young people went bathing, they noticed to their surprise that a fish kept them company: It was the dog. Every time they swam, the animal appeared and stayed near them. One day, however, it stopped coming, and they concluded:

Someone must have caught and eaten it.

The catfish is finally cooked. Kaōmawë unhooks the kettle and deposits the contents on a leaf. His children squat all around, detach pieces of steaming flesh, chew on a bone or pull off strips of nicely fat skin. Kaōmawë solemnly distributes portions, adding a roasted banana to each, and sends Remaema to bring one to each of his brothers and brothers-in-law. Then he feeds his family, giving a piece to each child. The head goes to Mabroma: It is a choice morsel, delicate and saturated with oil, and is always allotted to the women. Shōnikiwë at his hearth is distributing banana soup. Kaōmawë gets a brimming calabash full of it, which he pours into smaller containers while waiting to drink it. Each day everyone gives and receives food, and bad luck in the quest for it is always compensated by other people's gifts. Social life among the Indians consists mostly of exchanges, of a constant reciprocity of goods and services.

Everywhere people are eating, and everyone has given and received something. Yimotʰaushimi is carrying her infant who is busily sucking on a piece of banana. Suddenly annoyed, she takes the banana away from the child and provokes a tantrum. Shimiwë, her cohusband, hears it; he would have made fun of the incident if the baby had belonged to Turaewë, but since it is his child, the sobs make him furious. Yanomami fathers can't bear to hear their children cry, and many domestic quarrels have no other cause: If the little one is crying, it is the mother's fault, or else it is because she is incapable of soothing him, even if she shows great concern and tried to stop the tantrum by stuffing her breast into the child's mouth, humming to him, or shaking a rattle in front of him. As Yimotʰaushimi does nothing to calm the baby, Shimiwë's anger turns to rage; he grabs an axe and acts as if to strike his wife. She runs to take shelter under the low part of the roof. From afar, Turaewë, the main husband, orders his wife:

Don't run away, let him strike you! Let's see him strike you!

Thus challenged, Shimiwë turns his anger against the shaman. He sharpens a spear, puts it down as soon as it is ready, lies down in his hammock, immediately gets up again, rummages in his quiver, pretends to select his best lanceolate point to set it on an arrow. The shamming is obvious; Shimiwë is condemned to express violence in this manner, for he cannot act without committing something irreparable: killing his child, wounding his wife or his brother. He must simulate aggression so as not to lose face; he insults and threatens Turaewë, but he does not use against him the weapons he is making ready. Prudent, but undeceived, Kremoanawë confiscates his bow, his arrows, and his spear and carries them to his own hearth. Shimiwë makes a show of helplessness; he stretches out with his elbow under his neck, gazing vacantly at the central plaza.

The sun is declining. The parrots raise their annoying chatter, announcing the approaching twilight. When the sun is on the horizon, the *hōrema* bird says: "*were, were, were . . .*"

Later during the night, it is the toads and crickets that unleash their chorus until dawn. Toward morning, the *yōririmi* bird utters his "*yōriri, yōriri . . .*" Its song, slow and hesitant at first, rises faster and faster and ends in a cascade of trills.

Soon after, another bird, *hutumi*, says: "*hutu, hutu . . .*"

The bat scolds: "*irosisi, irosisi . . .*"

The animals tell time and set the hours; the Indians know their voices and hear their messages.

All are sleeping. Not a child is wailing, not a dog is barking. Sounds of snoring are punctuated by farts. The fires are burning low. Wishami awakes, thinking that she hears suspicious noises nearby. She shakes her husband and whispers to him:

There are Yanomami there, behind the shelter. I heard the rustling of leaves. It's sorcerers.

113

He hardly stirs, grunts, but does not open his eyes. She insists until he hears. Then he bellows:

Bei yö o!

And he goes back to sleep.

Men fight first of all because they are competing for the possession of women. The sorcery of the *ōka* is the second cause of wars: Should a community suspect another of having caused by such means the death of one of its members, it is obligated to avenge the dead person; the hellish cycle of warlike expeditions then begins, since each death inflicted by either side calls for retribution.

The different means of making war on the enemies are not necessarily exclusive, but they do frequently correspond to various degrees of hostilities; sometimes, too, they are a function of geography. Armed raids carried out by communities against each other represent the most violent form of aggression in the context of an open, public conflict and are preceded by an impressive ritual. Sorcery associated with a state of latent conflict is more discreet and more pernicious. Two types of magic must be clearly distinguished: the magic of the *ōka,* who use the *aroari* spell, and that of the shamans, who are endowed with supernatural powers. Both belong to men but are separated by mutually exclusive characteristics: The *ōka* work with substances; they are not specialists, their actions are kept secret, and they submit to the *unokai* ritual in case of success. The shamans manipulate symbols; they are specialists who work publicly, and they need not submit to any ritual if they succeed in their undertaking. Other distinctions are less sharply defined. The *ōka* may travel on foot to the community they are attacking and risk setting off a real war; the shamans aim their powers at communities with which they usually have no direct contact and which are often so far away as to prevent any actual war.

There is yet another kind of magic, without any direct relation to the two great types of magic just described: the small magic of daily life. This type usually does not aim at causing death, but at impairing physical well-being; and it is not associated with a state of war since it occurs within a given community, or else between allied communities. Numerous substances are used: mammals, insects, wild and cultivated plants. These products are not "blown" like the *aroari* of the *ōka,* but propelled with the flick of a finger. To use an evil spell against another, it is enough for a person to feel hatred, jealousy, envy, or even a vague and undefinable sentiment of hostility. This kind of magic is also enlisted in the battle of the sexes; plants known to women keep the husband at home against his will, others provoke a sluggishness of the male organism. Still others, when they are burned by women,

114

spread a noxious smoke that acts selectively: People with dark skins are affected while others are left untouched. Men control the power of aphrodisiacs; they can cause sterility.

The small magic is a source of mutual suspicion and makes it imperative to take a number of precautions if one fears an attack: One must conceal leftovers from a meal, and one must not leave footprints. When visiting, one must beware of proffered food, in which a harmful substance may be concealed. In allied communities, one often finds not only friends, but also members of hostile lineages who belong to groups that are at war with the home community.

The action of the shamans is of an altogether different nature, operating at other levels and toward other objectives. They carry out an endless struggle among themselves and inflict all sorts of damage thanks to their power over supernatural forces: They kill dogs, destroy dwellings and gardens, and take possession of souls to deliver them to demons. They are entrusted with the defense of their community against the same evils. A shaman's reputation can spread very far, but it is never founded on his successes in curing the sick; the more a shaman is feared because of his crimes and destructive deeds, the greater is his renown.

From the foregoing, it becomes easier to grasp how nothing would ever be fortuitous, how the incidents and accidents of life would necessarily be considered effects of other people's ill will. A snake bites someone, a jaguar kills a dog, a scorpion stings a child, a tornado destroys the shelter and devastates the gardens: Such events are not accidental but result from a deliberate intent to do harm. The forest animals are harmless; those that kill are supernatural beasts sent by enemy shamans. As for the wind, it is always a manifestation of the *hekura*'s movements; it becomes a tempest only if it is incited by an external hostile intent.

A long time ago, there was a shaman who was tormented by an ardent desire to make love. He went to the garden, where he met a beautiful young girl. He took hold of her arm and tried to draw her under the trees; but she bit him so cruelly that he released her. He was so furious that he wanted to avenge himself. One day, when she was in the forest cutting wood, he sent the *hekura*, who made a sharp branch fall on her foot. The wood was poisonous; the wound became infected and the woman died in agonizing pain. That shaman was abusing his power: Instead of attacking members of distant communities, he turned against his own. His companions, weary of his misdeeds, decided to kill him and pierced him with their spears. The *hekura* came to fetch his body and carried it away to the *makayo* mountain to place it into a recess in the rock.

Kaõmawë, who is recalling the story, adds:

I know the call song of that shaman, thanks to the spirits who deserted him and came into my breast. They help me cure little children.

Then he goes on to personal adventures:

115

The magical powers

We had gone hunting, and we were walking upstream along the sandy bed of a river. We came to a spot where the fish were plentiful, and we decided to shoot them in the clear water. I wanted to remain alone so as to be undisturbed. I told the others:

Go kill them upstream; I'll stay here.

While I was watching the fish, my dog was running in circles around me. He had probably scented an animal, and he was following it. Suddenly he started howling with pain; I knew that he had just been attacked by a jaguar. I started to run, but no matter how I searched, I could not find him. The ground was littered with cashews; I had noticed from afar the amaranthine color of their skins, which contrasted with the dullness of the dry leaves. I gathered a large quantity, crushed them in leaves, and I soon had a juice that I drank with relish. When I had finished drinking, I raised my head, and my eyes met those of the jaguar that had returned and was standing before me with the dead dog slung across its neck. I gave a start. When it saw that I was watching it, the cat let the dog's body fall to the ground. I had already grasped my weapons, and I pulled my bow. The lanceolate point sank into the jaguar's chest. The beast, wounded to death, snarled and crawled toward me. When it was dead, I stepped forward in order to take the dog, and I shouted to call my companions:

aë! aë!

As for them, they were having a good time. They had discovered a hole full of electric fish and had decided:

Let's see if the discharge is powerful.

They had formed a chain, and one of them had taken his position at one end to strike the fish with a machete. With each blow the electric discharge, transmitted by the metal blade and the wet handle, traveled along the whole chain through all the hands, arms, and shoulders. With every shock they burst into peals of laughter and jumped up and down without letting go of each other's hands. When they heard my call, they hurried toward me with a great deal of noise and banter. I told them of the dog's death; their laughter froze on their lips, and they started to weep. We cut off the jaguar's head and we carried home the dead dog. In the plaza of the *shabono* we built two fires; we burned the dog's body on one and the jaguar's head on the other. That is how one destroys the teeth to take revenge: They killed the dog.

I took some hallucinogenic drugs and discovered that *shamat^hari* shamans had sent the jaguar to kill my dog. I tried to take revenge; but they attempted to assassinate me with an *aroami* snake.

It was the season of high waters; we had left the *shabono* to escape the demons of disease that were persecuting us, and we had established our encampment on the bank of the "river of the *shitibori* trees." The first night after we set up our camp, I had a dream. I saw some *hekura,* very far away, who were carrying a snake. They flew over me, almost stopped, hesitated, then continued their flight: When I woke, they had disappeared without striking me.

At daybreak, most of the men and women went off to kill *yaraka* fish. "Mother of my daughter" said to me:

Let us also go and catch some fish; we'll eat them with roasted plantain.

I was uneasy about the dream I had just had; it was a bad omen, and I knew that I would be bitten if I ventured into the forest. I answered:

Let's not do this today. I dreamt about a snake, and I don't want to go out.

You never want to go; you always have an excuse. Moriwë's father, *he* went. Do as he did, and we'll offer food to the others.

116

Spells

You are stubborn. Let's go downriver; never mind if something happens to me.

We walked downstream along the brook; in a wide depression, there were quantities of small fish swimming about against a background of plant debris. I shot at them with a child's bow and arrows. They hid under the bank and soon disappeared. Mabroma went down into the water, where she caught them by sticking her fingers into the holes where they had taken refuge. The fear of the snake was not leaving me. I didn't want to remain alone on the bank, and I went to help Mabroma in the water. We killed a great many fish, and we soon had a shiny heap of them on the sand. We cleaned and washed them, then wrapped them in *bishaa* leaves. I said:

It is time to go back.

I still had a foreboding that I would be bitten, even after we had returned to camp. The others had caught almost nothing. We placed the bundle on the coals and put up some plantain to roast. Dusk was approaching, the forest was darkening. Frērema had found honey; one could hear the regular blows of his axe against the trunk. Presently the tree crashed, and its fall shook the ground. Mabroma said to me:

Let's go eat honey. We should hurry, otherwise none will be left for us.

I said:

Huu!

We drank the honey diluted with water; it was slightly tart, and I thought it was good. I did not want to linger, but the others proposed:

Come hunt partridges with us.
No, I won't go.

I returned to my shelter. At the encampment, other men were leaving on the hunt, who also asked me to accompany them:

Come with us.
No.
You won't go far away; we'll separate.
No, I prefer staying here.
Well, stay then!

They were already on their way; I don't know what came over me, but I suddenly changed my mind:

Wait, I'm going with you!

We made our way around a hill, we climbed a knoll, then we followed the bed of a brook; at each loop of the stream, the sand grew deeper. I announced:

I'm staying here; you continue without me.

I went the wrong way: precisely where the snake was. I squatted down, waiting to hear the clucking of a partridge to knock it down. A call presently sounded near me:

e, e, e, . . .

I placed my hand on my mouth to imitate the call; the partridge answered, and I was able to approach it; then I waited motionless until it came to rest on a branch. I was thinking:

It is right in front of me.

117

The magical powers

The forest darkened. When I was sure that the partridge was roosting, I crept toward it. I wanted to make out the exact spot where it was, and I left my weapons behind. I spied it on a low branch. When I went back to pick up my bow, I heard another partridge call somewhere else; I knew by its song that it was of the *yohoami* species.

It was almost dark when I stepped forward to kill it, my head thrown back, scanning the trees. I bumped into a nest of wasps; they stung me, and I ran to escape them. In order to get near the partridge and gain a good shooting angle, I had to cross the brook. I jumped and landed right on the snake, which was coiled on the sand. It was an *aroami;* it bit me on the leg, and I suddenly thought my calf would burst. I had the presence of mind to crush the reptile's head with my bow. I was in despair and wanted to throw my arrows away. I was thinking about the partridge: Should I return to camp without killing it? What would the others say?

I kept an arrow. I was stumbling and found it difficult to stay on my feet. Still, I managed to aim accurately. I tied the bird to my back, left my arrows propped against the trunk of a tree, and made my way home leaning on my bow. The muscles in my injured leg were hardening and stiffening; I was staggering and stumbling over roots, and several times I had to sit down because I was dizzy. It was pitch-dark when I reached camp. I said:

I was bitten by an *aroami* snake.

I was worn out. An intense pain wrenched my belly and I could hardly breathe: I thought I was about to die. I called Moriwë's father, who brought forth the *hekura* out of his chest, and they gave me back my soul that had been stolen by enemy shamans. I was unable to sleep all night and could not stop moaning, so great was the pain in my leg.

Two days went by. Moriwë's father came to care for me every afternoon. As there was little food in the neighborhood and our stock of plantains was running low, we decided to return to the great dwelling. I could not walk, so they cut a long, sturdy pole, hung my hammock from it, and took turns carrying me. We made it to the *shabono,* but not without much toil.

At night I dreamed. I saw the *hekura* shooting fiery darts at me. They stayed at a respectable distance, realizing that I was watching them. I scattered them with my hand. They kept on watching for some time; they were *shamatʰari* shamans. They are prudent and wary, and since they realized they had been discovered, they said:

Let's leave; there is no point staying here.

It was only a trick on their part: They pretended to go away. Their stratagem deceived me; I relaxed and went back to sleep. That was a serious mistake. They brought down from the sky an object unknown to me. The night was pitch-black; the moon had been "dead" for several days. When that unknown object was near me, I had a premonition and opened my eyes. My chest was glistening from a viscid, greaselike substance. I struck with the edge of my hand. I struck desperately, as hard as I could, for I had to drive them off, or they were going to kill me. Omawë's son helped me fight against them. Suddenly, the thing tore and dissipated. One last time I shouted:

Wau! wau! wau!
The *shamatʰari* shamans very nearly killed me.

Kaõmawë further explains:

When shamans want to cause death by means of a snake, they cut a length of vine and split one end to simulate the mouth. They paint designs on the body and glue

118

white down on the head. Then they stroke their creature, which comes alive and really becomes a snake. The shamans then take it away and set it down, coiled, at the edge of a path where they know their victim will walk. At other times, they send the *hekura* into the sky, to the land of Thunder and of the souls. They meet *hera* and ask him for a snake: He has numbers of them, coiled around him; they are his domestic animals. These are the snakes that attack us; those that live in the forest never attack people. The *hekura*'s snakes are frightful; their bite attracts worms and causes the flesh to decay. The *hekura* lie in wait near the snake they have set down and strike at the same time. Only the *kaomari* bird can fight them successfully.

Moriwë and Wakamoshiwë have just arrived at the old *shabono* of Karohi. They used to live there a few years ago, farther downstream on the "river of rains." Every five or six years, the Yanomami abandon their old dwelling and build another on newly cleared land. The old shelter has deteriorated: The vines of the roof, weakened by decay, give way under the weight of the leaves; streams of gourd creepers hang down from the structure and invade the central plaza, their yellow flowers sharply etched against the surrounding vegetation. The ground is littered with hard-shelled gourds that the women use to fashion calabashes. The two men reach the old garden and make their way through an extraordinary tangle of thorny bushes. A few banana trees are still producing; they cut two bunches that will soon be ripe. Moriwë walks ahead on the now-obliterated path; he bends down, suddenly alert, and stops short: Sharp, recent footprints are impressed in the earth. He signals his companion to come near:

Look, enemy warriors came through here this morning.

This discovery chills them; they prefer not to linger in this place.

As a precaution, they sleep some distance away in the nearby forest, without taking the trouble to build a shelter. A fire burns next to them; they hope that it will not rain. Moriwë sleeps and dreams. Morayema calls him:

My son, come and help me hang up the bananas.

He goes to her and they couple, standing. When he withdraws, he sees that his penis is red with blood. He asks:

Aren't you menstruating?
Yes, I am.
Oh, I'll never make love with you again.

A suspicious movement on the river wakes them in the middle of the night: Vague and strange splashes growing louder, suddenly followed by something diving into the water close by with a great splash. They take fright, imagining that a powerful animal is striking the water with its tail and is swimming in their direction. A *rahara* must have noticed the fire and is coming to swallow them. They flee under the trees, far away from the river, out of reach of the water monster. They stay there, squatting in silence until dawn, despite their sleepiness, the cold, and the mosquitoes. Moriwë recalls those men of Hasubïwë, whose story his father has told him: They were busy building a footbridge over the Orinoco to make it easier to reach their garden when a gigantic wave suddenly rose and swallowed them; they never reappeared, and it was certain that a *rahara* had eaten them.

Upon their return to Karohi, they recounted the events they witnessed. Shimoreiwë does not believe that the prints in the garden were left by raiders; he has just heard that visitors from Wayabotorewë have gone to Tayari, and it is surely they who came to steal from the garden on their way through.

Mabroma is cooking tubers on the coals; she turns them from time to time, and when they are done, she carefully scrapes them. Kremoanawë eats a few before picking up his arrows, checking the tips and making sure that they are straight by sighting along the shafts. He straightens one of them over the heat of the fire, then repairs the fraying strap of his quiver by rolling it on his thigh. Next he takes out his earlobe plugs: The bowstring or some vines could catch them and tear his earlobe while he is shooting or pursuing an animal. Finally he turns to Hebëwë:

Come hunting with me, little brother. You'll carry the game.

They walk into the forest and find caterpillar droppings; they examine them and notice that they come from the *maya* species and that the caterpillars are still too small to eat. They will come back later; they will inform those of Karohi of their discovery; they will publicly announce:

At such a place, on such a tree, there are *maya* caterpillars: They belong to us; we'll gather them when they are grown.

The two brothers proceed on their quest for game. They disturb a curassow that rises heavily and flies away, and they cannot find the spot where it alighted. A moment later they scatter a flock of agamis; but Kremoanawë hides behind a stump and imitates the call of a young one; deceived, the birds return trustingly and Hebëwë kills one. They cut out the bird's shimmering breast to make an armband; then they turn back.

They have just come home when the sky darkens. One of those brief and violent end-of-day squalls is in the making. A deep, thick, and dark cloud threatens on the horizon. The warm air is still, heavy and moist. Presently, there is a rumbling noise, indistinct at first, then swelling and crashing. A breeze rises, sends shudders through the foliage, and makes the banana trees rustle, then grows in volume and sings among the forest trees like a many-voiced organ. Thick drops splatter on the ground, few and distant at first.

The very next moment, the tornado is here, with its torrential rain and irresistible winds. The slow swaying of the trees has suddenly become uncontrolled; the forest is raging as if maddened. Tree trunks twist and burst, snapping like matchsticks. Branches are hurled afar.

All around one hears nothing but the noise of cracking posts, crashing masses, and roaring thunder. The shelter is overrun, despite the shamans who are hurling their fire darts, dealing machete blows, and fighting step by step in the plaza to repel the invasion of the enemy *hekura*. They are overwhelmed. A palm tree crashes through the roof over Moriwë's quarters, while the wind pulls off Shimoreiwë's roof in one swoop. The inhabitants have only time enough to jump out of their hammocks, which are ripped away from the supporting posts, and it is a miracle that no one is killed or injured. The shamans struggle until exhausted, lashed by the wind and the rain; women sob under shelters that no longer protect anything; children howl with terror, clinging to their mothers' arms.

The end is as sudden as the beginning. The storm subsides, the rain patters quietly, the thunder moves away.

An apocalyptic landscape now surrounds the destroyed shelter. In the garden, the banana trees are crushed against the earth. Of the beautiful drug-producing trees, source of so much pride, there remains only a tangle of branches. The *rasha* palms are devastated. In the forest, the wind has opened wide furrows lined with uprooted trees and obstructed the trails with branches and vines that will have to be cleared with machetes; mangled stumps point their long fibrous fingers at the sky. From time to time, a loose tree, tangled in another's branches, gives off a sinister crack. The rush of enemy *hekura,* manifesting themselves in the storm, has worked this destruction: It is the Spider Monkey Spirit that hung on the branches to break them; it is the Jaguar Spirit that pushed down the trees and shattered them; and it is the Giant Armadillo Spirit that uprooted them when digging its tunnel.

Turaewë denounces the enemy. The *hekura*, he says, were sent by Bukumariwë, a *shamatʰari* shaman, for the express purpose of destroying the dwelling and gardens of Karohi; they were so numerous and violent that the free spirits of the forest must have joined those sent by the shaman. Turaewë exclaims:

> I recognized Bukumariwë, it was he who led them. We shall take revenge!

Toward nightfall, those without a roof take refuge under the few parts of the shelter that are still intact. They retrieve their hammocks, dry them, and repair them. Conversations and commentaries pick up; everyone is talking about the storm.

The decision has been taken: The very next day, Turaewë will marshal the *hekura* scattered among the rocks and unleash them against the *shamatʰari* to avenge the destruction they caused. That night the shaman has a dream that confirms Bukumariwë's responsibility for the disaster.

The next day, toward noon, Kaõmawë fetches a strip of *ama* bark to prepare the drug required for the fulfillment of the ritual. He cuts it into pieces each about fifteen centimeters long, which he places on the coals and turns once in a while until they start smoking and catch fire. He then gathers them

Hunters' encampment and smoking grill.

in a broken earthen pot where, fanned into a sustained fire, they produce a light, very pale grey powder. Kaõmawë next unrolls the long wrapping that contains the hallucinogenic seeds; he tears off a piece, gets rid of the roaches that infest it, and carefully reties the package. On the ground he spreads a banana leaf over which he sifts the ashes; then he sits down on a log and squeezes his hands between his thighs to press the seeds and ashes vigorously together into a uniform mass. When he is satisfied with the mixture's consistency, he places the broken pot on the coals and waits until it is burning hot before crumbling the paste into it. The smell rises and spreads, heavy, suffocating, and nauseating all at once. When dry, the substance disintegrates easily; Kaõmawë can crush it with a flat stone until he obtains a perfectly fine, smooth powder.

When the powder is ready, Kaõmawë scours his tube, wedges it under his arm, and carries the drug toward the destroyed shelter. The other shamans assemble there, all of them painted and adorned to suit the occasion. The ritual of inhalation begins, with Turaewë leading and officiating. He utters the call to the *hekura,* gathers them near him, embodies them all in turn by characterizing them with some salient trait. Here are the Puma Spirit with his enormous testicles, the Giant Armadillo Spirit with his impressive penis and ridiculous gait, the Tamandua Spirit, the Sloth Spirit who gives orders to the others and stoically bears the cruelest wounds. Here also are Taisinakawë,

122

son of Thunder, and the Jaguar Spirit. When he has gathered his allies around him, Turaewë pauses for breath and asks for fresh doses of drug. Then he calls forth the beings of the storm: Ruwëriwë, Spirit of dark weather and thick, deep fogs, and Ihiroitʰawë, Spirit of clouds and mists.

All the shamans, the great and the minor ones, the powerful ones and the others, take turns marshaling their *hekura*. Mokaukawë performs last; his songs and imitations are particularly crude, and the young people who are attending the ceremony as spectators openly delight in mocking him.

Turaewë takes the initiative again. He digs a hole in the ground to fit a calabash filled with an imaginary liquid, *ami u bë,* a nourishing and intoxicating drink of the *hekura,* the juice of a legendary supernatural fruit, red as blood and sweet as honey; it causes those who drink it to lose their wits. The shamans then *are hekura;* they drink from the hollow of their hands or from a ladle to fortify themselves. With the remainder of the drink, Turaewë slowly passes near each shaman to anoint his body, spray it, and paint it with ceremonial motifs: The *hekura* would not go on an expedition without their feathers and their paintings.

When they are ready, Turacwë points out the path they are to follow and assigns them their final destination, henceforth convinced that, under the influence of the magic drink, they will accomplish the mission he is entrusting to them: to unleash the fury of the elements upon the community of Bukumariwë and bring it devastation. When vengeance has thus been satisfied, it guarantees future security, which is assured only if every blow is promptly repaid; to be unable to take revenge, or to neglect to take it, is to show oneself cowardly and powerless and to encourage renewed attacks by an enemy convinced that he can act with impunity.

6

Eaters of souls

Hostile demons, scattered in various locations, haunt the different levels of the universe. They are busy devouring souls, which they capture by surprise inside the dwellings. If they are vigilant, if they have knowledge and power, the protecting shamans recognize them immediately thanks to the fact that each demon has his own particular path and odor. The shamans know how to avoid the perils that threaten those who approach supernatural beings and how to restore their souls to the sufferers; if they fail, the soul is "eaten" and the body, deprived of its energy, of its "center," gradually wastes away and dies.

Transformed into *hekura,* the shamans travel through cosmic space to recover a soul from a demon or from enemies, or to steal one in order to "eat" it. They transport themselves instantaneously to distant places, traveling horizontally from one point of the compass to another, and vertically to reach the celestial disk or to penetrate into the underworld. They are able to describe unknown regions, to name communities or persons known to them only: Their knowledge is not limited to mythological and historical times but encompasses a three-dimensional space.

Whenever necessary, the shamans represent the souls materially: A bouquet of feathers, a bow, an arrow, or a scarlet passionflower stands for a man, a loincloth or a carrying basket for a woman.

Near rivers live dark-feathered, swallow-like birds with a two-pronged tail; they swoop over the streams, sometimes skimming the water, snatch insects in flight, and gather on the dead branches of trees that have fallen into the water. They are called *shoro,* and they constitute the *shorori,* a people of water demons who are also masters of fire; Kakamawë rules them. Under the water, their dwellings are identical to the *shabono:* When they are staying there, they put on a human appearance. It is advisable not to throw missiles at them when they fly above the rivers – as is done for fun with ordinary birds; they would take revenge for the injury. Children must not linger near stagnant waters in the evening, lest the *shoro* steal their souls.

Moriwë almost died at their hands:

124

Eaters of souls

I was still a child. I had an abscess on my thigh; the infection had spread to my entire leg, which had swollen enormously – and all because I had loitered near a swamp toward dusk. I was in such pain that I could not sleep but moaned through the night. My father decided to find out what I had; he inhaled the drug and discovered that the *shorori* had taken possession of my soul. He called down his *hekura*. I was sitting; in front of me had been planted a bow with a bouquet of feathers tied to one end. My father changed into a *hekura* and set out on the path of the *shorori*. This path is fiery hot; he was suffering from the torrid heat; the soles of his feet became covered with blisters; he grimaced with pain. He was about to turn back when Hebëwë's father came to the rescue; he cooled him with calabashes of water and struck him with boughs to fan him. My father could now better withstand the searing heat; he reached the bow, tore off the bouquet of feathers, and fled with it. He had just restored my soul to me when he collapsed on the ground with a great cry: The fire of the *shorori* was consuming him; he was about to die. He was quickly carried to a hammock; people poured water on his brow and splashed some over him; my mother whipped his shoulders and back with a handful of leaves. She was weeping, as was my little sister, for we all thought that my father would not survive. But he opened his eyes and soon arose from the hammock; he was saved.

As for me, I felt relief. The swelling disappeared and I stopped suffering. Now I never loiter near the water when night is near.

Moriwë speaks of his father's voyages:

The *waika* shamans never appear and do not cause us any injury. Only the *shamathari* shamans bother us: They send storms, hide snakes on the path, capture souls. Not long ago, Thoruwë, a shaman of Yeisikorowë, had captured the soul of Hebëwë's father. My father immediately took the drug. He traveled with Ritimi's father on board a long flying canoe. They flew so high that they almost touched the Milky Way; the heat was stifling. They swooped down on Yeisikorowë, rained fire bolts on the enemy shamans, and, taking advantage of the confusion provoked by their assault, they recovered the soul. In the meantime, the enemy shamans pulled themselves together and took their turn hurling fiery missiles. Ritimi's father, hit in the throat, was unable to regain his seat in the canoe. My father was out of breath and had to abandon him, and it was Bokorawë who went to deliver him on the occasion of a visit.

Another time, Mamokoriwë came to see us from Mahekoto to have his eye cured. He had excruciating stabbing pains and was afraid of going blind. My father called down the *hekura* and saw that the Sun Spirit had taken the vital principle of the eye in order to destroy it. To get to the land of Sun one must first reach a distant, embryonic, and diaphanous world of torrid heat, the Milky Way. My father changed into a spider monkey and climbed a supporting post. Other shamans joined him on the expedition; some were howling monkeys, others saki monkeys, others yet were squirrels. They started to climb toward the roof. The heat increased as they rose and was soon so violent that they had to be doused with water. When they set foot in the superior world, they again changed their natures; my father had become a hailstone so that the cold might protect him from the fire; Ritimi's father was an anaconda, Hebëwë's a *rahara*, and it was the water where these animals live that enabled them to bear the oven-like heat. Sun wanted to drive them off in order to keep the eye and eat it, and he aimed powerful rays at them. My father ordered us to place a carrying basket in the middle of the central plaza and to tie it to a stake. We did this while he was coming down from the roof. In that basket, Sun was keeping the eye. My father walked up to it, untied it, and carried it away. All the shamans had again changed into saki monkeys. They were shouting:

125

The magical powers

hōsē! hōsē!

They restored its vital principle to Mamokoriwë's eye.

Thunder is the master of the *morē* fruits. Formerly he was a tapir. He was killed by Fēifēiyomi's elder brother, who quartered him and carried him to his shelter. When the liver was cooked, they wanted to eat him. During the distribution of the portions, Fēifēiyomi had squatted down next to his elder brother; he was offered the pancreas. He was so angry at receiving such a bad portion that he flung it into the sky where it became Thunder. As for Fēifēiyomi, he changed into a bird; he is Thunder's son-in-law and lives with him in the shelter of the souls. Recently, my father went to Thunder to ask for the *morē* fruits. He prepared the drug, called Hebëwë's father, and they acted as if to climb the supporting posts; their feet were not leaving the ground, and yet they were already very high. My father advised Hebëwë's father:

Don't look down, or you'll get dizzy.

People who are dizzy let go and fall down. They were afraid, knowing that they were very high, and they shouted:

Hi-i! Hi-i!

They reached the celestial disk, set foot on it, and took a moment's rest. They first met Thunder's son-in-law, chatted with him, and convinced him to go to his father-in-law and divert his attention. Fēifēiyomi perched on the rope of Thunder's hammock and started to sing:

Fēi, fēi, fēi, yo!

That is how he sings in the forest. In the meantime, the two shamans entered the dwelling of the souls; they saw from afar Thunder with his curly hair and his eyelids heavy with warts. They took the *morē* trees and scattered their fruits over the earth, which was thus made fruitful. But they had seen the souls; among them they had recognized dead relatives. They burst into tears and lamentations. We were below and had understood what was happening; we started to sob at the thought of the departed. My father had seen his true parents: his father and his mother.

The rain has just stopped. A rainbow is arching over the trees; the Yanomami call it boa's belly, saying that it is the path where Omayari, the demon, watches human beings to send them diarrhea and other diseases and to capture their souls. The demon is split into an East Omayari and a West Omayari, just as rainbows appear sometimes in the east and sometimes in the west. For the Yanomami, a rainbow, like a red sunset, always has a baneful connotation; that is why they avoid pronouncing the name of Omayari when one appears. To pronounce the name of the demon is to call him; for the same reason, they do not speak of the jaguar in the forest, of the *rahara* near the water, of the ghost at the coming of night, or of anything that signifies danger or unpleasantness.

For a few days now the whole population of Tayari has been living at Karohi. The spacious *shabono* easily houses the two groups. The garden had yielded a plentiful manioc harvest, and many baskets are filled with cakes; the forest abounds with wild fruits; the busy and clever hunters rarely return

126

empty-handed. There is no lack of food. But the opposite was the case at Tayari. They had cleared the gardens too late; the new plantings had not matured in time to replace the old exhausted ones. That is why the inhabitants have come to their relatives and allies of Karohi to ask for aid, knowing that some day they will be called upon to give the same assistance in return.

As leaders of factions, Shimoreiwë and Kaõmawë compete with each other in their zeal on behalf of their guests. They take turns offering banana soup, send their hunters after game, organize great sessions of drug-taking and shamanism.

The people of Tayari are distributed within the dwelling according to their kinship ties with their hosts: Some are staying with brothers, others with married sisters and brothers-in-law, still others, settled at a decent distance, accept the hospitality of their sons-in-law.

The shelter hums with overflowing life. Long-sustained, shrill, and repeated cascades of laughter flare up everywhere, provoked by jokes or funny memories. News items are passed along, often amplified and distorted; tattletales take delight in gossip and scandalmongering. Plans are laid, never to be realized. Youths compete for the girls' attention, and jealous, suspicious husbands tighten their vigilance. Special friendships are strengthened, others are born. Personal alliances are formed, jealousies and hatreds are set off. What dominates, however, is the breath of friendship that circulates through the whole shelter, warm as a fire after a drenching rain.

To meet the sudden increase in demand for dye, Mabroma has gone to the garden to gather the hairy pods of the roucou trees. She takes out the seeds, boils them in water, then presses out the juice through a cloth and heats it again to a slow boil on a low fire. Squeezing her abdomen with her two hands, she pronounces the following formula:

Blood clot of a tapir, blood clot of a tapir.

The decoction will thus acquire the color and consistency of a tapir's blood clots. Meanwhile, Kaõmawë is burning a piece of resin. He covers it with a calabash, so that the soot will be deposited on the inner surfaces; he will only need to scrape it off and mix it into the thickened roucou to turn the dye from bright red to ochre-brown, which is the color used for body painting.

While his father is thus occupied, Hebëwë asks him:

Have you heard about that woman who became a shaman at S^huimɨwei?
No.
The news was brought by one of the visitors.
It's possible. Women cannot be initiated, but some of them are acute clairvoyants who sometimes receive the revelation of the *hekura*. There is a *hekura* woman among the Waika; her name is Wëikayoma. I don't remember where she lives.
Do the female shamans treat the sick?
They take hallucinogens, sing to the spirits, and are capable of going after a

patient's soul. Wẽikayoma kills children, whose souls she eats, and she is always on her guard: Every time a shaman comes to strike her, she detects him right away, wards off his blows, and pursues him.

During her stay at Karohi, Breimi falls ill. She has terrible abdominal cramps that make her cry out in pain. Turaewë, when consulted, does not immediately pronounce a diagnosis. He hesitates and takes his time. That night, the shaman has a dream that reveals the cause of the illness: He sees Titiri, the white-haired demon of the night, creep up to the sleeping Breimi, press her waist between his thighs, insert his monstrous penis into her vagina, and force the opening until the flesh tears. Hence the pain she feels.

In former days, endless daylight reigned over the earth. Titiri did not yet exist as a demon; he was only a gigantic curassow that "wept" endlessly, always sitting on the same branch that he never left. He wept and wept, and dusk did not come. So the Yanomami slept during the day; they went hunting, came back, ate their quarry, did not quarrel, and slept only when they were tired. They could hear the Curassow Spirit singing plaintively, saying: "*Titiri, titiri, titiri, wẽ!*"

And he went on singing, naming rivers, mountains, rocks:

> That way is the "rock of the ghosts,"
> that way the "mountain of the taro,"
> this way the "river of the *tʰoru* flowers,"
> here is the "river of thorns."

It is he who gave their names to the places of the forest.

The Yanomami thought that night would come if they killed him. They encouraged one another: "Go on, try! Try! The one we hear all the time, that one is a demon."

As they had no knowledge of night, they slept when the sun was high in the sky. Always Titiri was weeping. The branch on which he sat bent down to the ground under his weight. The elders incited the young people: "Try, my children!"

One day, they walked toward the source of the song. They saw Titiri flap his wings to shake out the parasites. They drew nearer. One of them shot an arrow that grazed the bird's feathers. At that very moment, the sky darkened and they thought night was coming; for the first time they heard the voices of the night: rustlings of insect wings, croakings of frogs and toads. It lasted only a moment; then it was daylight once more, and the bird resumed his lament. "We were right, my children; that is what we must do. Let us try again."

Hõrõnami declared: "*I* am going to kill him."

He was a good hunter and a good marksman; his arrow pierced the Curassow Spirit whose body, wounded to death, fell heavily. The noises of the night sounded a second time. Some white feathers loosened from the bird's lower abdomen and moved away in a long file after changing into demons of

128

twilight, the *weyari*. The night was pitch-black, and the Yanomami could not find their way. They asked one another: "Where are we?"

They were groping about and shouting to those who had stayed in the shelter: "Hey, you over there, come and get us!"

The others heard them; they made bundles of firebrands that they waved before them to light their way. They went back to the shelter and said: "I'm sleepy!"

They began to snore. Some ordered their wives: "Light a fire here; I'm cold!"

They fell into a deep sleep and dreamed for the first time. The birds announced the coming of daylight; it was dawn. The elders spoke: "Rise, my children, it is time to leave for the hunt!"

Since then, Titiri has changed into a demon and torments the Yanomami. His penis is inordinately long and thick. He couples with women and sodomizes men, without their knowledge, while they are asleep, tears their flesh with his member, and captures their souls after he has ejaculated.

The similarities between the dwelling's shape and the Yanomami conception of the universe have already been noted. The central plaza is the highest part of the sky; the supporting posts serve the shamans as ladders to climb into the superior world; they are links between one level and the next. Indeed, the superior world is conceived as a convex structure; its center is a flat disk, and its sides slope gently down to the horizon where they touch the earth – just as the shelter's roof gradually slopes down to the ground. And Titiri lives at the meeting point of the earthly and celestial worlds. If one keeps in mind the correspondences set forth above, that place, in the configuration of the dwelling, is the perimeter of the low side of the roof. Indeed, it is on that circle that Turaewë has someone hang a basket containing a log and a cotton loincloth – at a point diametrically opposite the spot where the cure is taking place. The log represents Titiri's penis, and the loincloth symbolizes the sick girl's soul.

The shamans of Tayari and Karohi join their efforts under the direction of Turaewë. Thanks to the drug, they have worked a change in their nature; they have become *hekura*. First they scatter, look for firebrands, which they tie into bundles, then line up in single file, preceded by Turaewë, who has found the path to Titiri's lair. That path is hidden in the most complete darkness and is studded with thorns. Turaewë is standing; he moves on tiptoes and clears the thorns in his way; the others are squatting, and the firebrands they are holding at arm's length enable them to see. The familiar *hekura* surround them and dispel the fog that envelops them. They cross the central plaza and injure their feet despite their cautious progress. To prevent them from reaching the soul, Titiri urinates on the firebrands; several times he almost puts them out, and they must pause to revive them. Still, they reach

129

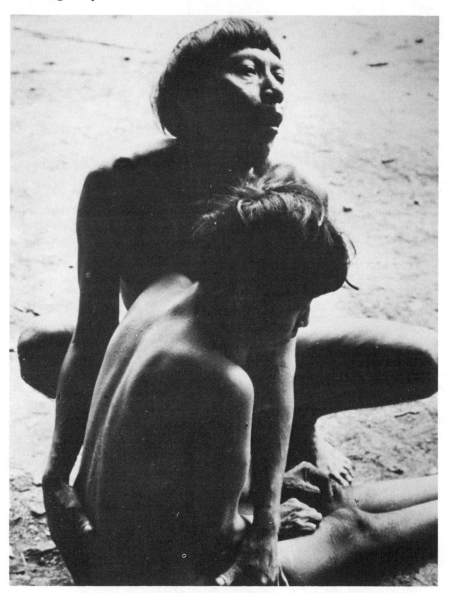

Turaewë cures Breimi who has been made ill by Titiri.

The shamans advance on the way to Titiri.

Turaewë carries the basket containing the demon's penis and his victim's soul.

their goal; Turaewë hugs Titiri around the body and snatches the basket, which he sets down in front of the sick girl. He removes the log and the cotton loincloth and simulates sexual intercourse. He handles the penis until he provokes ejaculation; the demon's sperm gushes forth in a copious flood, spills on the ground, and splashes over everything. Turaewë now only needs to draw out of the girl's body the "reflection" – it is also called "the image,"

132

the "shadow" – of the male member that is still contaminating her; then he gives the penis back to Titiri and sends him to Rumirumiyoma, his mother-in-law, so that she may watch over him.

One year ago, Turaewë's son, little Heturawë, died. For whole nights, the great shaman had fought to wrest the child from the claws of the devouring demons, but the young patient's cough had become deeper and harsher, his cheeks had hollowed. It seemed at one time that his condition was going to improve. That was a vain hope: He had died suddenly one night while his father was singing at his side to cure him. Turaewë had failed. Defeated, he could not hide his distress; his confidence in his powers had been permanently shaken; for many weeks he had not been able to free himself from an infinite sadness.

Since the arrival of the guests from Tayari, the allusions to his dead son have become frequent again: Few nights go by without Turaewë voicing long funeral lamentations; in the songs to the *hekura,* his reproaches burst forth and his desire for vengeance rises to the surface.

Here is what he is saying today, during the collective session of shamanism:

Ocelot Spirit, come down into me! *Hekura,* you did not help me. For whole nights I pondered my vengeance. I saw the Vulture Spirit and the Moon Spirit. Moon Spirit was struck by Suhirina's arrow when he invaded the dwelling, eager for human flesh; and from his wound, from his spilled blood, were born a multitude of flesh-eating vultures. Moon Spirit, Vulture Spirit, you are cannibals. Vulture, your head is polluted with blood, your nostrils teem with worms. The dragonflies gather in the sky. Omawë pierced the earth with his bow; out of the hole he made sprang a gusher of water that reached the sky and formed a canopy. Up there the dragonflies multiply; up there live the thirsty ones. Let them come down into me! Omawë has burned my tongue! Let them moisten my tongue and refresh it! Those who have ordered the demons to capture our children will receive my vengeance, wherever they may be. Already the *hekura* are advancing on them; already the *hekura* are rushing on them. Soon night will come, they will sleep soundly, and the little children's cries will ring out. They are many, the *hekura* in my breast! You, people of Hiyōmisi, *shamtʰari,* among you lives Breiwë, the murderer. May lightning unveil the sky, may thunder explode! However distant you may be, I shall reach you; I shall choose the most beautiful child, the one with the attractive smile, and I shall kill him. I, too, eat children. My *hekura* will come toward you, do not doubt it, and they will tear the birds' breasts and the decorative feathers; then my nostrils will fill with the strong odor of the newborn; they will breathe out the stale smell of mother's milk, and my breast will be like a carcass. That is how my breast will be!

Moon piles up the roots of rotten manioc with which he makes cakes that he cooks in old potsherds. When the cakes are ready, he prowls around the dwellings and calls to the children from afar, shouting:

Come to me, I am hungry for human flesh!

The scatterbrains go to him, and he carries them away to eat them with his cakes. Formerly, Moon was a true *hekura* who lived in the body of a great shaman. When

133

The demon's penis is removed from the basket.

that shaman died, Moon was liberated from his chest and wandered freely in space. Under the great roof there was deep sorrow as they grieved for the dead shaman:

What a great shaman he was! What grief, my husband!

His wife was sobbing. They built the pyre and burned the body. When the ashes had cooled, sobs and cries of grief swelled again. At that moment, Moon came down into the central plaza; he walked through the dead man's empty hearth and made his way to the ashes of the pyre and the bones, which could soon be heard cracking between his teeth. The deceased's son approached and thought that it was his father, for Moon looked vaguely like him. He said:

Father, father!

The other kept on eating the charred bones without listening to him. The son took a few more steps. When the child was near him, Moon rose and slowly walked away. Then they realized their mistakes: Someone they did not know had come to eat the charred remains of the dead man. Their anger flared forth:

Let's kill him, it's someone else!

They loosed their arrows, which whistled on all sides. Moon was already rising in the sky. They were on the perimeter of the shelter, but their arrows missed their mark. Suhirina, standing there, was smirking at seeing them such poor shots:

How is that possible?

They were shooting at Moon, who was rising without haste: The missiles flew up and fell back again before reaching him. Moon was about to disappear into the clouds. One of them came up to Suhirina:

Brother-in-law, isn't it true, as they say, that you are an excellent marksman? Will you remain here doing nothing?

Suhirina rose; his arrow was slender and bore a long, narrow point; he pulled his bow and took aim. Moon had become an imperceptible dot. Suhirina said:

Listen to the vibrations of the arrow; it will travel far.

Indeed, it rose, higher and higher, and sank straight into Moon. Blood gushed out in great spurts and spread in all directions, polluting the earth. Over there, toward the south, each drop of blood changed into a Yanomami of the *shamatʰari*, who are brave and fierce, and who began killing one another. Blood flowed everywhere. From that blood were also born Shãkinari, the cannibal demon, and the vultures, which are also cannibals. We, the Yanomami in this region, we do not come from Moon's blood: We are the sons of the Kanaboromi bird whose calf was impregnated by his companion.

Several more days go by. Turaewë grows gloomy and retires into an impenetrable silence; one can feel that he is concentrating. His resolve comes suddenly, during a drug-taking session that was so dull that it seemed it would not lead to any noteworthy event. The great shaman requests the help of those visitors who are capable of assisting him in bringing death to Hiyõmisi, where the culprit lives. They inhale the magical powder and become *hekura*. Turaewë says:

Moon Spirit, Moon Spirit! *Tei, tei* . . . I am working my transformation, I am changing my nature, I am other. My sons, see the evil demons prowling around us.

135

He imitates Koimawë, a falcon and great eater of souls:

Kakakaka . . . Eat! Eat!

A child comes near, his nose in the air. They shout to him from afar:

Go away, stay away!

Turaewë ignores the incident and asks:

Where does Breiwë live?

They answer:

Over there, upriver, at Hiyōmisi.

They show him the way with their hands. Meanwhile, an assistant shaman is bringing a bunch of white, red, and yellow feathers: It is a male child they are going to kill. Turaewë assembles those who are going to help him accomplish his purpose: the Ant Spirit, the *waroo* Snake Spirit, the Scorpion Spirit. Together, these will strike the child while Koimawë will capture the soul, which he will bring back to Karohi to be handed over to the cannibals.

Here is the Scorpion Spirit!

The chorus of shamans intones:

Moon Spirit! Moon Spirit! The time of the feast is drawing near.

The shamans start out. The scene they are staging at Karohi is really taking place in the enemy dwelling, at Hiyōmisi, where the shamans have now gained entry in immaterial form. A little *shamatʰari* has seen the spirit horde descend upon him. He is handsome. He entreats:

Father! Father! Do not do this, do not kill me! Oh, my father, take me back to where I was born!

It is Turaewë who imitates the young voice. The child has understood that he is about to die; he protects himself with his arms, and terror is in his eyes. All in vain: The Scorpion Spirit sinks his deadly stinger into his flesh, and the *hekura* all strike at once. The child collapses, dead, and the enemies' wails ring out. The little boy's mother sobs:

My son, my beautiful child! They have just killed him!

Breiwë, among them, has guessed. He takes his drug and wants to pursue the aggressors to recapture the soul they are taking away. But Turaewë has now become the Wild Pig Spirit; he scratches the ground, erases the prints that might lead to him and makes pursuit impossible.

The shamans are back at Karohi. Turaewë announces:

The scorpion has stung a child this tall. He is dead!

But the demons are waiting impatiently for their promised soul. The Moon Spirit is there, the Vulture Spirit, the Buzzard Spirit, the voracious Shākinari: the whole hideous crowd of great eaters of souls. Bokorawë is flat on his

136

Eaters of souls

back, embodying the Moon Spirit; his feet are drawn back to his thighs, a
dreadful grimace distorts his face, his teeth are bared, ready to tear the flesh.
In the awed silence of the *shabono,* one can hear the gnashing of teeth.
Koimawë finally arrives, carrying the soul; he delivers the expected prey.
The horrible meal then begins, orchestrated by a riot of sinister and confused
noises. When they are finished the demons stagger toward the plaza; they
have the hiccups; they vomit the child's blood, his veins, his bloody bones,
his fat, his hair. The loathsome regurgitations are wrapped in a leaf and
hidden in the back of the dwelling.

May your heart be at peace, Turaewë, your child is avenged; you have
finally repaid the evil and suffering that had been inflicted on you! The eaters
of souls have come by; tears have erased other tears.

137

III

War and alliance

7

The hunt

The season of visits, of long sojourns outside the great shelter and of wars, has arrived; it is the time of "low waters," and it is possible to travel quickly on almost-dry ground. The streams have shed their excess waters, and the swamps are reduced to modest, greenish puddles teeming with prolific fauna. Fishing, whether with poison, with harpoon arrows, or with hook and line, gives good results. Hunting is easier; the birds are mating, or else, surrounded by their offspring, they are more easily deceived by imitations of their cries.

At Karohi, the gardens are still producing plentifully; there is great abundance of all sorts of bananas, papayas, various tubers, and especially the beautiful, shiny *rasha* fruits that hang down in profuse clusters. That is why Kaōmawe and Shimoreiwë have persuaded the guests to prolong their stay; they want to invite the people of Hōkanakawë to a feast; the ashes of Sisiwë, a "son" killed by the warriors of Mahekoto, will be drunk. After the festivities, the ritual, and the funeral meal, all the able-bodied men will launch an expedition to avenge the dead man.

This war started several years ago, as often happens, because of a woman. Ohimi had just arrived at Wayabotorewë, accompanied by her husband and his elder brother. She had been living with her parents-in-law for a long time, and she wanted to see her mother and her brother again. The family reunion was a happy one. The visitors were well received; the hosts hunted for them and provided them with food and tobacco. Ohimi had hung her hammock near her mother, who did not weary of cuddling her little boy. The husband had remained a decent distance away from his mother-in-law, as is fitting: It was not proper for their glances to meet. All went smoothly, until one day the husband's brother lured Ohimi into the garden to make love. It was not the first time he had acted this way; she put up some resistance for appearances' sake, then she yielded. The husband noticed that they were both absent. He was usually tolerant, for it is accepted among the Yanomami that a man have access to his brothers' wives; but that day he was perhaps hurt in his pride because he was in a foreign group, and he wounded Ohimi in the

141

shoulder when she returned. Ohimi's brother was away; he was informed of the incident, and the mother sent word to him that he had to defend his sister. When he entered the dwelling, he had already fastened his best lanceolate arrowhead. He said nothing; his brother-in-law was turning his back to him, and he shot him at point-blank range. The wound was fatal, for the bamboo had pierced the vital organs; the man's blood poured out, and he soon died. His own brother burned his body in the central plaza, crushed the bones, and took the powder home. Those of Mahekoto lived nearby; when they heard about these events, they appeared, invoked their kinship with the dead man, and claimed one of the gourds containing the bone dust. Their request was granted, for they had a reputation for bravery, and they promised to avenge the dead man. A few months went by; then the ritual of the drinking of the crushed bones was fulfilled at Mahekoto. The very next morning, a group of impatient men started the war. Sisiwë was surprised and killed after a brief but violent encounter. He was a "son" to Kaōmawë and Shimoreiwë, and their grief was deep. They, too, obtained a gourd of ashes and promised to punish the culprits. Karohi was entering the war; the fatal cycle of retaliations, attacks, and counterattacks was set in motion.

When the decision to hold a feast has been taken, two messengers are dispatched to Hōkanakawë. They return after an absence of four days: The invitation has been accepted; the guests will soon set out to cover in easy stages the distance to Karohi. The travelers take pleasure in displaying the things they brought back from their visit: lanceolate arrowheads, curare, a ball of newly spun cotton, aphrodisiacs, and the *manaka,* a plant that makes women sterile.

Without further delay, the bunches of plantains required for the feast are brought back from the garden. Kaōmawë and Shimoreiwë hang them in rows under the roof, slightly in front of their hearths. Within a shelter, the rows of ripening plantains always indicate the quarters of important men who are influential in the political affairs of the community. These are leaders of factions, who are like small chieftains without any but moral authority, but endowed with eloquence, enterprising, competent in matters of hunting and war, and who take the responsibility of organizing long-term hunting expeditions. It is they, too, who provide the vegetable foods that accompany meat and who prepare the banana soup to be offered to the guests. When allied communities are visiting on the occasion of feasts and rituals, their economic role is of prime importance since they must have at their disposal an adequate surplus of food. Hence, their cultivated plots are two or three times larger than their neighbors'. They prefer to devote themselves to agriculture, leaving to younger men – their sons and sons-in-law – the task of providing game for daily consumption; they participate in long-term hunts only if their presence is indispensable. These leaders frequently have several wives. The advantages of polygamy are several: Women help with domestic tasks and with food gathering in the forest; they manufacture objects for barter; a numerous progeny makes it possible to establish a complicated network of alliances. The highest cleverness consists in acquiring wives for one's sons by negotiating whenever possible the briefest possible marital service and in seeking for one's daughters husbands who agree to settle permanently in the community (occasionally, they are granted two wives to persuade them to make that decision). The faction is thus increased, and daughters and sons-in-law are acquired who take part in the common tasks. The importance of these leaders without any power or coercion depends solely on the number of their followers; it can be reduced to nothing if a conflict or a quarrel provokes a split or a defection.

The *heri* hunting ritual begins as soon as the plantains have been hung. After dark, the young men and the older boys come together in groups of three or four to walk arm in arm around the perimeter of the central plaza. Then one of them intones a song, always brief, immediately picked up in chorus by the others. From time to time, they interrupt their walk to dance forward and backward. The melodies are beautiful, in spite of the confusion of voices and the singers' lack of unison. Each community has its *heri* songs; some are popular and, being known to all, are picked up without hesitation; others have just been invented or have been borrowed; these are badly sung, with syllables or words left out.

These songs evoke things imbued with simple poetry:

> Those of Kōbari carry their blowguns
> tightly under their arm.

> The *waika* imitate the *kirakirami* bird,
> like the *kirakirami* bird do the *waika* whistle.

> The macaw swishes its tail,
> its long blue tail.

> The moon tree has been called.

> The jaguar's tail unrolls,
> unrolls, unrolls.

Irrepressible fun, a thousand pranks, obscene jokes accompany the celebration of the *heri;* outbursts of shouts and peals of laughter follow periods of silence and prolonged conferences; then the song resumes, unexpected, lilting and mocking with its nasal tones.

For a long time now, the successive waves of participants have been turning around the plaza, their voices now rising, now falling. Everywhere people have fallen asleep despite the noise. While passing in front of his family's home, Hebëwë, before rejoining his companions, hastily gathers a supply of ripe bananas from the bunches hanging above his father's hammock. Then he chews great mouthfuls of the fruits, which he spits out into

143

his hands, and he flings this pulp, warm and sticky like sperm, onto the faces of sleeping women. That is the signal for a general wasting of bananas: All the boys rush to supply themselves with fruits furtively torn off here and there, and the women become the targets of gluey missiles aimed especially at the genitals, the buttocks, and the face. Sometimes, one of them, in exasperation, hurls a firebrand or some coals at a snickering shadow that jumps aside and is swallowed by the darkness.

The game goes on for hours, interrupted by songs. This mock fight represents not only the antagonism of men and women, but also that of day and night, of silence and noise. Its sexual connotation is obvious. The ritual, which started at nightfall, continues until morning; when the boys, exhausted from so much singing, shouting, laughing, and dancing, go to their hammocks, they are immediately replaced by the young girls. At the moment when their male rivals wish for a peaceful rest, the girls try to repay the outrages they have had to bear. Near dawn, when the first tentative bird songs rise in the forest, the young men again replace the women until the coming of daylight.

For three nights in succession, the same nocturnal scenes take place with the same gusto but with some variation in the pranks. Some young men have almost lost their voices, hoarse from so many excesses. Exhausted, the young people make up during the day the sleep they fail to get at night, so that the days seem more peaceful than usual.

Meanwhile, the color of the plantains has lightened, turning from dark green to yellower hues: It is time for the hunters to set out.

On the morning of the hunters' departure, Mabroma rises well before dawn to bake the manioc cakes that will feed the hunters. She prepares a whole basketful, intended not only for her sons, but also for other hunters, who will give their game to Kaōmawë. The women must accept such additional chores occasioned by a position of responsibility: A leader is expected to be generous and to grant portions of food to the people of his faction who offer their services. Mabroma is busy and efficient: By daylight, the cakes are ready, piled up in an open-work basket. A warm odor of roasted manioc floats all around like a promise of the feast to come.

Above Kaōmawë's hearth hang the bony remains of animals: heads of monkeys and wild pigs, breastbones of birds, armors of armadillos, tails of caimans, and fishbones. These trophies testify to the men's cleverness in the hunt and signify prosperity: In this place, there is always something to go with roasted bananas. These hanging bones, dusty, smoke-stained, and cleaned by the nocturnal nibblings of roaches, ward off the misfortune of becoming *sina,* namely a bad shot and bad hunter. Thanks to these trophies, animals do not flee from the hunter; that is what would happen, however, if they were thrown away. It is the women who thus hang them up, for it is they

144

who receive the heads to suck on, the tails, and the breastbones. When a dwelling is abandoned for another, these bundles of bones remain in place. They are thrown out only when they become too cumbersome or when they are replaced by others; they are then piled into a basket and thrown behind the dwelling on the household refuse. When a man dies, his hunting trophies are burned with him on the funeral pyre.

Mabroma grants herself a moment's rest. She looks absentmindedly at the bundle of old bones hanging next to her; unconsciously, her glance rises along the vine, up to the spot where it is fastened to the roof. Her eyes then fall on a kind of gecko that is holding fast to a dry leaf by means of the suction disks on its feet. For an instant she takes fright; when she collects herself, she warns her husband and her children, who prudently move away: It is said that the lizard enters into the body through the anus. Hebëwë kills it with a small palmwood arrow.

Meanwhile, Remaema has taken the basket of cakes to Ebrëwë. One last time, the hunters check the straightness of their arrows by sighting along the shafts and verify that their quivers contain everything they need: spare points, fragments of long bones, resin, and matches; they also make sure that the pins are correctly fastened to the lids and that the carrying straps are solidly attached.

Ebrëwë gives the signal to set out. They cross the river in an old canoe; then they begin the long trip through the forest.

On the way, the hunters kill a macaw and some agamis. When they reach their goal, Ebrëwë chooses the campsite, along a clear-flowing brook. Then everyone busies himself erecting his shelter: In a half-hour, the huts with their trapezoidal roofs are up and covered with *ketiba* leaves, which are similar to banana leaves. As for Ebrëwë, he merely puts up the frame of his shelter – three posts that support the roof – leaving to young Fama the task of laying down the covering of leaves. They store the food under the shelters and quickly pile up a supply of wood; the fires flare up, and wisps of light, bluish smoke filter through the foliage. They cook big caterpillars wrapped in leaves and boil the birds. This game is the last that the hunters will grant themselves: For the duration of the expedition, the men would feel dishonored if they ate of the animals they kill; they are permitted to have only insects, frogs, and the entrails of certain animals.

A little before nightfall, the young men build a short distance away an imitation smoking grill on which they place pieces of those black, rough-textured, egg-shaped termite nests that are often found hanging on tree trunks. It is said that these fragments represent the haunches of meat that will soon pile up on the grill. Through this propitiatory gesture, they ensure an abundance of game.

Moriwë and Kremoanawë share a shelter. While they are cooking their food, Moriwë narrates a recollection from his youth:

145

War and alliance

I was only a child, hardly bigger than Tiyetirawë. I had gone with my father on a hunt like this one. My father fell ill; his testicles began to swell; they were as big as this, and he could no longer hunt. He had the "giant armadillo testicles" [nat^heki wakabi]; he was in such pain that he decided to return home. We started on our way; I was walking in front; my father was following, leaning on a stick. Our dog was running around us and was straying farther and farther away: He smelled something. Suddenly he started to yelp: He had just discovered a tamandua cowering in a hollow trunk. At the thought that there was game nearby, my father started to run despite his condition. He said: "The dog has found an animal, let's go and see!" We came to the tree; we had to open the trunk with an axe to reach the beast, and my father started to hack away with all his might, moaning all the while. When we had killed the tamandua, we tore off a strip of bark, and it was I who carried the beast. We came to a river that we had to cross by walking on a tree trunk. It was a fallen genipap, and the humidity had made the bark slippery. I didn't watch my step, slipped, and fell in the water. The river was deep at that spot, and I sank down, still holding on to the beast. I did not realize it, but my father later confided to me that I stayed under some time before reappearing; he had feared a mishap.

Moriwë laughs when he recalls his father's face, filled with anxiety. They nibble on their caterpillars together with some cake. Then they soon fall asleep, exhausted after having spent these many nights playing games, dancing, and shouting.

Daylight is near when suspicious noises are heard on the side of the trail; first a sharp sound like that of a bowstring snapping against the shaft, then whistling noises similar to those the Yanomami make when signaling to one another. Those who have heard shake the others and say in low voices:

Wake up, we were followed by enemy warriors; they are lying in ambush on the trail.

They hastily scatter the fires and blow on the flames to put them out. They grope about in the darkness for their weapons, then noiselessly slip into the forest. To avoid falling into a trap, they form parallel files making their way through the trees on each side of the trail. They advance a few hundred meters in this manner before coming out on the trail. They notice then that it is still encumbered with cobwebs; with the firebrands they are carrying, they examine the ground, where no tracks are visible. No one has passed this way; they are reassured and return to the camp by way of the trail. The fires flare up again; they warm themselves and say:

It was a ghost that lurked thereabouts.

One must always beware of ghosts. Some are completely harmless; others, on the contrary, capture the "vital center" of people to make them die, or else, stealthily coming up to them while they are walking, apply their knees against their backs to break them in two. Near Tayari, on the other side of the Orinoco, there lives a ghost so fierce that people avoid the place where it dwells.

As daylight is near, they dilute peach palm fruits in water to make a liquid

146

gruel that they swallow with roasted manioc or plantain. Those who want to go fishing do not prepare a fresh quid of tobacco, but retain the old one: With a newly prepared cud, they would surely come back empty-handed; the fish would not bite. When on the hunt, certain actions are inadvisable. To use the specific names of the animals one is tracking or to point at them is to make them disappear. When one has just defecated, one finds only empty armadillo lairs; curassows fly away and remain hidden if one farts. It is as if there existed an equivalency between the rectum and the armadillo's lair, and as if farting were linked to the bird's flight. This relationship that the Indians establish between excretion and hunting is also found with respect to wild pigs; it is not without similarities with the link they establish on another level between copulation and eating.

At dawn, the signal to set out is given. The forest is still dark; spiderwebs stretch across the path, and wet boughs are like cold fingers on the hunters' shivering bodies. Ebrëwë is walking in front, following a faintly marked "hunters' trail." After traveling for a while, the hunters pause; they sit down, chat, then divide into three distinct groups, each heading in a different direction. Each group consists of three to five persons who are going to cooperate closely for a whole day. Before leaving, the men "close the trail" they are using by breaking off a few branches and placing them on the ground; they hope by this means to keep the animals inside their chosen hunting grounds.

Moriwë goes with Ebrëwë and two other hunters. It isn't long before they come upon recent tracks of a troop of wild pigs. Without hesitating, they hurry after them. Ebrëwë unties a ball of brown dye wrapped in a leaf and rubs some onto his chest and shoulders: One must be handsome and fragrant to hunt the pigs. The dogs are in their way, ill-tempered, undisciplined curs that run off in all directions, bark inappropriately, and do not respond to their masters' calls. It is to be feared that they will stampede the pigs during the approach. Yet after some hesitation, they resign themselves to their presence.

The hoofprints are more or less visible, according to the nature of the terrain or the humidity of the soil. Following the tracks of wild pigs is an exercise requiring great concentration and skill. Sometimes the animals move in a long file, tracing a veritable furrow in the ground; sometimes they divide into several groups, and the prints are less obvious. Sometimes they scatter and tear up the ground rooting for food; it is then necessary to find the place where they gather again. The troop may rush ahead in a straight line; at other times it may describe wide circles, returning to its starting point and scrambling the hoofprints; or else it may actually turn about and retrace its route. The hunters following such tracks may lose their way and spend precious time finding the true direction again; and when they do find it, the tracks have become so light, so imperceptible that they must read the ground step by step. The pursuers then scatter to unravel the tangle more easily, and they call to find each other again.

147

Hunting wild pigs is always an uncertain business. Sometimes the troop moves so swiftly that it is impossible to catch up with it. At other times it travels slowly and seems to loiter; the animals are not fearful, and it is possible to approach and kill them easily. At other times still, they charge their pursuers and disembowel the dogs, and there is nothing to do but to abandon one's bow and arrows to take refuge in a tree – which should be solid enough, for the maddened beasts hack at the wood with their tusks.

The bands of pigs appear and disappear in cycles; they constitute an element of temporality. When a troop is reported, the Yanomami say: "The wild pigs are coming to see whether humans have grown: They are checking whether children have become adolescents, and adolescents adults."

Of good hunters of wild pigs it is said: "Their arms have a value of wild pigs" (*bë boko no warebɨ*); it is asserted that these people are able to kill great numbers of pigs because they are generous to animals by offering them earlobe plugs: The pigs respond to this gift of an eminently cultural object by offering themselves as game. On the other hand, it is said of a poor hunter that he is miserly toward the pigs.

Hunting these animals requires a minimum of cooperation among the hunters. One does not attack a troop alone; that is contrary to the moral code. When someone has noticed fresh tracks or seen the animals, he must make sure that the beasts do not notice him; he hurries back to the dwelling to notify his friends. On his return, he uses a conventional formula in a prescribed tone of voice: "I have seen warriors" or "I have seen Yanomami." The others immediately guess what it is about. If by mistake he said, "I have seen wild pigs," the troop would surely vanish; one never names the desired object, for that would make it disappear. The hunters follow the hoofprints, locate the band, approach, and attack it. The best hunter places himself in front and shoots the first arrow; the others take positions at the center of the group of animals and shoot them as they are driven back. When the beasts are stampeding, it is again every man for himself; in any case, each hunter claims as his own the pigs that he kills.

Ebrëwë and his companions are drawn farther and farther away. Sometimes they think that they are nearing animals whose prints are still wet after fording streams; then they speak in low voices and avoid urinating or farting to prevent the pigs from detecting their presence.

As they are walking, one of them finds some honey. They stop to confer about what to do. The sun is visibly declining, and they are discouraged: The tracks no longer seem as recent as before; they have perhaps taken a wrong turn and are following the wrong tracks. Some declare that they should continue the pursuit; but in that case, they will have to sleep in the forest, and they have no hammocks and above all no food. One cannot ask empty stomachs to fast, and those in favor of returning easily prevail: "Let's eat the honey and return to camp," they say.

148

The hunt

The *yoi* bees are humming; the nest is in a hollow tree. They raise a plat-form and widen the opening to extract the honeycombs. Maddened, hundreds of blond bees rush into the hunters' scalps and pubic hair, biting furiously. Quickly, they tear off the layer of eggs, and the honeycombs over-flowing with golden honey are placed on a heap of leaves; greedy fingers plunge into it immediately, and tongues smack with delight. Moriwë has gone to fetch water at the bottom of a ravine, and the honey is diluted in large folded leaves that serve as containers. This delicately fragrant drink reinvigorates them after the long pursuit.

It is already night when they arrive at camp, exhausted and famished. They are given roasted plantain, caterpillars, and cashews. Hebëwë takes a turn around the smoking grill; there are only a few birds. This first day of the hunt has not been successful.

The next morning, Hebëwë, Ebrëwë, Frêrema, and Kremoanawë set out together after the frugal morning meal. They walk downstream along the brook that flows near the camp. They soon kill a curassow. Using a lanceolate point as a knife, Ebrëwë cuts out a strip of skin on the bird's head, starting at the beak, including the crest, and passing along the eyes to end at the base of the neck: Dried, this strip will be used to fashion an armband. He also pulls out the quills, which are used to feather arrows, and sticks the tailfeath-ers in a straight line into the ground, that they may testify to his skill as a hunter.

In the meantime, Hebëwë, alone, has approached a nearby waterhole. He remains a while on the bank, observing the fish teeming in the water. He shoots some, harpoons others, then, abandoning his bow, he steps into the water and strikes with his machete. Absorbed in the killing, he doesn't real-ize that in leaving the bank, he is nearing a hole infested with electric fish. A violent discharge courses through the metal of the machete; he cries out and drops the weapon, but his feet become entangled in a submerged root, and he stumbles. He is about to fall, sees that he is surrounded by electric fish, and is afraid of drowning. Then, with a surge of energy, he rushes to the bank and finally reaches it, exhausted and shaking with fright and cold. The others have heard his cries and come running:

What is the matter?
I was attacked by electric fish.
We thought a jaguar was eating you.

From shore, they shoot their arrows at the slithery fish that look somewhat like eels. Hebëwë silently makes a bundle of his catch, still shaken by his narrow escape from danger.

The brook they are following is now full of fallen trees and dead branches; they must make their way through particularly dense undergrowth. Ebrëwë seems worried; he asks:

Doesn't the *rahara* monster have its lair near here?

149

When plucking a curassow, the quills, which are used to feather arrows, are planted in the ground.

Frērema answers:

No, it lives much farther upstream.

The *rahara,* gigantic aquatic monsters, swallow those that approach them and rush ashore to devour those foolhardy enough to pronounce their name near the deep hole that is their dwelling. Frērema is mistaken; the place where the beast is supposed to be is very near. They sit down a moment, talking of the *rahara,* but since they are near the water, prudence dictates that they avoid the monster's name; they say "the beast." Frērema announces:

I'm going to continue downstream.

The others follow suit, walking on the bank. They come near the *rahara,* and it is Hebëwë, who has been here before with his father, who first realizes it. They are going to cross on an enormous trunk spanning the stream. Around them spreads a tapirs' feeding ground etched with countless hoof-prints and trails that the big herbivores use to come here and forage in the earth. Fear and foreboding rise in Hebëwë as he recognizes the place more and more positively. He is thinking: "This is it, the monster lives here." He is about to speak and warn the others, when Frērema, who is walking ahead, suddenly turns back. He makes hand signals telling the others to squat down and, in a low voice, warns them of the danger:

It is here, this is where it lives. Don't take another step; stay where you are.

They step back and sit down at a safe distance. Ebrëwë says:

It won't attack, we are too far away from it.

Hebëwë says:

I was just thinking that it was here.

Frērema, who is curious, announces:

I'm going to take a look.

He walks on all fours. At that very moment, two curassows alight near them. Ebrëwë says:

They are the "beast's" mascots; it uses them to draw us to it. These curassows always roost above the waterhole where the monster is hiding.

That is what they say, but they can't refrain from killing one of the birds; the other takes flight and disappears. As they are leaving, Frērema explains to Hebëwë:

When the *rahara* are in a friendly mood, they emit a kind of snapping sound; otherwise, when their intentions are evil, they remain silent to surprise the foolhardy person who approaches them. The *rahara* always have near them some pet animals, most often hoatzins.

On the way, Frērema notices a poisonous snake curled under a pile of leaves. A well-aimed blow with a machete lands on the reptile's head, and

151

the scales of the tail rattle in the death throes. Frērema breaks the poisonous fangs on a big root, then wraps the head to avoid being soiled by the dripping blood. The snake will not be smoked; it will be added to the hunters' evening meal. On a long-term hunt, only the biggest snakes – boas and anacondas – are smoked.

Further on, the hunters find urine left by a horde of howler monkeys; they smell it to make sure that it is recent. They search in the immediate vicinity, listen to the noises of the forest, climb the trees, but nothing indicates the animals' presence. The monkeys are probably out of reach; they stopped in this place, then swung from branch to branch toward an unknown destination.

Discouraged by the scarcity of game, the men resume their endless journey. They are already feeling hunger and fatigue. Kremoanawē has decided to give up and has turned back toward camp.

At one point their hopes rise again: The sharply defined recent tracks of a tapir run before them. They judge that they were made that morning and hope that the animal has remained nearby, asleep on the ground, waiting for nightfall. Silently, they scrutinize the ground step by step, following the tracks. Suddenly, a crashing of branches and shredded foliage is heard: A dog has just roused the beast, which has started off on a mad flight. Then they run as fast as they can through the thickets; thorns injure their bare feet, vines threaten to break their arrows, they bump against roots. They orient themselves by listening for the dog's howls; already the strong, penetrating odor of the tapir saturates the track. When they reach the dog, it is pointing to a trunk in which a peccary has taken refuge. While pursuing the tapir, the dog has dislodged the peccary and followed it, abandoning its original prey. The hunters are disappointed; they insult the dog, but kill the peccary.

The other group has had better luck; it came back with a tapir. When they are back together at the encampment, they set to building a wider, stronger smoking grill, on which they pile the haunches of bloody meat. The young boys bring large pieces of wood on their shoulders; they revive the fire, and on top of the tapir they place the small game: birds, monkeys, pacas, coatis, and armadillos. Despite hunger and fatigue, they are happy this evening, and a light, festive mood makes them look cheerful. Under the shelters they have hung green bananas in which they have stuck the feathers of the parrots they killed, to "heal" them from having been ruffled; these will be used for decorations. They carefully wrap the tailfeathers of the macaws, which will be used in the dance of presentation during the feast; they are already thinking that they will have to look their best.

It is time, however, for the hunt to come to an end. The hunters have been scouring the forest 'for five days, and the stocks of food have been reduced to almost nothing: not a single manioc cake; only a few plantains are left. To

152

The hunt

still their hunger, they have opened some palm trees to harvest the heart; but this food for hard times only bloats the belly without ever giving the pleasant sensation of being full. Despite the lack of food, they will have to wait one more day before the haunches of tapir meat are properly done. And it is a pitiful thing to feel hungry before this mound of meats that they do not touch for fear of losing face.

The next morning, they slacken their routine, setting out later than usual, out of a sense of duty, but without conviction: It is not fitting for hunters to remain inactive in camp, even when there is enough meat. Before leaving, Ebrëwë stirs the fire and says:

Ghost, ghost, you will stay to fan the fire.

That is the formula one must pronounce when one leaves the grill before setting out. It is a sentence full of cruel irony for the ghost, who is wandering eternally in the forest, shaking with cold because he does not possess fire.

When they return to camp, they find near their huts a monkey lying on the ground, still alive but unable to move. It has fallen there, probably sick and exhausted, incapable of continuing its jumps from branch to branch. Some youths pick it up and show it to their elders, who examine it. The animal bears no trace of a wound. They say it is *ōrihiyē* and that it is a bad omen: Some Yanomami have died for having foolishly consumed the flesh of such animals. *Ōrihiyē* animals are really tricks used by enemies to tempt scatter-brains. When hunters on a foray meet an *ōrihiyē* animal, it means that there is danger: The omen is most baneful, and they immediately turn back. The hunters now suddenly remember that this very morning, while pursuing a flock of agamis, they seemed to hear foreign voices and that the hoarse cry of *kōbari* birds sounded several times along the way – another unfavorable sign. Perhaps warriors or sorcerers are watching them. They begin to worry, and to protect themselves they surround the camp with a hedge of branches. To an intrepid young fellow who is nevertheless setting out to hunt partridges, they shout:

Watch out for enemies; don't follow the trail; walk through the woods!

A young boy who is approaching the monkey to examine it is ordered:

Go away, keep your distance; it's dangerous!

But the young people's desire to have fun by inflicting pain proves stronger than the threat hovering over them. They gather around the poor beast and take pleasure in injuring it repeatedly, sticking their fingers into the wounds and pushing sharp sticks into its eyes. And the monkey dies, little by little; its every contortion stimulates them and makes them laugh.

Night has fallen. In the distance, thunder is rolling. Frērema covers the grill with large leaves that will protect the dry meat. The precaution is not in vain; soon the storm breaks and the branches, broken by the violent wind, fall onto the fragile shelters.

153

War and alliance

It is not yet daylight when the smoked game, wrapped in leaves and secured with strong strips of bark, is distributed among the carriers; the bulky and heavy bundles are transported by means of headstraps. The division of portions and the selection of those who carry them home follow strict rules: Kaõmawë and Shimoreiwë are the organizers of the feast and, as such, they will receive the biggest pieces, which their sons and sons-in-law will carry to the dwelling. The other hunters will keep for themselves only the toucans, parrots, macaws, and other small catches.

Despite the burdens, the journey home is swift: All are anxious to return. Before crossing the "river of rains," they wash themselves and stick feathers into their earlobe plugs. They cross the central plaza with quick steps, without a word, without a glance for anyone. When they reach their hearths, the hunters hang their hammocks and immediately lie down.

Meanwhile, curious eyes have estimated the amount of game by the number and bulk of the bundles. Without delay, the women moisten tobacco in calabashes, pass it through hot ashes, fashion the cud by pressing the rolled leaves against their palms, and offer it to the brother, the son, or the husband who has just returned. Soon they can be seen undoing the bundles and hanging each piece of game above the fires where it will keep dry and protected from flies. All speculate as to the plumpness of the tapir, and their mouths water in anticipation of all that fat.

Kaõmawë distributes the banana soup as soon as it is ready, and he sends his daughter to take the portions to the other households. Already, drugs have been ground into fine powder, and groups form to inhale them; more than one will presently throw up the food he has just eaten.

Squatting near the hammock in which Ebrëwë is resting, Kaõmawë informs him of a noteworthy event:

During your absence, a visitor arrived from Batanawë. It was the relative of "mother of my daughter," the old fellow with white hair and beard. Batanawë and Mahekoto launched a common raid against Hasubɨwë. The warriors were already near the enemy dwelling when they were surprised by a group returning from the garden. A few shots were exchanged, but no arrow reached its target. Since they had been discovered, the warriors of Batanawë thought of returning home without attempting anything: An attack against enemies warned of their presence was too risky. They changed their minds, however, and made a long detour to launch their arrows over the roof. Some men of Hasubɨwë went out without being noticed and went to lie in wait on the bank of the Orinoco, at a place where they thought their assailants would pass. When the warriors broke off their attack, they did indeed fall into the trap. Arrows were whizzing near them; at any moment one of them could be killed. A warrior of Batanawë shouted:

Run as fast as you can and get beyond them, otherwise we shall be killed!

A group of men from Batanawë were thus able to overtake those of Hasubɨwë – one of them, as he was running by, broke an arrow that was aimed at him; the others stayed where they were, taking shelter behind trees. The men of Hasubɨwë were now

154

in the midst of their enemies, backed against the river. One could see their blackened, anxious faces; they wondered:

What are we going to do?

Arrows were beginning to fall all around them; one of them sustained a deep gash in the shoulder. They had no other recourse but to throw themselves into the Orinoco where the current carried them away. Recklessly, a man from Mahekoto swam after them, thinking that he could grab an enemy, but the fugitives stuck him with arrows, and he was forced to turn back, infuriated by the wounds he had just received. The men from Batanawë then started running along the shore, for those from Hasubiwë, being poor swimmers, found it difficult to gain any distance. A warrior from Mahekoto owned a gun, a gift from a missionary; he fired and hit a swimmer in the head; from afar, they saw blood spread over his brow. Others jumped into the water and, covered by their companions, brought back the wounded man, whom they dragged onto the bank. They all formed a circle around the man, lacerated him with the tips of their arrows, gouged his eyes by pushing the end of a bow into them; into his mouth they forced sticks that pierced his cheeks. The enemy knew he was going to die, but he was a brave one, a *waitʰeri;* he struggled and tried to return some of the blows. Then they riddled him with arrows and finally planted bows into his throat and chest. Before ending his narrative, the visitor added:

We had practically ceased our raids against them, but now we are going to resume the war. We'll make them flee far away from us.

Ebrëwë says:

The men of Hasubiwë are not cowards; they will take revenge; in the past, they did kill several of their enemies.

Night has come. A young man from Tayari draws a woman to him; she is not his wife. She doesn't want to give in and resists, holding onto the hammocks. As they are struggling, they accidentally upset the meat stew that Hoashimokawë was keeping for dinner. Hoashimokawë becomes angry and, in revenge, he warns the husband, who pounces on the youth and strikes him cruelly on the head with a log. Immediately two groups are formed; one wants to defend the youth; the other would strike him again. Everyone is shouting and milling around them. Young boys and youths are there, making much noise and brandishing clubs even if they are not taking part in the confrontation, out of sheer bravado; some carry pieces of sugarcane for weapons. Hebëwë joins Moriwë, who is carrying an axe; he laughs and asks:

What are you doing with that?
I couldn't find a club; I took the axe so as not to come empty-handed.

Meanwhile, Shimoreiwë is walking about trying to separate the combatants. He keeps repeating:

Go away, break it up!

No one listens to him. Furious women shout at the young man, urging him to return the blows; but he is groggy, does not hear, and staggers. Blood is flowing over his face and chest. A woman runs up and places a club in his hands, but he can hardly hold it. She yells into his ear:

Avenge yourself, go on, avenge yourself! Return the blows you received.

Rabema and Mamikiyima are facing each other, each lifting a long club with both hands, ready to strike. There is extraordinary confusion. Hebëwë, quite excited, shouts with the others and says anything at all to make noise and put on a show of courage, a mocking smile on his lips. Kremoanawë is having fun.

When the volume of shouting abates, some people go back to their hammocks. Soon the injured youth returns to his hearth. Kremoanawë comes to him to stanch the blood that is still flowing and to scrape the skin with a stick. A long gash runs deep into the scalp, framed on each side by a smaller one. Kremoanawë picks the matted hair out of the wound with a twig. Some women are still shouting, but a general fight has now been avoided.

One last time, the young people perform the *heri* ritual of the hunt, but without indulging in the usual pranks. During the hunters' absence, the women alone had fulfilled it at nightfall.

8

The pact

While the hunt was in progress, the guests traveled the distance that separated them from Karohi. The women shouldered the heavy burden of domestic utensils and green plantains, of little children running at their side or riding on the baskets. Now the guests are camping in the forest, near Karohi, waiting to receive the official invitation, the *teshomomou,* before entering their hosts' dwelling to participate in the festivities and the rituals.

The temporary camp occupied by the people of Hōkanakawë – that is the name given to their *shabono* standing at the very top of the mountain of the same name – includes about eighty persons. The shelters, with their triangular bases, have been built in a circle within the forest; the undergrowth in the center has been cut and thrown to the outside. Around the camp rises a hedge of branches planted in the ground and secured with vines, for protection against warriors, sorcerers who "blow" their poisons, and ghosts who steal souls. For longer-lasting roofs and for better protection from rain, they have selected *miyōma* leaves instead of the usual *ketiba* leaves, which deteriorate too quickly.

The morning sun slanting into the forest strikes the huts with its blinding shafts. On the transverse poles of the shelters are displayed long strips of red cloth as evidence of both the group's wealth and its generosity.

The place is infested with bloodsucking insects, and the Indians are continually slapping their sides and backs to drive them away; only the coming of night puts an end to this constant torment.

That morning, as the stock of bananas and plantains is about to give out, the women go to ask for some at Karohi, accompanied by little girls and a few small boys. Under their hosts' roof they stretch out in the hammocks of their relatives for a chat. They are offered ripe bananas; the children play in the central plaza. After chatting to their hearts' content, the men of Karohi take their machetes and head for the garden, followed by the visiting women carrying baskets. In the garden, they cut down as many banana trees as necessary, and the women pluck from the bunches small clusters of fruits, which they carefully pile into their baskets. Before going, they also ask for ripe

157

bananas, which they place on top of the loads. They leave, walking heavily through the forest, each carrying about sixty pounds; the little girls and boys also carry loads, secured by a strap around their foreheads. Humoama has her period; as she is walking, the blood drips onto her thighs and mingles with streaks of perspiration. They stop to bathe at the brook near the camp. When they enter the enclosure, they are greeted by the sarcastic remarks of the youths, who ask them with whom they made love, and by a swarm of greedy relatives who run up to them and quarrel over the ripe bananas.

Humoama offers a fruit to her little boy; his older brother immediately snatches it away from him; the little one breaks into tears and remains in the middle of the path, howling and rubbing his eyes, deaf to the voices telling him to move away. The older brother squats down in front of him and, mocking him, eats the banana with much noise and snickering. To calm her son, the mother detaches another banana and holds it out to him, but the child pretends not to see it. Ten times at least, she repeats:

Here, take this banana, it's yours.

Her patience is praiseworthy. Finally, with an angry motion, the child snatches the fruit out of his mother's hand and begins to peel it without even looking at her.

In the meantime, Shëyërewë has gone hunting. He is walking through a part of the forest full of waterholes into which he wades in order to avoid the dense undergrowth. Several times he takes out, without success, the small fishing line wound around a piece of wood that he carries in his quiver: The fish do not bite. In one waterhole, the bottom of which is covered with a thick layer of dead leaves, his foot touches something hard; he probes with his bow and finally dislodges a caiman, motionless as in the state of hibernation. At that moment, Shëyërewë realizes that he has forgotten his machete; he climbs back on the bank and cuts a heavy stick with which he fells the beast. To quarter it he uses a bamboo point that he inserts under the abdominal plates, opening the belly and disemboweling the animal. From time to time he renews the edge by stripping away the bamboo fibers with his teeth. To loosen the limbs, he breaks the joints with his stick before cutting the ligaments. He washes the intestines and wraps them separately, but ties together the other pieces: the head, the four legs, the trunk, the tail, and the belly.

On his way back, Shëyërewë finds a tree bearing Brazil nuts; he puts down his load, climbs the trunk, and knocks down the thick, heavy shells that contain the nuts. To crack them he inserts the pointed end of his bow into the shell at the end opposite the stem, so as to widen a natural opening; then he forces a pointed stick into the hole, using it as a handle to break open the tough shell by knocking it as hard as he can against a root. On his return to camp, Shëyërewë shares the caiman and the Brazil nuts with several relatives. He notices near his shelter a thick branch lying on the ground. His wife asks him:

> Didn't it rain where you went?
> I heard thunder, the wind blew, but it didn't rain.
> Here lightning fell. We suddenly felt that we were going to be flung to the ground; our bodies were shaken, our legs gave way. Then we heard a fearful crack; a branch broke, and we rushed out of the huts to avoid being crushed by it.
> It's the *shamat*ʰ*ari* shamans, who sent the *hekura* upon us to look at the *bei kë mi̇ amo* [souls] of our children; they will come back later to take them.

Shëyërewë sits down. He is the only man in the region who has become a shaman without having been initiated; he received the revelation of the *hekura* one day while he was hunting in the forest. Since then he has been able to spit out the disease-causing objects that the sick have in their bodies – the magical plants, for instance. He is an excellent hunter, and this is proof that he enjoys the favor of the *hekura*.

His wife cooks some plantain for him and boils a portion of the caiman. But Shëyërewë will not be able to eat this meat: A hunter never partakes of the game he brings back; if he did, he would violate the rigorous moral code that enjoins exchanging with others; he would become *sina,* a bad hunter, and would no longer kill any animals.

After he is rested and has eaten, Shëyërewë calls Barikiwë; he shouts:

> "Father of Wëkërawë," come sit here!

The old man approaches, offers him a few Brazil nuts, and speaks of the young boy in a neighboring community who was bitten by a *Bothrops* snake. The flesh rotted away, and the bones loosened below the knee. Now the young man hobbles about on one leg. They speak:

> These snakes, I fear them more than anything else; I wouldn't want to be bitten by one.
> That one could have died; he has only one leg and leans on a bow to walk. Yet he still hunts game; he is a good marksman. The days after he was bitten, he was howling with pain; his neighbors could not sleep.
> Me, I'm afraid of snakes, jaguars, and sorcerers. Yet I don't fear warriors: That's not the same thing.
> At Karohi, "Hebëwë's father" was once bitten on the leg. Since then he no longer participates in the long hunts nor in raids: He cannot run.
> When I was little, a jaguar one night came inside the shelter. I was walking in the central plaza and turning its big head toward us. We didn't dare shoot it, for fear of hitting a relative; we threw coals at it, and it calmly walked away.
> It is raining a great deal lately; I walked in water the whole day.
> Another moon is going to "settle" soon, and the weather could change.
> Do you know whether there is any tobacco at Karohi?
> They say that they do have some.
> I'll ask for some; I have an "empty lip." My wife cannot stand to have an "empty lip"; she substitutes green cotton leaves for tobacco.

His wife is spinning cotton next to him; he says to her:

159

Hurry up, "tongue" ; make a big ball, and I'll ask those of Karohi to give us a dog.

Meanwhile Kiyēkō and a few others have gone to harvest honey nearby. Kiyēkō is fulfilling at Hōkanakawë his premarital service; that is why he has been assigned this unpleasant and arduous task. The bees are of the *ōi* species; their nest is fastened high on a big tree. To cut the trunk, Kiyēkō raises a platform about three meters from the ground. While he is making the first cuts with an axe, the children play and keep a casual eye on the fire, which they feed by throwing dry twigs into it. A boy of about twelve is drying dead leaves near the flames and keeps them ready for burning. Kiyēkō works a long time; his body is streaming with sweat, and several times he asks for water. Finally, the tree makes a cracking sound, and Kiyēkō cautiously steps back to the edge of the platform. Soon, the trunk begins to lean visibly, and Kiyēkō, judging that the tree is going to fall by itself, comes down from his perch. Slowly, the trunk leans more and more. Suddenly, there is a terrific noise; the wood splits all at once, the tree crashes down, and the ground trembles from the violence of the shock. Kiyēkō sets the leaves afire and rushes to the nest, followed by a band of enthusiastic urchins. Many bees are burned, but they keep coming out everywhere, fastening themselves to the skin, biting with their mandibles and getting tangled in the hair so that they have to be pulled out; hundreds of insets pinch their skin. Only the most courageous reach the nest, which they hastily break up and carry some distance away where the bees are less numerous. They are then able to extract the honey and secure it in leaves, frequently interrupting their work to lick their fingers.

Kiyēkō's wife is no more than six years old; she lives with her parents. When Kiyēkō returns from the forest, his parents-in-law send the little girl to him with a bundle of roasted plantains. She can be seen timidly crossing the encampment, losing her way among the shelters, fearfully looking up at the adults who are showing her the way; she hands the bundle to that fellow, her husband, nonchalantly relaxing in his hammock, and goes back without a word.

Meanwhile, at Karohi, they are busily getting ready. Some men are completing the job of feathering their arrows; some are repairing a bow or rolling a rope on their thigh. Women are finishing the edges of basketwork, spinning some more cotton, or making dye: These things will be used in exchanges; they must be ready on time.

At the insistent urgings of the elders, the central plaza has been cleared of grass and swept in front of the hearths. Here and there have been planted sticks topped with tufts of multicolored feathers. In front of Kaōmawë's and Shimoreiwë's hearths have been placed large troughs made of bark, their sides supported by stakes; in these will be poured the banana soup offered to the guests.

The day before, some people went to the "old women" gardens at the old site, downstream on the "river of rains"; they came back heavily laden with the red fruits of the *rasha* palm. Following Mabroma's example, the women gathered to loosen the fruits from the clusters; then they started to peel the green plantains with their teeth. All night long, young people took turns cooking meat and vegetable foods on large fires set out of the way. They have filled open-work baskets with boiled plantains, taking them out of the kettle with sharpened sticks to avoid burning their fingers.

For a long time now, Kaõmawë and Shimoreiwë have been preparing the banana soup: They peel the fruits and split them in half before putting them into the water. After the fruits have simmered for a long time, they untie the kettle and blend the contents with a many-branched stick, thinning the liquid from time to time with cold water. When the soup is ready, they pour it into the bark troughs. Kaõmawë can be seen wiping his sticky hands by rubbing them against the supporting posts, then through his hair.

Some men cross the central plaza carrying enormous logs on their shoulders; others get rid of old stumps or are busy splitting tree trunks.

While going about his tasks, Hebëwë tirelessly keeps up his gossip and banter; now it is Hewakema he chooses for a victim. During the night, the child was bitten by a bat without even being aware of it; when he awoke, a streak of dried blood could be seen on his temple. With the coming of dusk, bats, which are particularly numerous this season, flutter continually under the roof, brushing against people and things with their quickly beating wings, clinging to ripening bananas to feed on them. Sometimes they alight on the foot or the temple of a sleeper to suck blood, and the often painless bite does not waken the person.

Kaõmawë oversees the cooking of the ripe plantains while narrating a dream to his wife. At the end he adds:

Lately, I have been dreaming throughout the night. I don't stop dreaming, and I don't know why.

Mabroma answers:

I'll give you a tarantula to eat; to stop dreaming one must eat a tarantula.

She calls Hebëwë and asks him to sit down to be deloused; she crushes the parasites with her teeth to take vengeance for the discomfort they inflict and pulls the hairs to loosen the eggs. She laughs suddenly and searches for a louse she dropped into the dust and cannot find again. Giving up the search, she says:

It will go into the dust; soon it will be a scorpion.

It is believed that lice that fall to the ground change into scorpions.

Near them, Remaema takes out of the fire some plantains she has roasted.

161

Basket filled with boiled plantains for the guests.

She scrapes them with a stick because they are slightly burned: The Indians dislike the bitter taste of charred food.

Both the hosts and the guests have gathered new, light green palm fronds; they have split them in two along the central vein and have lacerated the leaves. These palms, called *hoko siki,* are indispensable for the dance that opens every festivity, and they also make up the ornaments of the *hekura.*

Everything is finally ready at Karohi, and they debate the selection of the person who is going to carry the ritual invitation, the *teshomomou,* to the guests' camp. Ubrawë and Wakamoshiwë are prevailed upon to go; they promptly get ready, dye their skin with roucou, thread macaw feathers through their armbands, and hang toucan skins on their belts. One of them borrows a bead necklace, the other a machete, which he rubs into the sand to brighten the metal. Thus adorned, they set out and reach the encampment of Hōkanakawë where they are greeted with whistles and frenzied shouts. Then they quickly recite fragmentary, staccato sentences to which an elder gives replies. The visitors do not wait for them to finish before getting ready and stuffing their hammocks into baskets: The next few nights will be spent under the great roof where the feast will take place. In a trice, a haircut or tonsure is perfected, body decorations are checked to make sure that nothing has been forgotten.

All finally set out in a long file winding under the trees along the narrow trail, and they do not stop until they come to the brook near Karohi. There they halt and delegate two strapping fellows, painted and adorned like their counterparts of Karohi, to take their stand in the central plaza and reply to the invitation. When they have finished the conventional declaration, they are given a calabash full of soup, which they swallow in long gulps, and two baskets filled to the brim with boiled plantains and portions of meat, which they take back to the brook, bending under their burden.

During this time, the people of Hōkanakawë have begun painting and adorning themselves. Their bodies are already decorated with varied patterns, armbands are in place, bird skins and feathers have been inserted into the earlobe plugs, monkey tails are wrapped around the men's brows, and white down is laboriously glued to them. Some people can be seen carefully smoothing a skin; others, working in pairs, are tracing body designs. A youth displays a magnificent new cotton bracelet that he had been assiduously fashioning for several days; squatting next to him, his mother is tracing circles on his skin. Everyone is checking the condition and the appearance of the palms that will be used in the dance. The object is not only to be handsome, but also, if possible, to be amusing in one's costume and decorations. A young man has cut himself a skirt out of a palm frond; another hangs the dried legs of a heron on his back, a third a collection of toucan beaks; a boy of about twelve has fashioned a three-holed flute from a bird's thighbone,

163

Young visitor adorned for the feast.

The pact

while another owns a panpipe; two or three young men have their bodies completely blackened, and on that background they are speckled with white clay.

Two elders untie the gift baskets from Karohi. Leaves are placed on the ground and the food is spread out. The meat is distributed, and every head of a family, every youth, receives a portion together with some plantains. The fathers distribute what they receive among their wives and children – which is not always easy, since a whole category of animals is forbidden to young people between the ages of twelve and eighteen, boys as well as girls. Thus, pacas, peccaries, agoutis, the whole deer family, coatis, howler monkeys, saki monkeys, and capybaras are prohibited, and other meat must be found for them.

The reasons for the restriction concerning the eating of game by the young are not apparent: No logical connection seems to link the designated animals. What is more, the forbidden animals change according to the region. The Indians claim that the skin of those who violate the prohibition becomes covered with ulcers and that they risk death. Perhaps they believe that these meats are too strong for the organism during the critical period that precedes and follows puberty; but if one considers only the tangible results of the interdiction, one cannot help noticing that it is as if the older members of the population, those who wield authority, had the prerogative of controlling to their advantage the consumption of game by the younger, more active members, the very ones who devote themselves to the hunt most energetically if not most skillfully.

They eat without haste, put the finishing touches to their costumes. Then, when they are finished, the group moves forward again, only to stop just behind the shelter of Karohi, near an entrance: The moment has come to perform the dance of presentation.

As soon as the presence of the guests is known within the shelter, a deafening concert of shouts and whistles rises to greet them. This is the beginning of the *braiai* ritual, the dance of presentation that the visitors perform around the perimeter of the central plaza. Five or six persons appear at the entrance to the dwelling; three of them dance around the plaza in one direction while the others take the opposite direction. They jog along, carrying the palm fronds with their arms extended or pressed close to their bodies, waving arrows decorated with down, a machete, or an axe. The thin strips of the fronds wave with a faint rustling sound. From time to time, the dancers stop in front of a hearth, dance in the same spot, and mumble an incomprehensible song while maintaining as expressionless a gaze as possible; then they move on. Unusual costumes sometimes draw admiring exclamations interrupted by remarks laced with subdued irony. Some, misjudging their stamina, find it difficult to go the whole distance and reach the end of the circuit

165

At the beginning of the festivities, a guest executes the dance of presentation around the shelter.

quite out of breath. Small children, terrified and clumsy, stumble, make wrong gestures, and provoke laughter; one of them is about to take the wrong exit and has to be shown the way. When the dancers have completed the full circuit of the shelter, they disappear and are immediately replaced by others.

Some women participate in the ritual, but their steps, quite different from the men's, are heavy, almost ungainly; most of them, especially the older

Groups of dancers shake the palm fronds.

ones, prefer to enter the shelter discreetly and go straight to a relative's hearth.

After the men have thus presented themselves, they wait outside a moment, then, all together this time, they again enter the enclosure of the shelter and dance around it once more. They form a colorful file that stretches out in a striking harmony of gestures, forms, colors, and mingled odors of dyes, fresh palm leaves, sweating bodies, and smoke. When they have finished, they stride to the center of the plaza where they remain standing; some place the palm fronds on the ground and cross their arms on their chests; others hold an axe or a machete aloft; still others cross their bows and arrows. All are gazing toward the peak of the roof in an attitude of defiance, waiting motionless to receive a formal invitation to settle down at their assigned hearths, the very same where their mothers and wives have already preceded them. The paint, the monkeys' tails, and the white down mask their faces, so that they are not always immediately recognized. The hosts approach, carrying palmwood clubs that they brandish above their heads as if to strike their guests. They study their faces. One of them exclaims: "Here is my brother-in-law! Do come this way!" And the man thus addressed follows him, carrying his hammock, in which he then lies down without a word.

One after another, all the guests have been invited to a hearth, and the

167

A group of men.

central plaza is now deserted. The newcomers have been offered cuds of tobacco and calabashes brimful of banana soup: This offering of food and tobacco precedes any verbal exchange. During this time, the children and adolescents have gone to the tubs of soup, squatting around them, shoulder to shoulder, their downy heads softly swaying; they stuff themselves, burping loudly and contentedly to indicate that they are eating their fill.

After a while, when all the guests have received tobacco and are sated with banana soup and palm fruits, Shimoreiwë advances toward the central plaza and takes his stand there to address them. He says:

You are visitors, aren't you? I have warned our women not to be tempted in case you should desire their pubis. We are adults; we dominate our desires. Why should you take the women by the arm and draw them to you? Do not lead them astray! Do not lead them astray! Your women have painted their eyelids and have adorned themselves for the feast; they have all painted their eyelids. You are here, lying peacefully in your hammocks, aren't you? Do not go to the women then, if you did, you would have to leave. Brothers-in-law, do not think that you will be attacked. Do not say

168

The pact

A boy whistles and dances.

that! Do not say that! We are truly friends. I am a friend to you. Why should we become enemies? Are we going to fight one another over women? No! You will have all the food you will need, even though some of our people have damaged their gardens out of anger. Come here! Brothers-in-law, stay here! We are friends. This is an influential man who is speaking; do not speak evil of me, brothers-in-law! Do not think that we are going to draw your women away by that path which leads away from the dwelling; do not think that you will be attacked; let not that fear make you rush out in a crowd. We shall share our food; do not fear for your women. Women, do not be afraid! No one will take you by force! My sister, who is sick, is here. Among those of Hōkanakawë, a man and a woman have come, who said:

We are going to make love.

They were mistaken. No, no, no, we shall not copulate! You, my sons of Karohi, your wives are miserly because they are not offering tobacco to their guests. We shall have cuds of tobacco. Are they going to think that I am short of tobacco, that I went round the hearths to beg for some? Did they think that? I did not go from hearth to hearth! I am generous! As for tobacco, I shall offer a full basket of it. I have asked the women to prepare some. Put your cuds under your lips!

He keeps talking, but hardly anyone is listening to him: All are pursuing their own conversations and activities. Near Turaewë's place, they are gathering to inhale drugs. It is Shokoriwë, a shaman from Hōkanakawë, who begins to sing to the spirits; his way of dancing, of invoking the *hekura*, and

169

A group of children.

his dialect, which are peculiar to "those upstream," provoke laughter. He pronounces the names of beings unknown at Karohi; the teenagers push each other with their elbows, snicker slyly, and make disparaging remarks about the length of his scrotum: The Yanomami who live upriver have it hanging low, with sparser hair than is the case with the Yanomami of this region. When Shokoriwë has finished his performance, he is replaced by Turaewë. His song, as always, is solemn, his steps slow and supple. First he calls down into him the familiar *hekura*; then, sometimes singing, sometimes speaking, he recalls a mythical tale:

The souls wander in the forest until the time when the partridges take their flight. Then the souls follow them to heaven: That is where they gather.

One day the souls returned to the place where they formerly had lived. The inhabitants had been decimated, and only part of the shelter was left: The circle was not closed; large spaces remained empty. The souls arrived in great numbers; their faces were recognized. In the dwelling, they had just burned a young girl who had died the day before; the mother, crushed by grief, kept the ashes in a gourd near her.

When they saw the souls come down in such great numbers, they said:

We must rebuild the dwelling so that everyone will be able to live in it; let's make it as spacious as possible.

Some souls went to gather long poles; others cleared the ground. The soul of the girl who had just been burned presented itself with the others; she had inserted into

170

The oldest of the visitors receive banana soup in a calabash.

The visitors gather around a bark container and eat the banana soup.

her earlobes flowers red as blood. How beautiful she was, thus adorned! She had the same appearance as when she was still alive. She sat down next to her mother, in the same hammock. She had noticed the location of the funeral pyre and was examining everything:

Mother, why is the earth burned and cooked here, in front of our hearth?
It is because your brother burned the grass there.
Mother, why are your cheeks blackened?
Your brother rubbed them with coals.
What is in that gourd?
The ashes of a bark that I am keeping as a condiment.

The dead girl's son had started to suck on his mother's breast again; his father, alone at another hearth, was happy about the unexpected return. Everywhere people were busy raising the supporting posts. They were calling to each other; mothers were calling to their sons, and the sons were answering their mothers. There was a great bustle. Little by little, the circle of the shelter was closing: It was a true *shabono,* with its central plaza neat and clean. They had brought from the forest the trees needed for construction; all had now returned.

The mother was rejoicing at her daughter's return. Near her were a couple of parrots, roosting on a perch. The daughter was truly a great beauty. She had just asked whose were the ashes she saw. Oh, that cannibal fire, that fire in which she had been consumed! Her nose and her eyes had become fiery, and yet her features had not changed. The men were working. The daughter was near her mother when suddenly the partridges took flight. The chattering parrots had just answered the soul's question:

172

Women discreetly go to settle down at the hearth that is assigned to them.

A young participant in the festivities.

The pact

They are your own ashes.

At that precise moment the souls disappeared. The mother tried to hold on to her daughter, but she was left with only a handful of charcoal.

The souls go with the partridges. That is where they are: in the celestial world. The souls hear the partridges cluck, and they wonder:

My children, my children, why are they invisible? Why isn't it possible to meet them? We can hear them, we know they are all around, clucking near us.

But the partridges are invisible to the souls. The birds stay near them, in full sight, yet the souls' glances do not rest on them but are directed elsewhere.

While they are entertaining themselves, telling the adventures of the ancestors who lived in primordial times, night has fallen. A few children are still playing, throwing and catching the inflated bladder of an anteater. Mabroma, who needs water, turns to Hebëwë:

My dear, go fetch some water at the river.
I'm already busy picking my teeth.

That is what one says to dodge a request for a service.

Wishami's baby is sick. They say that he has lost his "image" (*noreshi*), embodied in a small lizard. The women walk about the rear of the dwelling and in the central plaza, emitting piercing cries and shaking boughs in front of them, hoping that the lost "image" will return into the child's body and that he will be cured. The "images" of small children are represented by a tiny, blue-tailed lizard; they are unstable and therefore have a tendency to get lost frequently, so that they must be sought. As children grow, their "images" become embodied in other animals. These "images" are inherited: Boys take their fathers'; girls usually receive their mothers', but that point is uncertain, for some people think that a woman takes the animal of the group where she lives after her marriage. However that may be, all the male descendents of the same ancestor have the same image animal, which is, so to speak, the emblem of the group they form. Two emblematic animals are represented at Karohi: The spider monkey belongs to Kaõmawë and his brothers, the jaguar to the others. All the women of Karohi are otters. At Hõkanakawë the men are jaguars, spider monkeys, or harpy eagles and the women otters or snakes.

Among the central Yanomami, a whole class of animals includes the emblems assigned to the men, namely the capuchin monkey, the spider monkey, the harpy eagle, the jaguar, the toucan, and the macaw. A completely different class, distinct from the former, includes the animals reserved for women: the otter, the snake, the toad, and the tapir.

There is a direct relationship between a person and his or her emblematic animal, something like an unbroken, organic solidarity; if one is sick or dies, his or her counterpart immediately falls ill or dies. The animals live far away from the humans whose images they are, so that the two can never meet. Hence, a man whose counterpart in the animal world is the spider monkey can without qualms kill and eat spider monkeys; he need not be afraid of

175

slaying his image animal and losing his own life. The only exception is the harpy eagle, which lives quite near the men whose "image" it is. And that is why the man who kills one is bound to submit to the *unokai* ritual, like all murderers: By killing the bird he has caused the death of its human double. The "vital principle" (*bei kë no uhutibɨ*) of harpy eagles, like that of people, can come back to torment the murderer; but that of other animals never does.

A person who loses his or her "image" becomes weak, falls ill, and may die if the situation is protracted. To cure him or her, friends and relatives imitate the cries and attitudes of the "image." It is possible that in past times the emblematic animals served to identify matrimonial classes. One can sometimes hear people say: "Spider monkeys marry only otters" or "Jaguars do not marry snakes." In fact, as things are now, there are no incompatibilities, and a man may marry a woman of any image, as long as her kinship to him is that of a cross-cousin or the like. If a man respects the rule, he can obtain a wife only from a person whose emblematic animal differs from his own.

Shokoriwë has received Kaõmawë's hospitality; they are brothers-in-law – Shokoriwë was the husband of Kaõmawë's sister before she was carried away by measles. They chat about this and that, especially about war. Shokoriwë asks:

> What is the matter with Rakɨrawë? They say that he is losing his mind.
>
> That's true; he is unbalanced. When he takes drugs, he wants to break everything and must be tied up. He gets up during the night, wanders about the dwelling, wakes others to insult them and fight with them; dogs bark at him and want to bite him.
>
> It is probably because of Katarowë, whom he killed.
>
> Yes. Katarowë's "vital principle" entered his body, grew in him, and is tormenting him: His victim has taken possession of him, and that's what is unsettling him.

For a moment they observe Hiyomi by the light of the fires. Her child wants to drink. She is carrying him astride a piece of bark that she is holding with her left hand; not strong enough to lift with only her right hand the big gourd full of water, she squats down, slides her free hand under the container and raises it by sliding it along her body. She drinks from the opening, filling her mouth with water, then puts her lips on the child's lips so that he might drink.

The two men have resumed their conversation. Kaõmawë remarks:

> Wars are no longer as fierce as they were in the old days. One day, our men captured a baby whose mother they had killed. It was a boy; they didn't know what to do with him, so they drowned him by holding his head under water.
>
> When lightning flashes in the sky when it is not raining, it means that, at that precise instant, warriors are sending their arrows against enemies. When warriors leave on a raid, one can hear the sound associated with the bamboo points they are carrying. The points of the *sikorobirimmi* species go: *sei, sei*. The others go: *wẽh,*

176

wëh. If they are alert, those who are about to be attacked can hear these sounds at night. Then they shout to the others: "Be on your guard, this is the sound of the arrowheads that comes to us!"

Once I clearly heard the sound associated with the warriors' arrowheads. I didn't pay any attention to it. The next morning, I was still in my hammock. I had just eaten a banana, and I was reaching for another. Suddenly I heard the noise of an arrow leaving the bowstring. I made a sudden movement, and the arrowshaft grazed me; it bore a curare point. We immediately rushed to our bows to drive off the attackers.

It was after such an attack that a man of Shibariwë was killed, you may remember. They were returning after having unsuccessfully attacked Mahekoto. The warriors of Mahekoto had made a long detour, running all the way to surprise the aggressors on their return trip. So the assailants were returning without suspecting anything. Their group was preceded by a man who had ignored prudent advice and had hurried ahead. An enemy faced him, an arrow ready on his bowstring, and killed him. When they found their companion dead, the men of Shibariwë feared for their own lives and abandoned the corpse. Later, when they came back to look for him, he already smelled bad, and they burned him on the spot.

I myself almost died because of a similar lack of caution. Some women had gone fishing; they were surprised by enemies – two of them were killed, two others wounded, and a little girl that was with them was taken captive. As soon as we were told, we rushed on the trail of the aggressors. We ran to post ourselves along their route, saying:

They are in that direction; they are in that direction.

But we were warned:

Don't go this way; the forest is "empty"; they went in that direction.

We went to take positions somewhere else. I squatted down, making myself as small as possible. But we waited in vain; the enemies did not appear where we were waiting for them. I left with a companion. We came to the hill "of the white stone." There we heard the voices of our enemies who were shouting: *hōhō, hōhō!* I was crawling with my companion to get near them. We were soon so near that we could hear their voices distinctly. They were saying:

Let's strip the bark off this tree to make a rope.
Walk in silence; we could be pursued.

To make faster progress, they carried the little girl on their backs. We were very near; I rose slowly and pulled my bow with all my might, but the knot of the bowstring slipped along the wood, and the arrow did not fly. My companion's arrow hit its target: We heard a great shout among the enemies. Later we were told that the arrowhead had made a hole like this, very big, in the chest, and that the wounded man's eyes had widened enormously. I fled, all alone, running straight ahead and right into the group of enemies, who had turned back. They were aiming their arrows at me; I took to my heels again. Suddenly my bowstring became tangled in a branch; I pulled to free it, but it would not loosen. The others were already surrounding me. They were taking their time, knowing that I could not escape, and were calmly fitting their curare points. I was thinking of my coming death. Suddenly I heard a muffled noise in the forest. It was approaching and growing louder at a terrific pace: It was a storm. The wind started to blow violently, with a great uproar; dead branches were falling all around me. Then it rained. Then I made up my mind; I ran straight ahead, like a tapir, as fast as I could, with all my strength. I stopped only when I was out of breath and exhausted. I listened for noises, but all was silence: The wind had ceased, and the rain was slowly dripping down. No one was near. Thanks to the storm, I had succeeded in escaping from my pursuers. I very nearly died that day.

At irregular intervals, the night was disturbed by sobs and funeral songs. But at daybreak people slowly wake up, sleepily stretching their stiff limbs. The sun is rising. People converse from one hammock to another, peel palm fruits, and nibble them lazily. A burst of laughter, a dog's bark, a child's weeping are the only noises disturbing the morning peace.

The sun has passed its zenith and is already declining toward the horizon when Ebrëwë shouts in his powerful voice:

> Young men, start on your way without delay; now is the time, you must go.

Then youths carrying bows and arrows stride around the perimeter of the central plaza, along the extreme edge of the shelter's roof, from left to right when facing away from the forest. They advance in single file, snapping their bowstrings against the shafts with a dry, cold sound. While they are circling, Kaōmawë takes the gourd containing the ashes of Sɨsɨwë, who was killed by Mahekoto, and reddens it with roucou. The wax seal is broken. Presently the adult men arrive with their weapons and quivers; they stand up, pressed against one another; the women have come to sit down at their right. All are weeping and singing, and tears can be seen rolling down their cheeks. Kaōmawë pours the remainder of the ashes into a large calabash half-filled with soup. When the mixture is ready, he hands it to Mabroma, then to Kokobirama and to Motʰokama; the women drink in quick gulps, without taking breath. No male consumes the ashes; only women may "drink" the remains of a man killed in war.

When they are finished, the empty gourd is broken and the fragments are placed on the fire. Other objects that once belonged to the deceased are brought out, some still wrapped in dirty old pieces of cloth. Down is glued on the lanceolate arrowheads, and an old woman dances with them in the central plaza. A quiver is broken with great blows of a machete; the sheath made of palm spathe, containing the bird skins and feathers with which the deceased adorned himself, is torn apart. The arrowheads are broken, a bead necklace is undone, fishhooks kept in a matchbox are taken out. Everything that can burn is placed on the fire; the rest is thrown into the river. A machete that must be made to vanish is placed on an anthill: The insects will bury it in the center of their dwelling.

The fire has not yet consumed these modest relics when a great shout rises inside the dwelling, so mournful that it chills the heart. Immediately, the young men pick up axes and machetes, and one of them ties on his back the large sheet of tin on which drugs are usually crushed; another carries the inhaling pipe and the little packets of fine powder. They dance around

178

the plaza, but their gestures are unbearable caricatures: They are unhinged puppets of death with turned-up eyes. Their whole attitude inspires fright, and indeed, everywhere people are deathly silent watching them go by. They presently stop in the center of the plaza, place the sheet of tin on the ground, and blow into each other's nostrils massive and repeated doses of hallucinogenic drugs. Erasiwë goes berserk under the influence of the drug; he throws logs at the dogs and nearly walks into the fires. The women turn him aside and put out of his reach everything that can cause injury.

At that moment, starting at the fire where the funeral ashes were "drunk," the adults advance toward the unconscious youths. They make slow progress, not walking, but crawling on the ground, purposely soiling themselves with dirt, which they fling about by the handful. They mingle with the youths and in their turn take copious doses of drugs. Meanwhile, on Kaõmawë's orders, a whole section of the shelter has been cleared: The hammocks have been taken down and the household utensils carried somewhere else; the space is deserted and empty. That is where the men are now heading, squatting and waddling like ducks, still flinging handfuls of dirt. They can be seen turning their eyes up to the sky, holding their elbows spread out from their bodies, fiercely beating their chests with their hands and letting their tongues hang out of their mouths in a dreadful grimace. When they reach the place under the roof where the fires are, they scatter the ashes without minding the still-glowing coals they contain, fling into the air all the remains of the fires, and roll into the hearths without fear of burns, seemingly oblivious to pain. When the fires, the embers, the coals, and the ashes have been scattered and extinguished, the men, now gray from head to foot, sit down in the plaza facing one another two by two, with their legs entwined, a host with a guest, and promise one another friendship and alliance. By doing this they seal a pact of mutual assistance: The enemies of one become the enemies of the other, and the visitors commit themselves to joining their hosts in taking vengeance for the deceased. The very next morning they will together launch a warlike expedition. This is the *haõhaõmou* ritual.

Dusk soon falls, and Ebrëwë again raises his booming voice:

Children, have fun! Have fun, here comes the night!

At this command, all the older children and adolescents, about twenty persons, once again go round the perimeter of the central plaza with bows and arrows raised. After a full turn they discard their weapons and form a compact mass of bodies, advancing arm in arm. As they are turning, adults throw hot ashes on their exposed backs, knock firebrands above their heads to loosen glowing coals, and set dry leaves afire. The young people turn without stopping; their feet crush red coals, their bodies sustain cruel wounds, but they must remain stoical and hide the pain they feel. At times, it looks as though the group were about to break up: It hesitates, falls apart

179

for a moment, only to come together again immediately – a moving mass on which falls a hail of fire. Women's voices yell encouragement from afar, exhorting the young people to be *waitʰeri*. In the deepening dusk, the sparks fluttering around the bodies streaming with sweat in the oven-like heat, the movements and the shouts make up a fantastic spectacle.

A new day is dawning. The women gather together the cakes they have baked during the night. But the warriors do not hurry; they are familiar with the route they will travel and know in advance where they will sleep: It is no use leaving too early. The men check their arrows, intending to take only the best; they take off the points to reset them carefully, sometimes replacing a lanceolate or harpoon point with a poisoned tip. They remove all superfluous things from their quivers. They betray no nervousness, though their faces are more serious than usual.

Mabroma is preparing tobacco, while next to her Ebrëwë's wife is piling manioc cakes into an open-work basket. Children are playing. Kremoanawë, who has slightly injured his foot, declares that he will not participate in the raid. He says:

I'm in pain; I don't feel like going.

His father answers:

If it weren't for the snakebite that prevents me from running, *I* certainly would go. But I can't. Yet one of us should go. This time we'll kill the sons of Kasiyewë.

The sons of Kasiyewë are the inhabitants of Mahekoto: the enemy.

The men eat roasted plantains. Frërema fastens his quiver; Ebrëwë rolls up his vine hammock. All those who are participating in the raid blacken themselves with charcoal. There is no aesthetic intention in the designs: The face is crudely blackened, and the color is smeared over the body by hand. It is an identifying sign, which the warriors wear like a garment, black symbolizing war and death. Kremoanawë, too, finally blackens himself; his insignificant wound was too slim an excuse.

When they are ready, Bokorawë harangues the warriors. They must, he says, take implacable vengeance, kill as many enemies as possible, and exact from Kasiyewë – twisted mouth – the price of death. No sooner has he finished speaking than a hoarse clamor suddenly rises throughout the dwelling; the men of Karohi line up in a single rank at the extreme edge of the high part of the roof, resolutely turning their backs to the nearby fires. All the able-bodied men are there except the oldest ones. The men of Tayari have assembled in a compact mass facing them; when they advance, they utter piercing cries, cross their bows and arrows in a challenging posture, knock their arrows one against the other, or snap their bowstrings. They take their places to the right of the warriors of Karohi, while those from Hōkanakawë place themselves to their left. Together they form a straight line of naked,

Lined up in the central plaza, the warriors are ready to leave on a raid.

181

black-smeared bodies, of proud, impassive faces. There are nearly forty of them. They remain motionless for a moment; then, upon a signal from Ebrëwë, they solemnly raise their weapons, giving them a slow, undulating motion as of reeds bending in the wind.

Discreetly, the women have placed the provisions at the edge of the path they are soon going to take; little girls wait there to hand them the bundles. As they pass, they take without stopping the food prepared for them and vanish into the forest. They follow the trail at first, then, after a halt, continue through the woods, guiding themselves by the streams, the accidents of the terrain, and various long-familiar obstacles. They have regained their good humor while walking and from time to time exchange jokes. Nor do they refrain from hunting or gathering: They stop to eat Brazil nuts, to collect caterpillars or dig out a toad; they pursue a band of monkeys and kill a bird. The expedition will become truly serious only the next day.

They stop when the sun is declining on the horizon; at this time light is scarcely penetrating the thick, tangled foliage; then the forest darkens and night falls all of a sudden. They set up camp on the bank of a brook. In no time, they build shelters and cover them with leaves. Most of them have no hammocks, but fashion them out of strips of bark. Those who have brought their usual hammocks or their machetes will leave them here the next day, to be recovered later: Objects useless for the attack are only a burden.

They are aware that, since their departure, the shamans at Karohi have sent the *hekura* to damage the enemies' arrows; the risk of being killed is thus lessened. The next morning they will continue with extreme caution their progress toward the enemy group. When near enough, they will fashion a manikin, a crude human effigy, toward which they will shoot their arrows. This ritual is supposed to further their plans. They will spend another night in the forest, but this time they will stretch out on the ground, without fire, and will stay awake. In the morning, even before daylight, they will lie in ambush in a garden or at the edge of a path, waiting motionless for an enemy to come by, on whom they will loose a volley of arrows; then they will take flight to escape the enemy counterattack.

The fires are bright. Bundles are cooking on the embers. When the bird's entrails were removed, blood flowed too thickly for the warriors' liking: It is a bad sign. At dusk, all around the camp garrulous macaws are jabbering, toucans utter guttural cries, different from their usual song; a band of monkeys passes overhead; these are so many unfavorable omens, for these animals are not true animals, but emissaries sent by their enemies to spy on them.

Ebrëwë spends the night under the open sky, in his hammock stretched between two strong poles transversely joined. When he wakes, he gravely announces that he dreamt that a jaguar was drinking from the brook. The vision does not bode well, and Ebrëwë thinks they should turn back. He has no difficulty convincing the others, who are not anxious to push on when everything is warning them of the risk they are running.

At Karohi, no one is surprised by their sudden return; it is the fate of three raids out of four not to be carried to conclusion. No one blames them for their caution; the omens were obviously unfavorable, and people are glad to see them return alive. During their absence children were forbidden to play, fires had not been allowed to burn too brightly, people refrained from delousing each other, and the trail they had taken on their way out had been prohibited to women.

No chieftain leads warlike expeditions; it is the wisest and the boldest whose opinion prevails and who convince the more timid. Indeed, disagreements about the best course of action are not unusual. The fewer the participants, the better the chances of success; it is difficult to maintain a large group's cohesion when no one is in command, and the attempt then fails before it is carried out. Participation in a raid is not mandatory, for no one has enough authority to enforce it; it depends solely on the prevailing moral code. Young men need to solidify their reputation for valor, and war is for them the ideal means of demonstrating that they possess that virtue. Those who are fulfilling their marital service participate without exception in their allies' wars, else they lose face and may be rejected as cowardly. A good warrior – a *waitʰeri* man – enjoys a superior status; people respect him, fear him; he is influential in the political affairs of his community, and his opinion is taken into consideration. War is a means of self-assertion; one must be brave, fierce, cruel. Every mature male is duty-bound to punish the outrages perpetrated against his relatives and to avenge the dead; otherwise, despised and weak, he will encourage new blows and will always be the loser in the subtle and perilous game of matrimonial or economic exchanges.

That night, the men fulfill the *wayamou* ritual, for the guests will leave the next morning. As soon as night has fallen, a visitor utters the prescribed call; a host approaches and answers him. The visitor leaves his hammock to face his partner in a dizzying verbal competition, a ceaseless interchange of short, staccato sentences uttered and repeated alternately. Each has his turn taking the initiative. In this verbal jousting, they must constantly keep up the spirit of repartee, never make a mistake or commit a slip of the tongue. The stereotyped sentences are cut up into short sequences, and circumlocutions and metaphors are the rule: It is a particularly formalized discourse. Every Yanomami dialect has patterns of speech suited to this way of speaking; hence, the *wayamou* ritual does nothing to promote mutual comprehension when the dialects are too far apart.

Long before they are of age to participate in a *wayamou*, the youths, even the children, regularly practice for it, repeating the formulas, which they

183

hum to themselves on rainy days or at night before falling asleep. It is a great event for them to participate for the first time, almost as if they thus attained manly status.

Indeed, the youngest go first, at the beginning of the evening; wisely cautious, they often limit themselves to the formulas they know by heart, reeling them off with great verve. As the night progresses, older and older men enter the lists to battle with words. Their mastery is greater, and the tone changes; they are able to improvise and may slip a message into their discourse, or a bit of information, or a request. With them the ritual calms down, the sentences acquire meaning. Sometimes they compete in a singing mode, in a detached manner; sometimes their voices become almost inaudible, confidential, and then they are conversing; then, suddenly, the rhythm changes and the delivery picks up volume and strength.

The *wayamou* begins at nightfall and ends only at dawn, when all the male voices are hoarse from excessive use.

After a brief rest and a frugal meal, there only remains to initiate the exchanges that always precede the departure of visitors. There is no alliance without trade. To conclude a political pact means that one implicitly accepts entering the cycles of matrimonial and economic exchanges. Neutral relations are inconceivable; either they are peaceful and involve commercial and matrimonial exchanges, or else it is war: One can only be friends or enemies. In some communities, to declare, "I will not give anything" or "I will not give what you are asking" is to risk a clubbing; to refuse a gift is inevitably insulting and is understood as a sign of hostility.

Every celebration, like this carnival of alliance, necessarily ends with commercial exchanges that commit the partners.

The bargaining, however, does not proceed without bitter disputes. The partners stay at the brink of rupture, but it is precisely the risk of the game, the zest of the confrontation that appeal to them. The Yanomami have a passion for barter and bargaining, not so much for the sake of the object itself, which is after all of only secondary importance, but for the social and spiritual element involved in every exchange. They also appreciate the pleasure of quickly giving away what they have just received. Since exchanging is an obligation, hoarding is impossible. The only vice that Yanomami morality recognizes is avarice, and they have devised for it a punishment comparable to the Christian punishment for sin: fire – with the difference, however, that the Yanomami fire is celestial and consumes souls apparently without pain. If the Indians strive for profit, it is then not for the pleasure of accumulating wealth, but for the prestige and the private satisfaction involved in the division and redistribution of possessions.

In this male game, the women play a significant role. They restrain male prodigality on the side of the hosts, and, on the opposite side, they push for maximum profit. For example, this very morning Mabroma hid behind the shelter a pot she does not want to give. It is she again who urges Kaõmawë not to give a dog in exchange for the cotton that he is offered; if she finally gives in, it is on the strength of the recipient's promise to send a basket of tobacco at a later time.

While the men linger behind engrossed in conversations, the women set out, with baskets crammed full of utensils, hammocks, and provisions swaying on their backs. They walk with heavy steps, with that gait peculiar to the Yanomami when they carry heavy burdens, turning their feet inward, the better to keep their balance and cling to the ground.

The visitors rise; they have suddenly fallen silent, and without a parting glance, they cross the threshhold of the *shabono* to vanish among the trees as if swallowed by the forest. Inside the great shelter now emptied of its crowds, there is felt suddenly, albeit briefly, the weight of an absence, the sadness of being once again with the usual people, the prosaic prospect of daily chores.

APPENDIXES

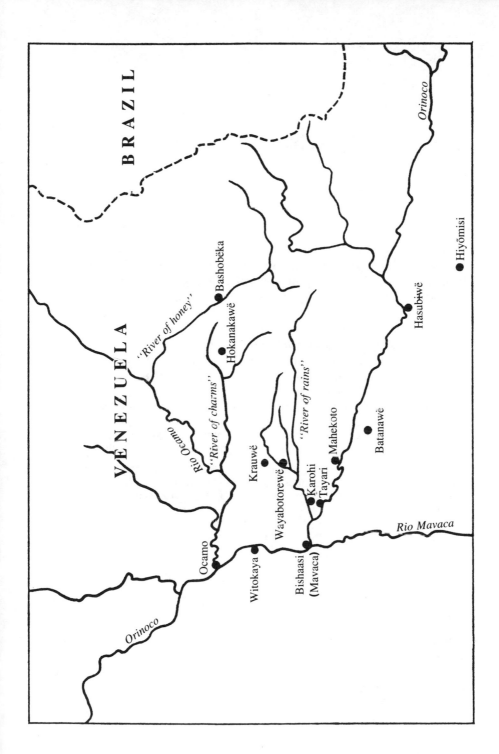

Notes on phonetic transcription

The orthographic symbols used for the transcription of Yanomami words have approximately the following phonetic values:

    a   [a]   a low central vowel as the *a* in Spanish *casa* (closest American English sound is between the *a* of b*a*t and the *a* of f*a*ther)

    e   [e]   a mid front vowel as the *ai* of b*ai*t but without the high glide

    i   [i]   a high front unrounded vowel like the *ee* sound of f*ee*t

    o   [o]   a mid back rounded vowel as the *o* of n*o*te but without the glide

    u   [u]   a high back rounded vowel similar to the *oo* sound of p*oo*l or the *u* of r*u*de, but short

    ë   [ə]   a mid central vowel similar to the *a* sound in the word *a*bout or the u in j*u*st

    ɨ   [ɨ],[ï]   a high central and sometime back unrounded vowel, similar to the *i* of b*i*rd, approximated by pronouncing *u* as in p*oo*l with spread lips

In Yanomami, vowels may be *nasalized* (i.e., pronounced with the air escaping through the nose). Nasalization is indicated by a tilde [˜] over the vowel.

Vowel *clusters* (e.g., *ee*) are pronounced with a glottal stop between them (e.g., ee ⇒ [eʔe]).

Consonants are pronounced as in English with a few exceptions: p, t, and k are never aspirated and are pronounced as in the words s*p*in, s*t*em, and s*k*in.

tʰ is a [t] followed by an aspiration [h], always pronounced as the initial t in English *t*ime, *t*ill, and *t*one.

r is an alveolar flap; although not trilled, it resembles more the Spanish r than the English r.

sh [š] is a palatal voiceless fricative and is pronounced as the English cluster *sh* in *sh*ell.

To avoid confusing the reader, the author has taken certain liberties with phonetic transcription: In contrast to accepted usage, he has used capitals at the beginning of names of persons and places, and he has not italicized them, as is standard practice. All names of communities are followed by the suffix -*tʰeri* (*karohi-tʰeri*), which is omitted in the text to simplify matters.

Note: The publisher would like to thank Ernest Cesar Migliazza for his assistance in the preparation of this appendix and the glossary of Yanomami terms.

190

Glossaries

Yanomami terms

ama: Tree (*Elizabetha princeps*), bark used as a hallucinogen

amahiri: Beings of the underworld; they are hairless and look like the Yanomami; *also* decomposed and phosphorescent vegetable remains

ami kë u: Red, intoxicating beverage obtained from a mythical fruit; the
hekura use it for food and to paint their bodies

ami u bë: Intoxicating, sweet, and red drink of the *hekura*

aroami: Poisonous snake (*Bothrops atrox*) whose bite can be fatal

aroari këki: Bulbous plant of the genus *Cyperus*, used in black magic

baushimi: Species of banana with pink, starchy pulp

bë boko no warebi: Describes a person who is expert in hunting wild pigs

bei kë maki: Refers to the rocks where the *hekura* come to live

bei kë mi amo: This is the "soul," the "center" of a person; its loss brings
about the death of the body; it is, so to speak, the "vital principle"

bei kë no uhutibi: Synonym for *bei kë mi amo*

bei yë : Interjection used to show potential enemies that the speaker is on his
guard

bëna: Small rodent (unidentified), with a reddish pelt, that lives in the mountainous regions of the central Yanomami; its pelt is used as a charm in
black magic

bishaa kë henaki: Plant (*Calathea altissima*), the leaves of which are used
for wrapping and for cooking on coals, and sometimes for roofing forest
shelters

bore kë hi: Unidentified species of tree (tree of the ghost)

bore koko: Imaginary bird belonging to the supernatural world of the *hekura*

braiai: Ritual of presentation performed with a dance step during festivities

eeeeri: Small species of toucan, probably *Pteroglossus flavirostris azara*

fëifëiyomi: Bird (*Lipaugus vociferans*)

habrabiwë: Refers to the migrating *hekura* who leave the body of a dead
shaman to settle in that of a living shaman

191

hama: Visitor

haōhaōmou: Daytime ritual, performed in pairs during a festivity, to seal an alliance and promise mutual assistance

hayu: Tree (*Pseudomedia* sp.); also, its fruit, the size and color of a cherry

hekura: Supernatural beings of the imaginary world of the shamans; spirits of plants, animals, or natural elements; the *hekura* come to dwell within the breast of the shaman to whom they lend their powers

hemare: Tree of the same family as the cocoa tree (*Theobroma* sp.)

hera: Demon who lives with Thunder in the dwelling of the souls in the celestial world

heri: Nocturnal ritual of the hunt associated with the consumption of funeral ashes in banana soup.

hiima: Mainly used in the third person, possessive case; refers generally to any tame or domestic animal, particularly the dog

hoko: Palm tree (*Oenocarpus bataua*), the fruit of which is used to make a very rich beverage that is drunk with roasted plantain

hoko sikɨ: Leaf of the *hoko* palm, used during the dances of presentation

hōrema: Species of bird, probably of the family *Tinamidae,* whose song is associated both with floods and with wild pigs

hutumi: Bird (*Momotus momota aequatorialis*)

kakuru (kakuruwë): Milky stone, hard as quartz; Kakuruwë is the spirit associated with this stone

kanaye: Tree (*Tachigalia paniculata*)

kaomari: Bird of prey (*Micrastur ruficollis*) that feeds on snakes

kareshi: Palm tree (*Maximiliana regia*), the fruit of which is edible, as are its nut and its heart

këkɨ: Abbreviation applying to the rocks where the *hekura* live

ketiba kë henakɨ· Leaf of *Ravenala guianensis,* used to cover shelters

kirakirami: Kind of parrot (*Deroptyus accipitrinus*)

kōbari: Bird (*Buteo albicantatus*) whose cry is a bad omen

kōmishi kë henakɨ: Leaf of *Geonoma cf. baculifera* (Poit.) Kunth

kowahito: People of demons of the waters and the savannahs

kreōmari: Species of toucan (*Ramphastos vitellinus*)

kumato: Oil-rich nut of *Caryocar villosum*

kumiti: Vegetable attribute of the *hekura*

kunamaru: Unidentified species of toad; the Yanomami believe that its urine, when sprinkled on the chests of sleepers, can cause death

kushë ha: Formula that is spoken to obtain the desired effect

makayo: Big belly (as in name of mountain)

manaka: Herbaceous plant cultivated in gardens and used in black magic to cause sterility in women

mārāshi: Bird (*Pipila cumanensis* Cracidae)

192

miyõma kë henaki: Plant with broad leaves and thorny stem; the leaves are used for cooking and for roofing forest shelters

momo: Tree (*Micranda rossii* Euphorbiaceae), the fruit of which is poisonous, but made edible by parboiling and prolonged soaking

morē: Tree (*Dacryodes burseraceae*) that fruits every four to five years; the Indians believe that Thunder is its master

morõ: Small species of armadillo (unidentified)

mraka nahi: Unidentified tree

nabë: Has a range of meanings, depending on the context: foreigner (non-Yanomami), enemy, different; it stands in opposition to the word *yanomami* (human being)

naiki: Someone who has a desire to eat meat; is opposed to *ohi*

naikiri: Those who are hungry for meat; cannibals

natʰeri wakabi: Literally, "testicle of giant armadillo"; it characterizes a condition of the testicles that makes them grow to abnormal size

nii: Refers to any vegetable food; stands in opposition to *yaro,* game

noreshi: Image, shadow

nosi: Used up, without value

nosiyemou: To ask someone to do something; to have something done; *also* name given to a festive ritual during which trials are inflicted on young men who thus demonstrate their resistance to pain

ohi: To be hungry in general; refers mainly to hunger for vegetable food; it is opposed to *naiki*

õi: Species of bee

õka: Sorcerers; applies to persons who go to "blow" deadly substances on enemy groups

õrihiyē: Refers to sick animals lying on the ground; they are said to be bad omens, and must not be eaten

oshe: Large termites (*Bellicositerme*) eaten by Yanomami; also, a young person or animal

rahaka shiiwë: Name given to a lanceolate arrowhead; it is supposed to cause the effusion of fecal matter and certain death

rahara: Large, mythological, aquatic monster

rasha: Palm (*Guilielma gasipaës*), the fruit of which, much relished by the Indians, it not necessarily associated with festivities

ruwë: Prepubescent (green, unripe) female

shabo: Women's invocation to avoid an illness or some misfortune

shabono: Circular dwelling with an open central plaza, whatever the type or materials of construction

shāki kë na: Species of black bee that likes to feed on decomposing matter, salt, and urine

shamatʰari: For the central Yanomami – the subjects of this work – this word designates the southern Yanomami who live beyond the left bank of the Orinoco. *Shamat^hari* never applies to any well-defined subgroup, nor does it anywhere appear to be a self-denomination; it stands in opposition to *waika*

shanishani: Tree (*Miconia acinodendron*)

shawara: One of the names given to demons responsible for diseases and epidemics

shitibori: Tree (*Jacaranda copaia*)

shobari kë wakë: Blaze in the celestial world, in which the souls of the avaricious are lost

shoko: Species of tree-dwelling edentate (*Tamandua tetradactyla*), *Shokoriwë* is the spirit associated with this animal

shoro: Swallow-like bird, probably *Chaetura cinereiventris*

shorori: The *shoro* people: water demons and masters of subterranean fire

sikorobirimi: Species of bamboo; *also* the arrowheads fashioned from it

sina: Referring to a bad marksman or a bad hunter

tabitabirimi: Species of banana, short and round; its pulp is sweet and aromatic

tat^he: Ripe, referring to bananas; is said of banana soup and of a pubescent girl (in the latter case, the word stands in opposition to *ruwë*)

teshomomo: Official declaration opening every festivity

t^horu: Plant (*Amazonia arborea*)

tirirou: To assemble in great numbers

tirurou: Shaman's action in invoking the *hekura;* his way of singing

tokori: Tree (*Crecropia orinocensis*)

unokai: Condition of a murderer; the set of dietary prohibitions and obligations he must observe; *also*, those that a girl who has her first menstrual flow while living with her husband must follow

ushu: Formula that is recited to ward off a misfortune

ushuweimawë: Spirit associated with a fish

wabu: Tree (*Clathrotropis macrocarpa* Ducke), the fruit of which is poisonous but edible after boiling or soaking in water for a few days

waika: Word that the central Yanomami apply to their northern and eastern neighbors: The word is derogatory, and no Yanomami group or subgroup acknowledges being *waika;* in no way a defined cultural entity, it stands in opposition to *shamat^hari*

waima: Species of palm tree, the leaves of which are used to cover temporary forest shelters

wait^heri: Describes a fundamental value in the Yanomami moral code: It refers to both physical courage – the capacity to bear great pain – and the ability to return blows

wakrashi: (Onomatopoeia)

waroo: Unidentified species of greenish, tree-dwelling snake

watoshe: Diadem that is placed on shamans' heads during the final phase of their initiation

watota: Cotton armband (worn by males)

wayamou: Complex, nocturnal ritual of oratory that emphasizes metaphor and circumlocution, pitting a guest and a host against each other for a variable period of time (until they are replaced by companions); the *wayamou* is in no way a *lingua franca,* as has been reported

weyari: Demons of dusk

witiwitimi: Unidentified species of gregarious bird with a forked tail

yahetiba: Electric eel (*Electrophorus electricus*)

yaiyo: Funeral lamentation without precise meaning

yakõana: Refers to hallucinogenic drugs derived from the bark of trees of the *Virola* family – *Virola elongata,* for example.

yanomami: Simplification of *Yanõmami* (dialectical variants are *yanõwami* and *sanɨma*), a cultural and linguistic grouping: It means "human being," the "folk," and it is the Indians' self-denomination

yaraka: Flat, silvery little fish living in brooks

yaro: Game, meat, animals that are considered edible

yei: Palm tree of the genus *Attalea,* the fruit of which is edible

yɨbi kë henakɨ: Bush (*sorocea guyanensis*), the boughs of which are used to construct the booths in which menstruating girls are secluded

yohoamɨ: Species of partridge (*Tinamidae* sp.)

yopo: Plant cultivated in garden for use by shaman

yõririmi: Unidentified species of bird

yubuu na: Kind of condiment made from the ashes of a tree bark

yuri: Refers to the whole class of fishes

South American flora and fauna

agami: Trumpeter bird (genus *Psophia*), somewhat like a crane

agouti: American rodent about the size of a rabbit

cacique: Black or colored oriole with base of bill serving as a frontal shield

caiman: Kind of crocodilian

capybara: Large (often over four feet long) rodent, mostly aquatic (*Hydrocoerus capybara*)

caribe fish: Piranha

coati: Mammal of genus *Nasua,* related to raccoon

cotinga: Bird of brilliant plumage, related to the manakin

gecko: Small insectivorous lizard of family Gekkonidae

genipap: Tree (*Genipa americana*) or its edible fruit

hoatzin: Crested bird (*Opisthocomos cristatus*), smaller than a pheasant, with

195

olive plumage marked with white, and claws on first and second fingers

liana: Climbing vine that roots in the ground

mauritia: Genus of lofty palms

paca: Large, common, edible rodent (*cuniculus paca*)

peccary: Piglike mammal of genus *Tayassu*

roucou: Annatto tree; also, the red or yellowish red dyestuff made from annatto tree seed pulp

saki: Monkey (family Cebidae), usually bearded, with bushy, nonprehensile
tail

tamandua: Aboreal anteater (*Tamandua tetradactyla*)

tanager: Passerine bird of family Thraupidae; males are brightly colored

Other works on the Yanomami

Note: Ph.D. theses listed are available from University Microfilms International (UMI), 300 N. Zeeb Road, Ann Arbor, Michigan 48106 and 30/32 Mortimer Street, London W1N 7RA, England.

Biocca, Ettore. *Yanoama: The Narrative of a White Girl Kidnapped by Amazonian Indians* (as told to E. Biocca; translated from Italian by Dennis Rhodes). Dutton, New York, 1970 (paperback, 1971).
Chagnon, Napoleon. Yanomamo Warfare, Social Organization and Marriage Alliances. Ph.D. thesis. UMI, 1966.
　　Studying the Yanomamö. Holt, Rinehart and Winston, New York, 1974.
　　Yanomamö: The Fierce People, 3rd ed. Holt, Rinehart and Winston, New York, 1983.
Cocco, Luis. *Iyëwei-teri: Quince años entre los Yanomamos.* Escuela Técnica Popular Don Bosco, Caracas, 1972.
Fredlund, Eric Victor. Shitari Yanomamo Incestuous Marriage: A Study of the Use of Structural, Lineal and Biological Criteria When Classifying Marriages. Ph.D. thesis. UMI, 1982.
Lizot, Jacques. *Diccionario Yanomami–Espanol.* Universidad Central de Venezuela, Caracas, 1974.
　　El Hombre de la pantorilla prenada: Y otros mitos Yanomami. Fundación La Salle de Ciencias Naturales, Caracas, 1975.
Melancon, Thomas F. Marriage and Reproduction Among the Yanomamo Indians of Venezuela. Ph.D. thesis. UMI, 1982.
Migliazza, Ernest Cesar. Yanomama Grammar and Intelligibility. Ph.D. thesis. UMI, 1972.
Ramos, Alcida Rita. The Social System of the Sanuma of Northern Brazil. Ph.D. thesis. UMI, 1972.
Shapiro, Judith Rae. Sex Roles and Social Structure Among the Yanomama Indians of Northern Brazil. Ph.D. thesis, UMI, 1972.
Taylor, Kenneth. *Sanuma Fauna: Prohibitions and Classification.* Monografia No. 18. Fundacion La Salle de Ciencias Naturales, Caracas.
Zerries, Otto. *Waika: Die Kulturgeschichtliche Stellung der Waika-Indianer des oberen Orinoco im Rahmen der Völkerkunde Südamerikas.* Klaus Renner Verlag, Munich, 1954.
Zerries, Otto, and Schuster, M. *Mahekodotedi.* Klaus Renner Verlag, Munich, 1974.

197

CAMBRIDGE STUDIES IN SOCIAL ANTHROPOLOGY

Editor: Jack Goody

199

Cambridge Studies in Social Anthropology

200

Cambridge Studies in Social Anthropology

* Also available as a paperback
† Paperback available in USA only